provide a direct in your face Christian confrontation of where the Black man has gone and what it will take to bring him back in harmony with God, himself and his family. I hope to supply the reader with sound biblical advice on several issues related to human dysfunction. I hope to demonstrate to the reader the effects of family dysfunction when the presence of the husband is absent. Furthermore, we as African-Americans must confront the dysfunctions within the Black church also, you see, we can't separate the two. The Black man and the Black church were as one.

The ultimate hopes of this book is for each person that picks this book up and read its pages; I hope the Lord's Holy Spirit will convict you of your sins and transgressions against Him and your families. I pray that you will take these written words and seek God's face by committing yourself to a personal relationship with Him through His Son Jesus Christ. This book is ultimately about RECONCILIATION. It was God's original design for the human race to be in perfect relationship with Him, thus ourselves and each other. We are out of relationship with God and therefore with everyone and everything else. God is calling us to reconcile with Him and each other through His Son, Jesus Christ. If we don't, what kind of world will our children and children's children live in? And where does our responsibility lye? Will today's Black people be responsible for the annihilation of tomorrow's Black family?

Rev. Avery Bolden PhD.

"Fathers"

The Missing Component in the

African-American Family

(A Christian Perspective)

By Rev. Avery Bolden PhD.

"Fathers"
The Missing Component in the African-American Family

By Rev. Avery Bolden PhD. Publisher

© 2006 by Rev. Avery Bolden PhD. Euclid, Ohio 44119

-All Rights Reserved-

No part of this book may be reproduced, stored in a retrieval system, or transcribed, in any form or by any means—electronic, mechanical, photocopying, recording, or otherwise—without the prior permission of the publisher, Rev. Avery Bolden PhD 394 East 200th Street, Euclid Ohio 44119- except for brief quotations.

Rev. Avery Bolden PhD is founder and clinical director of Dove of Peace Christian Counseling Ministries LLC. For counseling needs; theological education, Christian counseling education, prevention education, and speaking engagements, call:

Rev. Avery Bolden PhD
Dove of Peace Christian Counseling Ministries LLC
291 East 222ND St. Suite 21
Euclid, Ohio 44123
(216) 731-7580...Fax (216) 731-7587
www.doveofpeacecounseling.com

ISBN- 978-0-6151-3878-7
Rev. Avery Bolden PhD.

Printed in the United States of America

"FATHER'S"
The Missing Component in the African-American Family

Table of Contents:

	Page
Preface	3
Chapter One: *A brief historical view of African slavery and the Black church*	7
Chapter Two: *The dysfunctional church*	14
Chapter Three: *African Americans and addictions*	45
Chapter Four: *Christian conflict resolution*	63
Chapter Five: *The father connection*	100
Chapter Six: *"Let my people go" Breaking free from a mind of bondage*	142
Chapter Seven: *"And the two shall become one flesh"*	177
Chapter Eight: *Raising children for the Lord*	215
Chapter Nine: *Reconciliation*	244
References	259

"Fathers"
The Missing Component in the African American Family

Preface

What has become of the African American husband, father, male role-model? As many Black mothers and children look around them, they see that something is terribly wrong within their line of sight. They rub their eyes and bat their eye lashes hoping to clear what has invaded their vision. Soon the countenance of Black mother's and children begins to fall as we, the African American race of God's people have noticed the fact that many of our husband's, fathers and once inspirational Black role models have nearly disappeared. The sad fact is; we can see clearly now the pain is gone. We've become cold, detached, selfish, and very, very angry. There's nothing wrong with our eyes. Our eyes are not the problem, but our heart is!

The Black skinned little girl waits for her father to call her on the telephone, because he doesn't live with his daughter any more. And neither does he place the telephone call to his anxiously waiting daughter. So the little girls cry in pain and disappointment, again! It's Saturday morning and the Black skinned little boy is up early, washed up, teeth brushed, and have already enjoyed breakfast. You see, this little Black boy is waiting for his daddy to come and pick him up and take him to the ball game. But to his surprise and just like the Black skinned little girl, this little boys daddy didn't show up again either, and now the Black face little boy is also weeping with great sorrow and pain. This Black face little boy does not understand why his daddy did not pick him up, or call him.

Later that very same day, the telephone rings and it's the little Black face boy's daddy. The little boy answers the telephone, and before he can ask his daddy why didn't he pick him up? His daddy says to him; put mommy on the phone! The little boy's mother picks up the telephone and before she can let him have it, the little boy's daddy says; I need you to come bail me out! Why? The boy's mother asks. The little boy's daddy says; the police arrested me, they said I had some crack in my car, but you know it wasn't mine!

The Black face little girl and the Black face little boy both weeps with pain. These children weep because they're hurt. They don't understand the proverbial why? They ask the question; doesn't daddy love me? Doesn't daddy want to be with me? I just wanted to spend time with my daddy!

Where is my daddy? How come my daddy does not love me? How come my daddy uses drugs? Why is my daddy so angry all the time? Why did my daddy abandoned me? How come my daddy didn't marry my mama? Why is my daddy in jail? Who is my daddy? Why did my daddy hurt me? Whey isn't daddy living with us? Did I do something wrong? Did I chase daddy away?

This is the reason why I wrote this book. This is not the book I initially wanted to write, but the Lord placed in my spirit the need to write this book. So, I present to you what I believe is a strong statement of the current condition of the Black man and the Black family. The Black man is the key to success of the Black family. Statistics prove the serious decline in Black marriages. Because of this great decline in Black marriages, and the separation and discontinuity within the black family structure, it is my opinion that the Black family is in a state of crisis.

Black people have turned away from God and the order and structure God commanded for all His people. God has made the man to be the head of the wife and family. God is a God of order, thus without God's order intact, we have disorder. Disorder is the product of dysfunction in the Black family. Where there exist a family, there must also exits a husband and a wife. Thus, this is the purpose of this book. I hope to address several important areas where the Black man has been led astray by his own choices. I hope the pages of this book will

Chapter One
A Brief History of African Slavery and the Black Church

"This was not a distant, far-away God in some king of institutional church, but it was a God, said the evangelicals, involved in the daily lives of people, involved in every thought and every deed of your life. …There had never been anything like it. Here's a meeting of 3,000 people out in the fields, blacks and whites together, listening to a preacher who says, "Here in my message is a new life for you, here's a new chance for you. Here's a God who had your interest at heart. Here's a God who may deliver you."
-David Blight, historian-

The 17Th and 18TH centuries have recorded the capturing, imprisonment, and forced slavery of the African peoples to Europe. During this time salve trade was the primary source of European wealth. Hundreds of traders made fortunes on the shipment of live human beings from the great continent of African. Philip D. Curtin in 1969 estimated that approximately 9-9 ½ Million Africans were imported or stolen from their native lands. How many Africans died trying to keep themselves free from those who sought to shackle and enslave them for the benefit of the oh mighty dollar? After being enslaved by African slave traders, Africans were forced to walk in slave caravans to the European coastal forts, sometimes as far as 1,000 miles.

Shackled and underfed, only half the people survived. Once boarded upon ships, the Atlantic crossing took some 60-90 days and lasted up to four months. Africans were often treated like cattle during the crossing. On the slave ships, people were stuffed between decks in spaces too low for standing. The heat was often unbearable, and the air nearly unbreathable. Many African females were sexually molested and raped. Men were often chained in pairs and shackled by their wrists or ankles. These Africans would lie on their backs with their heads between the legs of others. Africans had no choice but to urinate, defecate, and bleed on each other, as sicknesses such as smallpox, dysentery, and yellow fever grabbed hold of their bodies. The diseased Africans were sometimes thrown overboard to prevent wholesale destruction of human cargo. Some reports have African human losses between one and two million. A lack of food, water and care was the menu of the day as these great ships sailed the waters with their African cargo bound for trade.

Tribal families of slaves were quickly separated as slaves were sold for a host of labor responsibilities. Tribal languages and mannerisms were soon broken down by slave masters as these transplanted Africans soon lost cultural and social bonds with each other and their homelands. African customs, religion, social structures and kinships were all destroyed as these characteristics would create dangers for the slave masters. The attitudes towards slaves by their slave masters in most societies were less than the appreciation for cattle and other livestock. Throughout history slaves were often considered stupid, ignorant, childlike, lazy, untruthful, and cowardly. Slaves were forbidden to engage in occupations that might demonstrate their capacities, intermarriage almost never occurred, and manumission was almost unheard of as the reigning publicists proclaimed ever more loudly that blacks lacked any capacity to maintain themselves as free individuals. Meg Greene in her book entitled "Slave young slave long," she writes: "Some merchants displayed slaves in their homes, where potential buyers could come and inspect them. Slaves could be purchased with small down payments, and traders offered credit on "reasonable terms" to finance the remaining cost. An advertisement in 1726 offered buyers "3, 6, 9, or 12 month's credit terms.

O, where has mother gone, papa?
What makes you look so sad?
Why sit you here alone, papa?
Has anyone made you mad?
O, tell me, dear papa.
Has master punished you again?
Shall I go bring the salt, papa,
To rub your back and cure the pain?
--Former slave W.H. Robinson, 1913

Slaves had no legal rights. They were not allowed to learn to read or write. These restrictions were among many called "Slave codes." Masters had complete control over their property. Slave master's named their slaves and their children, which mirrored the names of the master's own family. Some slaves master's allowed the slaves to court and mate. However, some slaves rejected the courtships out of fear of heartache as a slave could be sold to another plantation. Other female slaves could not bare the physical punishment placed on their mate by the slave master's and thus decided not to court.

Brethren, arise, arise! Strike for
your lives and liberties. Now is
the day and the hour...
Rather die free men than live to
Be slaves...Let your motto be resistance! Resistance!
RESISTANCE!
--Henry Highland Garnet,
African-American abolitionist

Slaves used the wisdom of folktales and songs to teach other slaves important lessons of the times and to encourage one another while going through difficult days. It was the slave's desire for a separation from the lifestyle that had been forced upon them. This experience deeply involved the dehumanizing of the African person in its totality. However, this degrading, soul ripping experience was not enough to stop the life force of the African, now American slaves.

Arising out of the experience of slavery for Africans grew the genesis of the Black church in America. Quakers, a religious group established originally in England were seeking to worship without boundaries in North America. Quakers believed strongly that all men were created equal, thus many Quakers along with the Puritans worked to end slavery, as these religious groups strongly objected to slavery on moral grounds. A myriad of church denominations joined together with free blacks and slaves to offer religious education. Cotton Mather, a Puritan minister argued that African slaves should be taught about

Christianity. This type of message often brought wrath from slaveholders, as slaveholders resisted the conversion of their slaves. Many slaveholders feared that Christianity would make their slaves not only proud, but rebellious. Rebellious slaves might get the idea they could fight for their freedom and win. Insurrection from slaves was the greatest threat feared by slaveholders.

The "Great Awakening," was the name given to a spiritual revival led by minister Jonathan Edwards in the 1730's. Out of this spiritual revival grew several Black preachers who were received by white congregations. Richard Allen, a Black minister and former slave traveled with white ministers in Delaware and was given ministerial assignments by then Bishop Asbury of the Methodist church in 1786. It was Minister Richard Allen, in Philadelphia, that proposed a separate church for the African-Americans there. After being forcibly removed from his seat in a Methodist Episcopal church, so a white congregant could be seated, Richard Allen and other Black leaders then formed the Free African Society in 1788.

Members of the Free African Society began to organize churches in various cities. In 1816 they met in Philadelphia and established the African Methodist Episcopal (AME) church. Other small church denominations also formed during this time; however they were not as well organized. The first African Baptist church was established by a handful of free Blacks between 1733 and 1755 on the William Byrd plantation in Mecklenburg, Virginia, and the Bluestone church was established by a slave named George liele. During what was called the "Second Great Awakening," whereas Christianity began sweeping through the South near the end of the 18th century. This sweeping spiritual awakening came to be through Methodist and Baptist clergy.

The teachings of the second "Great Spiritual Awakening" was simple, clear, and easy to comprehend. These teachings emphasized a personal experience with God, thus leading to repentance and a change of heart. A personal relationship God through Jesus Christ spoke to the issues of the slaves. The message of the gospel reinforced a message of self-worth that was purposely taken away from slaves using strategies designed to humiliate and control the spirit of the slaves. The slaves found themselves entranced with the music of worship to God that emphasized hope and freedom. Leading up to the Civil War, most slaves had come to experience the gospel's message. Out of distrust for the slave master's, preachers and slaves began to hold secret worship meetings. Slaves continued to meet in secret to praise and worship God at tremendous risks and costs to their health, as slave owners who caught their slaves serving God would beat, punish and whip them. But the slaves continued to meet in secret places without fear of punishment and retribution by their slave masters. The slaves were strengthened by various prayers, preaching, songs and fellowship that counteracted the extreme difficulties of their day to day living realities.

The Christianity of the slaves was not the same Christianity of most whites and other Christians. Black slaves were encouraged by the gospel of liberation. The gospel message that spoke of self-esteem, respect, love, value and worth, pain and suffering for a higher calling, and other issues of the times, even if many of the slaves would not be a part of the reality of liberation, they held on believing that their children would be set free by the Jesus of liberation. Black slaves Christianity was a Christianity of freedom, whereby their shackles would be loosed and Jesus would restore unto them humanity, equality and liberty. Preachers preached messages of "Jubilee," the anticipation of freedom from bondage and degradation. The message of jubilee was suitable to the slave's needs, wants, goals and desires. As songs became an intricate part of the slaves Christianity, songs and hymns called spirituals began to develop and grow. These spirituals were specific songs aimed at encouraging one another to hold on, that change was coming. These spirituals emphasized patience and perseverance as the God of liberation who once freed the Israelites from bondage, would one day free them also.

Worshipping God for many slaves represented great personal risks, because of these personal risks slaves created an ingenious mode of communication that was unknown to their slave masters. Slaves would sing songs such as "Steal Away to Jesus." As a slave started to sing the song, other slaves would understand that there was a worship meeting planned for that evening. Many slaves taught themselves how to read and write, while others secretly were taught by some whites. The slaves that could read and write would read the Bible to the others who could not read. Slave masters were fearful of slaves learning to read and write as literacy would lead to revolts.

When people accepted the faith, it did not make them content to be slaves. What it did was, it opened up to them the possibilities that are available to those people who see themselves as children of this eternal and almightily God.
-Rev. Jeffrey Leath

...We are now encouraged through the grace and divine assistance of the friends and God opening the hearts of our white friends and brethren, to encourage us to arise out of the dust and shake ourselves, and throw off that servile fear, that the habit of oppression and bondage trained us up in.
-Absalom Jones

Chapter Two
The Dysfunctional Church

What is the African American Church?

What is the African American Church today? It would be a very difficult task for me to suggest to you that I completely understand the question I presented. You only have to look around you at those who call themselves Black or African American. We as a people are a melting pot of diversity, even within our own race, which today is not pure. I myself have a White Irish grandfather. So, in order to answer the question: What is the African American Church Today? We must first begin to look at who we are as a Black people living in America. We are a blend of many races, cultures and nations. Not only are we the product of racial blending that was forced upon us beginning in slavery, we are also a race of people who have now journeyed beyond our skin tone to find relationships with many other races of people.

As many races as there are in the world, perhaps a Black man or woman have procreated with, thus blending, stretching and enhancing our racial makeup. So, the Black race is truly a cornucopia of racial and ethnic diversity. With that said, we have to look at how far we've expanded in our ecclesiastical journeys. In slavery times Blacks were primarily Baptist or Methodist. As we converse with other Black people today, we often find out that they worship in the Islamic faith, Catholic faith, Episcopal faith, Seventh Day Adventist faith, Presbyterian faith, Jehovah Witness faith, A Holiness Church faith and so many others. You cannot take it for granted today that just because you're Black you must be of one or two denominational faiths. Black people have opened their hearts and minds to enjoy many rewarding new experiences with other peoples.

"Now in this that I declare unto you I praise you not, that ye come together not for the better, but for the worse. For first of all, when ye come together in the church, I hear that there be divisions among you;

and I partly believe it. For there must be also heresies among you, that they which are approved may be made manifest among you"
1 Corinthians 11:17-19.

The Black church was and is still a house where God's glory is revealed, worshipped, praised, magnified, reverenced and adored. The Black church has and continues to do great and wonderful works for the Lord and His people. I personally take my hat off to the many great Black Pastors and leaders of the church. I have personally witnessed the sweat, blood and tears' flowing from the brow of God's anointed men and women. The timeless dedication and service to God's flocks should not be minimized or underappreciated. *"Let the elders that rule well be counted worthy of double honour, especially they who labour in the word and doctrine,"* 1 Timothy 5:17. *How beautiful are the feet of them that preach the gospel of peace, and bring glad tidings of good things!"* Romans 10:15.

Worthy of high honors are many of our church leaders, but they are still men and woman clothed by the flesh, and therefore come under subjection of the flesh and not the Spirit. We are still flesh and blood; therefore we battle daily with the flesh we wear. With this said, many of our church leaders are dismissing many of the needed ministries of the church. Let's look at a theological definition of the position of Pastor. The Pastor is the feeder, protector, and guide, or shepherd, of a flock of God's people in New Testament Times. This term implies the nourishing of and caring for God's people. The Pastor is to emulate Jesus as the Good Shepherd (Nelson's New Illustrated Bible Dictionary).

Sin is abiding in our church leaders and congregations, as media exposes the sins and shortcomings of some of our leaders. **Sins of sexual immorality, lying, the greed of money, abuse of God's authority over His sheep, anger, mistrust, insecurity and control.** The identified sins of the flesh are seemingly weighing heavy in our churches today as seemingly more and more people are becoming disenfranchised with the administration of the church. Some Pastors and church leaders are taking advantage of the subjective authority giving to them by God's people and God Himself. Some Pastors are only **preaching how to get rich off God, while others have turned church membership into members only social clubs.**

Let's not forget that the Pastor represents a spiritual gift of the Holy Spirit, so why should some of these gifts get exercised while other gifts go undeveloped, underutilized and dismissed by some church leaders that have decided, not God; that the church is not in need of the gifts given by the Holy Spirit for our edification. Moreover, how is an associate minister ever going to utilize his/her gifts, training and calling, if their Pastor's view them as a potential threat to their ministry? After all, who decides what Spiritual Gifts get utilized by the church and what gifts get ostracized. I thought Scriptures said that all gifts were given by the Holy Spirit and is to be used for the edification of the body of Christ. If this is indeed the truth and it is; then why is the modern church so led by human thought instead of spiritual will?

Have many people, including myself misinterpreted the meaning of Scriptures as it relates to the awarding of Spiritual Gifts. Or perhaps I and others have not misinterpreted Scriptures as it relates to Spiritual Gifts. God's Holy Spirit has indwelled each believer with at least one Spiritual Gift. This (these) gifts are to be used for the building up and perfecting of the church of Jesus Christ. Paul wrote to the church at Ephesus 4:11-12 *"And he gave some, apostles and some, prophets; and some evangelists; and some, pastors and teachers; for the perfecting of the saints, for the work of the ministry, for the edifying of the body of Christ."* Let's look at what Scriptures identify as Spiritual Gifts according to Bruce Bugbee's book entitled "Discover your Spiritual Gifts the Network Way."

Administration	Apostleship	Knowledge
Craftsmanship	Creative Communication	
Leadership	Discernment	Encouragement
Mercy	Evangelism	Faith
Miracles	Giving	Healing

Prophecy	Helps	Hospitality
Intercession	Interpretation	Teaching
Shepherding	Tongues	

Of the gifts of the Holy Spirit, as Paul wrote, these gifts are to be used for the perfecting of every believer. Let's take a closer study of the term perfect as defined in Nelson's New Illustrated Bible Dictionary: "Perfecting- without flaw or error; a state of completion or fulfillment. God's perfection means that He is complete in Himself. He lacks nothing; He has no flaws. He is perfect in all the characteristics of His nature. He is the basis of standard by which all perfection is to be measured. By contrast, human perfection is relative and dependent on God for its existence. As applied to a person's moral state in this life, perfection may refer either to a relatively blameless lifestyle or to a person's maturity as a believer."

By definition, God gave believers spiritual gifts so the body of Christ (we the church) does not lack anything, but instead is complete within itself, as we continue to be perfected in our Christian walk. God provided believers with all the individual characteristics of His nature for the continual perfecting of each believer. With that said, each believer must seek the Christian church for spiritual perfection in the flesh. However, the issue is, how can a believer go to his/her local church seeking a perfecting ministry of, for example, Christian counseling, when the leader of that particular congregation does not believe, nor support Christian counseling. Instead, practices referring congregants to the secular counselor who does not believe in God, or uses the power of Scripture in his/her approach to counseling. How is that believer being perfected when he/she is being referred to the world and the world's solution to the perfecting of the Christian?

Christian counseling, using the above example utilizes the primary gift of encouragement; in addition, knowledge, wisdom, teaching, and shepherding may be utilized as minor gifts. But again, how can this gift be used if the gift or the believer with the gift is rejected. In a case like this one, not only is the gift of encouragement not being utilized for the perfecting of the body of Christ, in addition, God's Holy Spirit is being rejected, as it is God's Holy Spirit that awards each believer with spiritual gifts. So the problem being stated here is deserving of the question: are the leaders of today's Black church rejecting God? Statistics tell us that Christianity in America is in the decline. Moreover, there are more and more believers holding on to their faith in God through Christ, but their not believing in the physical church as a holy place of worship. Have the church lost its credibility? Why are so many associate ministers starting their own flocks? Could it be that many of them could not answer their call to ministry in the Black mainstream church? In this same way it is my belief, which many others share, is the Black church and the Christian church in American preauthorizing who is entitled to membership in the church?

Let me encourage the leaders of all Christian churches to maintain the integrity of the Holy Scriptures. It is not our responsibility or duty as church leaders to dismiss or omit the teachings and instructions of Scriptures unto the body of Christ, Instead, it is our responsibility and duty to spiritually grow each believer's gifts, so that the body of Christ will not be found wanting for anything. In this way, believers will not become disenfranchised with the church because a leader decided out of his/her own sin that God's commandments do not apply to the shepherd, only to the sheep. Moreover, it is the responsibility of the Pastor to grow each believer's spiritual gift (s) that's in their flock. One of the worst feelings for anyone is the feelings that accompany rejection; but how much greater are these negative and painful feelings, when one is rejected by the church! Many will view this type of rejection as rejection directly from God.

In addition, Pastors, please understand that God did not give us all the spiritual gifts, nor did He give us all the knowledge and wisdom of heaven. I do not say this to be sarcastic or demeaning, but to encourage all church leaders to use the wisdom of God and the nurturing of God to nurture His flock. Every believer need to feel apart of something. Each believer need to know that their labor is not in vain, but will be rewarded by God. More so, church leaders, please don't let anger, pride, control, and self-sufficiency become the cornerstone of your ministry. If you decide to lead God's people by the roots of human sinfulness, then I fear the success of your ministry. Remember, humility over pride and control. Pride will cause believers to leave your flock and find another, but humility, honesty and genuineness keeps salvation within all's reach.

Sins of the Flesh

My fellow brothers in the ministry, I'm reminded what Paul said to the Colossians: *"Put to death, therefore, whatever belongs to your earthly nature: sexual immortality, impurity, lust, evil desires and greed, which is idolatry. Because of these, the wrath of God is coming. You used to walk in these ways, in the life you once lived."* Colossians 3:5-7.

My brothers, the flesh of a beautiful woman is still a snare unto the depths of depression, anger, resentment, grief, confusion, disappointment and failure for **ALL** heterosexual brothers.

"Hear me, you who know what is right, you people who have my law in your hearts: Do not fear the reproach of men or be terrified by their insults" Isaiah 51:7.

My brothers, we all know the desires we fight with involving sexual attraction towards the sisters. Married, engaged, divorced, separated or single; we all find ourselves engaged in sexual immorality in our thoughts. The Bible teaches us that we've already sinned. However, it is much worse if we manifest our hearts desires into the natural. In other words, don't do what you're thinking. Many of today's Black Pastors are falling to temptation. The Apostle Paul spoke to the subject of our thoughts in Romans 12:2, Paul states: *"Do not conform any longer to the pattern of this world, but be transformed by the renewing of your mind. Then you will be able to test and approve what God's will is-his good, pleasing and perfect will."* Again, Paul speaks about this subject in 2 Corinthians 10:4, 5: He states *"The weapons we fight with are not the weapons of the world. On the contrary, they have divine power to demolish strongholds. We demolish arguments and every pretension that sets itself up against the knowledge of God, and we take captive every thought to make it obedient to Christ."*

Brothers, Paul is saying to us that we must take control of our desires. Our desires come from within us; our hearts. Therefore, we must not allow the flesh of a woman to enslave and entrap us into the snares of foolishness. We clearly understand through the teachings of King Solomon in wisdom literature of the Bible that foolishness is equal to death, but wisdom is greater than all the material wealth of the world. Solomon says fools despise wisdom. Paul teaches us that the sin we do comes from our desires within us therefore, we must kill every thought that sets itself up against the righteousness of God. We must kill it! If we don't, Pastor's will continue misrepresenting holiness and living by a higher calling as members of the congregation will continue to think that living by the flesh is acceptable for a Christian. The church cannot continue living in the church and doing what the world does, and think that this behavior is OK with God. These types of examples we present to the world may be the reason why many people claim that theirs no difference in church people and non-believers. We, the body of Christ live in the world, but we're not of the world. We must decide if we're going to be true to God, after all, God knows our hearts and we cannot hide them from Him.

The Gospel of Matthew 15:19 states: *"For out of the heart proceed evil thoughts, murders, adulteries, fornications, thefts, false witness, blasphemies."*
Colossians 3:5-7 *"Put to death, therefore, whatever belongs to your earthly nature: sexual immorality, impurity, lust, evil desires and greed, which is idolatry. Because of these, the wrath of God is coming. You used to walk in these ways, in the life you once lived."*

Scriptures clearly state the reasons why we do those things that are pleasing to us and not Him. But God has saved us from those things which were leading us to death.

1 Corinthians 6:11 *"And that is what some of you were. But you were washed, you were sanctified, you were justified in the name of the Lord Jesus Christ and by the Spirit of our God."*

Paul reminds us that we were once captivated by the sins of our flesh, but now that we've accepted Christ, God's Spirit works with us to continually wash and sanctify us. Paul tells us in 2 Corinthians 7:1 *"Having therefore these promises, dearly beloved, let us cleanse ourselves from all filthiness of the flesh and spirit, perfecting holiness in the fear of God."* Paul states in Romans 6:18 *"Being then made free from sin, ye became the servants of righteousness, I speak after the manner of men because of the infirmity of your flesh: for as ye have yielded your members servants to uncleanness and to iniquity unto iniquity; even so now yield your members servants to righteousness unto holiness.*

Remember my brothers; there is no temptation uncommon to man that God has not made a way of escape. My Black brothers, God has called each of us to live holy as He is holy, therefore, we must not yield to our temptations. The Apostle Paul reminds us that the "Wages of sin is death, but the gift of God is eternal life," Romans 6:23.
Church leaders must hold to the teachings of Scriptures. Pastors, if we're struggling with sinful sexual desires, we need to first speak to God about it, then to a Christian mental health counselor who has been called and prepared through God's instructional institutions to provide wise counsel to **all** members of the body of Christ. There is no shame in the truth. However, a lie creates the illusion of truth, and the illusion of truth keeps us held in bondage. Counselors need to be counseled, Pastors need to be Pastored, and Believers need to be in fellowship with other believers. Because we have all sinned and fallen short of the glory of God. Therefore, it is our duty to face the truths of our sins and desires, and address them Scripturally. Confess our sins one to another…

To my sister's reading this book, if your skirt clearly shows off the pimple near your anus, your skirt is probably too tight and up too high. My sister's, if when you sit down your skirt rises up and becomes a halter top; your skirt is probably too short. Sister's, if your blouse fails to cover your twins; your blouse is probably a napkin and not a blouse at all. Sister's, you must come under the conviction of the Holy Spirit and present your bodies as a living sacrifice, holy and acceptable unto the Lord. Let me share with you this brief true story. One day after church services, I stopped by a drug store to get the Sunday newspaper.

Now there had to be about four or five men in the line with me waiting for the lady in front of me to be served by the cashier. I was fully garbed with a suit and clergy shirt. The man directly behind me was a priest, and thus he was fully garbed in a suite and a clergy shirt. When it was my turn to pay for my newspaper, I looked up from a position of glancing down at the newspaper to notice a young black sister (probably 17-20 years of age). My eyes were immediately opened wide as this beautiful young Black lady had a half something on (some kind of one piece stretchable fabric) that exposed all of her stomach and supported her perky, full, half exposed breast.

When I attempted to shift my eyes from her breast, my eyes caught hold of her pants, or lack of pants. Now, I know that ladies like to wear clothing to expose their cleavage, but something should be left to the imagination. This young lady had a pair of pants that were cut in a V shape at her groin, exposing pubic hairs. I felt so shame to look at her again, that I turned my head away from her and looked back at the other men and the priest who shared my feelings of shame, the men all looked back at me and each other, and then turned their eyes away. When I left the store, I wondered why the store manager would allow this young lady to dress that way. When I thought just how inappropriately dressed she was, my sinful nature kicked in and I thought to myself, WOW! I struggled with the image of this young lady's body for the rest of the day. I had to go to war over the images and thoughts of my sinful nature, and so I used this Scripture to help me fight against my thoughts: *"We take captive every thought to make it obedient to Christ"* 2 Corinthians 10:5.

Paul wrote to the church in Rome 7:20-21: *"Now if I do that I would not, it is no more I that do it, but sin that dwelleth in me. I find then a law, that, when I would do good, evil is present with me."* This is what I felt as I drove home from Sunday worship services after stopping by the drug store to buy a newspaper with clergy attire on. What if I had dwelled on my memory and thoughts of this young lady's body? What testimony would I give to others about resisting temptation and fleeing from sin? What would become of another Black Baptist preacher? I can tell you that I fought the images in my mind and the true desire to dwell on the possibilities. I did not want to succumb to the desires of my flesh and thus have to experience the fall-out from giving in to my desires. It was truly God's Spirit that held my emotions in check, along with my desire to please God and not the flesh.

I told you this story for the purpose of sharing some truths with some of the sister's. Some of you sister's must share in the responsibility for the backsliding of men trying to live for the Lord. I have heard some women say that I don't want to dress like a Quaker, I'm only keeping up with fashion, and because I dress like this don't mean that I'm responsible for what others do. We'll sisters, if any of you have stated anything like this, I'm disagreeing with you. You are responsible for how you present yourself before others. What you wear can be the catalyst for some Brother trying to get his life together, by sliding back to the ways of the world and giving into temptation. Would you offer a recovering alcoholic a drink? I hope not. Would you feed a newborn baby BBQ ribs? In the same manner, you should present all of who you are as a living sacrifice, holy and acceptable unto the Lord. Teasing men with your flesh, and unholy gestures is not acceptable unto the Lord.

How many men and women today are battling sexual addictions? Yet, society at large, offers every piece of temptation to the sexual addict. It's OK not to tempt a recovering alcoholic, or drug addict, but it's OK to constantly bombard the sexual addict or the person struggling with sexual fantasies with real live images of young, hot, sexy, firm ladies who can care less about how they present themselves and what kind of messages they send. No woman wants a man to disrespect them by them calling her a hoe. Well, in likewise manner, a respectful woman of any age would never shame and degrade herself by what she wears. She has too much respect for herself to present herself as anything else but a child of God. So if you dress like a hoe, maybe, just maybe … After all, it's only fashion, right!

And another thing, the language from some of you sister's is atrocious. It's a shame to walk down the street and hear young and not so young sisters saying: @#*$&*&^%$#@@$%^*&^#* (I don't have the heart to say it). I would like to know why Black children all the way from elementary school to grown folks, male and female, think it's OK to sound like you just got off the submarine after being out to sea for the last six months. Why do our people feel as if it's cool to talk like a fool! Our mothers and grandmothers never spoke the words we now hear as a part of our daily language. It's not acceptable to hear female teenagers swearing like they have a penis in their pants. Moreover, it's not OK for our teenage males either. How disgusting it is to see many of our youths smoking freaked cigars, girls and boys, with sagging pants. If it wasn't for a pronounced set of breast, I would not be able to tell the girls from the boys. I don't know about you, but I want a female to be a female. I don't want an intimate relationship with a woman who acts like a man. Quite frankly I don't need the competition; it's hard enough just to be a man, let alone a Black man.

My young and not so young Black sisters, please change your ways. It does not mean that you're weird if you decide to live a life that's pleasing to God. After all, we have enough jail cells filled with us and not enough college desks occupied by us. There is a better way; there are better choices you can make. It's time young people for you to own up to your responsibilities and renew your mind, renew your hearts, and renew or begin a right relationship with Jesus Christ. For me and many others like me; it's weird not to walk with Christ. You are special people to the Black family and especially to God. You have to decide to make a change in your lives. You must choose to present yourself with dignity, honesty, respect, and class. It's time to stop opening your legs and begin to open your minds. It's time to shut your mouths of the filth that comes out from them and begin to listen to the truth. It's time to put on morality and put off worldliness. It's time to get hip to the ways of loser boys and shut them down. It's time to leave the clubs, marijuana and crack cocaine and begin to get filled up on Jesus. I guarantee you, if you try Jesus, you'll never need to light up another blunt.

    My young Brothers, why do we abuse our young sisters? Just because you witnessed mom being abused don't mean that you have to repeat the same stupid actions. God did not make the female for us to enslave, bully and control. There is more to females than their orifices. Females are not on earth just so Brothers and some sisters can get their swerve on and then get tossed out with last week's turnip greens. Many of our sisters are your baby's mama. Yes, it's no headline news report that many of our female teenagers are becoming pregnant at ages 13, 14, 15 up to age 20, at alarming rates (refer to chapter seven). And just as many of your daddy's impregnated your mama's and left her; many of you young Brothers have turned right around and done the same thing to someone else. Brothers, our young sisters are not your bitches and hoes. Why is it that when you're engaged in conversation with one of your friends, many times you refer to a sister as "That bitch" or "That hoe?" If that's what you think of them, then you should stop for a minute and realize that if that's the term you give to identify a female, and then you must consider your own mother as perhaps a "Bitch" or "Hoe?" I truly don't believe either of them are any name other than a child of God.

    I contend that all Black males and females are precious in the site of God. God did say after he made all things that was made; *"God saw every thing that he had made, and, Behold, it was very good."* Genesis 1:31. If the creator was well pleased by our creation, why is it that seemingly, we are displeased with ourselves and each other? Why is it that we try to degrade and persecute all things good? Perhaps we should begin to reconcile our personal sins with God first and let His Holy Spirit begin a good work in us and then, we can begin to affect positive change in others, our families, our communities, our government and our world. But we must start with our self. A mirror will only reflect back what is presented in it. So if you don't like what you see, change it! If you're OK with what you see, then keep living and don't die.

Just in case you thought I got off my subject of the Black church, I did not. You may not witness young people openly swearing in church; (may be not until they get outside), but the worldly descriptions of reality I just presented to you, is coming from the church. How many couples attending your church are married? How many teenagers in your congregation have been or are currently pregnant? How many members of the congregation light up a cigarette as soon as they reach the outer doors of the church? How many women in the church have suffered from physical or sexual abuse? How many members of your congregation is still going to bars and clubs and drinking? So you thought I was referring to someone else, and not the body of Christ, called the Christian church?

The church is made up of former members of the world. The church is a microcosm of the world; what's in the world is bound to be in the church. Did I forget to ask you how many down low brothers and sisters are sitting in the pews of the Christian church? Or maybe serving as a church officer? I'm not hating, only stipulating the truth. The church is neither hot nor cold; but it's lukewarm. There are many Black folks sitting in church pews and standing behind the pulpit playing church, and not living church. I'm not judging, only stating my observations. We each must work out our own soul's salvation. There is no better place for a sinner to be than in the church. In the church God's Spirit can speak and change hearts, minds, situations and circumstances. The church of Jesus Christ is where the blood of Christ drips and what His blood drips upon, there is victory!

Insecurity in the Church

"And the Lord added to the church daily such as should be saved"
Acts 2:47

Many of our church leaders have disallowed various gifts of the Spirit to be utilized in many of our local church assemblies, and congregants to serve in various ministries because some of our leaders are insecure in their positions as leader. The fact is, some of our Pastor's and church leaders may have been called by God, but they failed to continue to perfect their skills. If I know I don't have very good leadership skills, perhaps I should improve my skills through continuing education. Moreover, maybe I should assign certain duties and skills that I don't possess to someone who does. Because I delegate duties to others does not mean that I am an inefficient leader of God's church. It only means that God did not give me all knowledge, wisdom and spiritual gifts. Administrative leadership in many of our church hierarchy's may look something like this:

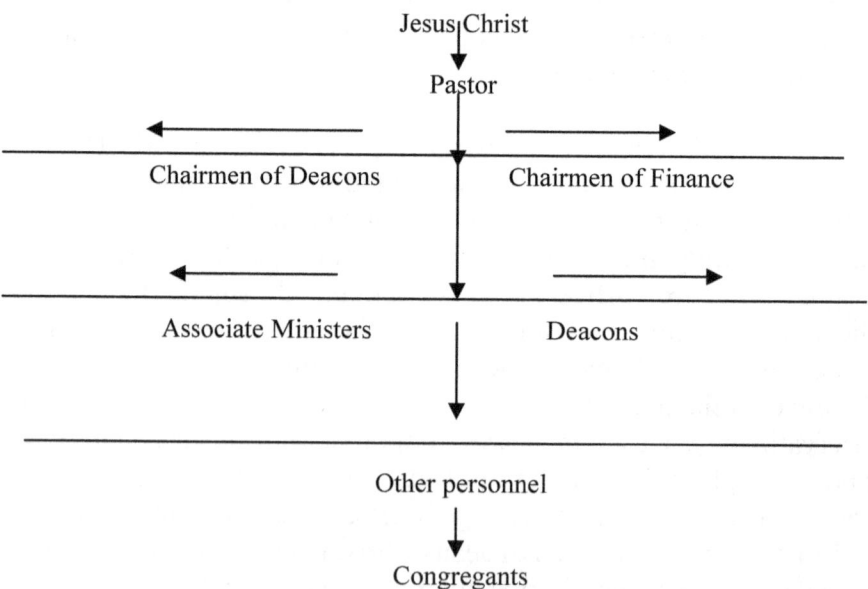

In this graph the Pastor is the chief administrator of the church. The only person above him is Jesus Christ. This chart represents one of many hierarchal structures in the church today. However, I contend with the leaders of the Christian church to operate according to this chart:

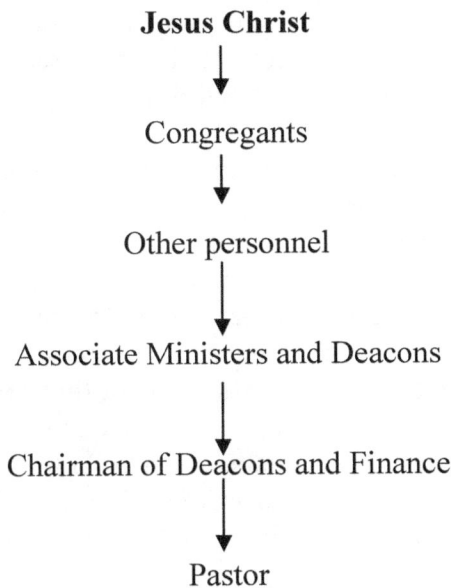

In this hierarchal chart, we see that Jesus Christ is still on the throne over His church. But the primary difference here is that the Pastor, who must immolate the life and ministry of Christ, has dropped to the bottom of the structure. Thereby the pastor has now become the chief servant of the people. If you were to study what the term minister or deacon means in the Greek, you'll find the term 'diakonos', when interpreted means servant. Jesus said to the people of His time, I did not come to be served but to serve. Jesus is saying the same thing to us today, Pastors we don't have to worry about position insecurities, God has sent us all we need, if we only grab hold of His blessings and do our parts to grow and nourish the blessings God has already given to the church., remember God said He would add to the church such as should be saved.

Think about this: why would God bless a ministry with greater numbers when some of us have not been faithful over the few He's already given us to shepherd. When we're faithful over the few, God promises to bless us with many, but we must remember that the higher your position is in the church, the greater is your service (humility). The true Christian leader does not lead by being served, but by serving, in heart, mind, spirit, gifts, talents, time and from his soul. Therefore many of the leaders of the church today must rethink their service to the Lord. Pride has interfered with humility.

Control is another factor in the dysfunctional leadership of many of today's churches. When you think of the term control, we understand that control means to regulate or direct, to exercise authority over. However, we must also look at another meaning of this word. Control also means to restrain, which means to hold back, suppress and to limit or restrict. Scriptures record that Jesus exercised this type of control when the crowds became overwhelming or threatening to him. This type of servant leadership is rarely exercised in today's church. There are times where church leadership must yield human thought and desire for spiritual direction. In other words, when church leadership is faced with a situation, instead of relying on human intelligence, which is often clouded and shrouded by dysfunctional, selfish and sinful thought patterns, church leadership must search the Scriptures for answers and spiritual direction.

Relying on Scriptures for spiritual direction involves humility, wisdom and subjugation to yield human direction for spiritual truth and direction. Effective church leadership involves knowing when to push an issue and when to allow others freedom to follow wise counsel. For example: Some churches have verbal and physical disagreements between Deacons and the Pastor. The question of control for church leaders is to know how to yield to righteousness instead of maintaining an ineffective and sinful position of self-righteousness that's not supported by Scriptures. Disagreements in leadership views must always be decided on through biblical solutions, principles and presuppositions. Leaders must access situations carefully and ask questions of themselves and others to ascertain proper direction. Pastors and other church leaders must never allow sinful human emotions to cloud spiritual issues of the church. Disagreements will come, but arguments are sinful as they come from one's heart which is the center of sin. Too many times today, the church's administration resembles more like the worlds, when the church is called to a higher standard of administrative relationships.

The Fight for Souls; or Money?

An unfortunate practice today in church leadership involves the failure to collaborate. If the church is one body with many branches, then the question must be asked of the church; how are the branches receiving its nourishment? We know that without the proper nutrients life cannot exist. So why isn't the Lord's churches pooling together their resources to provide for greater effectiveness and increased ministries within the church. We all know that not every church congregation is equipped with the financial resources and spiritual resources to effectively minister in a host of needed ministries. Some of our church leaders have decided that they are not going to fellowship with other churches in any context because some of their members might see or experience something greater than they have provided, and thus they may want to leave their flock for another. Some Pastor's may view each member of the congregation as representing dollars to the financial life of that church.

We also have heard that Christianity is declining in the United States, while it's booming in other nations. Why is there not more unsaved Black folks coming to Jesus? Why do we hear people state that they believe in God and in His Son, but don't believe in the church? Millions of Americans and Black folks have become disenfranchised with the church community. Why do so many brothers view the Black church with disgust? I don't propose to have all these answers; there are more questions than answers; but I do propose to have an opinion.

First, many Brothers view the church as places for the "Preacher" to gain riches while the members financially suffers. Well, the fact is Satan is busy everywhere. There are some Pastors that have been on the news that were entangled in disputes over the church's finance. The reports suggest that the Pastor has misled the flock and has suggestively mishandled the church's finances to his/her personal gain. However, I don't believe this is the norm. A few sinful preachers should not suggest total corruption in the church. In that same vain, I believe Brothers should not only view what the preacher has gained such as a Cadillac car, fine suits, bling bling, and other stuff. The vast majority of our leaders who may have these material things are worthy to have them.

Perhaps, some Brothers view what the preacher has and correlate that to "Pimping the flock," but I don't believe this is the norm either. A few of our mega churches can afford nicer things, including the preacher, and he/she is worthy of his labor. However, the vast majority of our Black churches cannot afford to pay a salary deserving of the Pastor. Thus, many Pastors have to be bi-vocational. Many Pastors must work outside the church to earn a living and meet his/her financial goals, but the church still demands all of his time, talents, skills and gifts. In this case the salary of the preacher does not parallel the church's expectations of his/her performance and neither will you hear this in the media. The media only sensationalize on negative events, rarely, if any, will they report on positive happenings.

I understand that image plays a very important role in the life of the Black Christian church. The church's leaders are always scrutinized by the public; therefore they must always present themselves appropriately. Now, think about this Brother's; if you worked a job all day long, day and night, you were always on call and never got overtime pay. Don't you feel like you deserve some of the nicer things life has to offer; after all, you earned the right to have some nice things. It's no different when you look at a Pastor. He or she may like to wear nice clothes and drive a nice car as well. Not many Preachers actually have the financial opportunities to live a life of financial comfort, despite what you may see on television.

Still, some of our church leaders equate church membership with financial stability or lack of it. Because of this view, our churches do not come together to perform ministry. Many of our smaller congregations are barely holding on to their existence because of this. As a Christian counselor I am personally appalled by the lack of ministry vision. There are many church leaders who do not see the various needs of the community or the congregation. There is a wide spread need to provide ministries to those suffering with various addictions, parenting skills, pre-marital and marital ministries, financial ministries, mental health ministries, senior ministries, youth ministries and others.

I understand that some of our congregations are too small to support these ministries; this is where collaboration comes in to assist, however, many of our congregations can support these ministries, but church leadership doesn't see the need for them. Open your eyes and see what's around you. Refer to the statistics I provide you in chapter seven and come up with the same conclusion. This is not an issue of finance in these churches, as it is an issue of leadership insecurity that suggests to these leaders that they should be able to do all things well, and if they can't; if another minister is better at it, congregants may view the associate favorably over the Pastor, thus the Pastor uses control to deny others the use of their gifts and skills, thus the church and the community suffers.

Church leaders, Jesus said *"Preach the kingdom of heaven is at hand."* Whatever we preach (as long as it's in the Bible), the point of every sermon must be Jesus and Him crucified; that is the good news; the gospel message of Christ. Salvation is at hand; Jesus said call upon Him while He may be found. I and others, have some concerns about prosperity only preaching. I do not find where Scriptures supports getting rich off God as the gospel message of salvation. There is nothing wrong with preaching all of Scriptures, but if you're only preaching one message; you, as the preacher need to check your spirit with God's Holy Spirit. Jesus said preach salvation. I personally preach a number of help me topics as it relates to reconciliation and suffering of Christ's body, but the hook to every message is Jesus and Him crucified. My father in the ministry made sure all of his Timothy's understood this foundational truth about expository preaching. If we don't preach Christ, we've lost the meaning and purpose of the gospel; Jesus Saves!

Preaching vs. Administration

Let me be clear, preaching and church administration are two sides of a coin. A good preacher is not necessarily a good church administrator; and a good church administrator is not necessarily a good preacher. Why is this important? One of the dysfunctions of today's church is the fact that there are lots of good vibrant preachers that the Word of God is truly like fire shut up in their bones. However, when it comes to church administration or Pastoring, a good preacher may not possess good leadership and administrative skills. I have known great preachers, but not necessarily great administrators. What is a Pastor? A Pastor in the New Testament church is a feeder, protector, and guide, or shepherd, of a flock of God's people. Jesus in Ephesians 4:11, as Paul wrote, *"Jesus gave some to be apostles, some prophets, some evangelists, and some pastors and teachers."* A Pastor is both a spiritual gift and a position within the church.

Let me take this point a little further. A Pastor can be a truly anointed person of God that has been endowed with the spiritual gift of Pastoring or leading God's people. Also, a Pastor is a position within the church that the church uses to officially call a Pastor into this position. A church called Pastor may or may not have been endowed with the spiritual gift of Pastoring. This is why I made the earlier statement that a good preacher is not necessarily a good Pastor. The Pastor is the Chief Executive Officer of the church. However, if the Pastor does not have the necessary skills to be an effective leader and administrator over the affairs of the church, the results will be conflict, foolish pride, insecurity, control, mistrust and misguidance. I'm sure that as you read these words, some of what I'm saying is playing like a song in some of your minds, because you are now picturing what I'm saying. This is a problem within the church; a dysfunction within the church that leads to problems within the church.

Search committees must be very careful not to select a potential Pastor because he or she has a good reputation as a preacher. Preaching by far is just one of the many responsibilities a Pastor has. Therefore, preaching is not the only skill a search committee must look for. How about a candidates knowledge and experience with finance, policy and procedures, building management, capital asset management, personnel management, event planning, budgeting, and ministry training. What are the candidate's special gifts? Does the candidate have formal seminary training and if so in what discipline? When a search committee considers a Pastoral candidate, please consider some of these points and then some. Not every Pastor standing behind the pulpit was called by God to be there! The church called them, and when this happens, the church must deal with any aftermath of a bad decision. Please note: I'm not suggesting or inferring that every Pastor is a problem, that's not what I'm saying. I'm simply describing the difference in a church called Pastor and a truly anointed Pastor.

The church must provide all of its officers and ministry leader's ongoing theological training. An anointed Pastor is not a Pastor that knows it all, but a Pastor that understands why God gave the church spiritual gifts. A truly anointed pastor is an administrator over the official affairs of the church, not a control freak. An anointed Pastor is one that grows and develops the people of the church towards spiritual perfection and human excellence; while fully understanding that he/she will never accomplish neither task successfully. A truly anointed Pastor understands that he/she has many human weaknesses and works toward his/her own perfection, in other words this person is real. This person is truly a leader of people and has a heart for where people are at in their lives. If you're a good preacher and an anointed administrator, then you've met the qualifications of the position and gift of Pastor. If not, you can still be a good Pastor, but understand that you must be engaged in ongoing theological and administrative training.

Choose ye this day

Brothers, despite the fact that you may believe the old cliché "One apple spoils the whole bunch," this is not the case in the church. Do you stop supporting a member of your family because they have a problem; I think not. Likewise, don't let your perceptions skew the facts. Many of you Brothers do not attend church because you are afraid what other dysfunctional Brothers will think of you. Other Brothers may not view a man in the church as being strong. Some Brothers believe that church is for females only, only gay men go to church. If you're one of these Brothers who are labeling us Brothers who do go to church falsely, let me say to you that the reason you don't believe in God through His only begotten Son, Jesus, is because your head in stuck in the mud of worldlyism.

You Brothers don't believe and won't support the church because Satan has a hold of your mind, your heart and your Spirit. Real men go to church. Perhaps the church is two-thirds females, because most females are smarter than most of us Brothers who don't attend church. Perhaps you Brothers who shun the believing Brothers are the ones that are adding to the continuously negative statistics that's placing Black folks at the top or near the top of most negative social indicators. Perhaps some of you Brothers are the ones stealing from us; murdering us; raping us; selling drugs to us; impregnating and leaving us; disrespecting us; dropping out of school and acting like a fool! Perhaps you're looking at the men who's attending church as weak men, but the truth is that no man is perfect *"We've all sinned and fallen short of the glory of God,"* but the Brothers who do attend church truly have better lives than you Brothers who reject Christ and His church, simply because we are kept by God and you're not.

Joshua wrote in 24:15 *"Choose you this day whom ye will serve."* The prophet Joshua asked the Israelites to make a choice what god they were going to serve. Were the Israelites going to continue to serve the false gods of drug addiction, baby making, stealing, murdering…or were they going to commit to Jehovah, the one true living God. We'll my Brothers, are you? The reason why so many Black families are dysfunctional is because the man who's supposed to be its holy covering is "Missing in action." Some of you Brothers can continue to make excuses for your behaviors, but the bottom line is that you have to decide who it is you'll serve. I'd rather be called a chicken eaten preacher any day, but know that my family has not suffered by my absence, than a renegade Brother in disrespect of human life. Moreover, when God called me for salvation, I eventually gave in and accepted his gift of salvation, in addition, He called me into ministry and I've attempted to serve Him in spirit and in truth. This is the reason why I am writing this book.

Brothers, you can't be an effective husband and father if you're locked behind bars for doing stupid stuff, like using and selling drugs, robbery and many other stupid crimes. If you're taking drugs because you can't stand the emotional pains of life; then I beg you to talk with a Christian counselor. There's hope and help available, if you want to commit to it. My young Brothers and Sisters, get your head out of your behind. You're not the only people suffering with the "Lack of's." It's time you face reality, whatsoever your sow; you'll reap. It's time for you to start being a positive member of the family you have and the society you live in. People are tired of wondering what young people are going to get themselves into next. If you sincerely want a life of crime, sex and stupidity, then keep doing what many of you are already doing. But if you want a way out; it starts with a commitment to follow Jesus. Jesus says, *"We can do all things but fail."* The world is one big opportunity waiting for you to reach out and grab it. It's yours for the taking; if you're properly prepared.

"It is God's will that all be saved." My Brothers and Sisters, the dysfunctional state of the church does not lye within bricks and mortar,

but within the body, spirit and soul of each human being. I'd rather join a dysfunctional church that is attempting to do the best it can for the Lord, than to serve Satan and the destruction of the family in America. None of us is perfect, but God is still asking us the question, *"Whom will you serve."* Pastors and church leaders you must live in spirit and in truth if you are to be effective in ministry. Realize your faults and shortcomings, after all, we all have them, and utilize every perfect gift that comes from above. My unbelieving Brothers, it's time to get out of the physical jail cell and the human jail cells of our minds and hearts and begin to understand that we are wanted and needed. There is a host of single mothers struggling to raise your bad and unruly children. These mothers need your help; these kids need their dads; the church needs your leadership and the world needs your skills and talents.

The Christian Church; Members Only Please

Romans 10:13 *"For whosoever shall call upon the name of the Lord shall be saved."*

Calling on all sinners, yes, you right there; the drunkard, the sexually immoral, the liars, the murderers, the thieves, the money changers, the rich, the poor, the Black, the White, who ever wants salvation can enter into the Church of Jesus Christ. Isn't this the way it's suppose to be? If you said yes, then why are many of today's Christian churches setting boundaries for the "Whosoever will." Why is the church of Jesus Christ refusing to accept gays to praise, worship, be changed and perfected by the Holy Spirit? Yet, we allow the sexual immoral, liars, thieves, murderers, molesters, abusers and many others worthy of death to enter into His gates with thanksgiving and into His courts with praise.

I used to work at a country club as a young chef's apprentice. I understand the country club mentality. The country club is a place of luxury, fine linens, imported furniture and fixtures. The foods served at a country club are of the finest ingredients, chef prepared by the best local, national and international chefs. If a member doesn't feel like cooking today, he or she can come to their club and dine, have drinks; play golf and sip on fine brandies and enjoy immeasurable amenities. But remember, not just anyone can enter into a country club. This type of social club is restricted to those persons who meet the rigid qualifications for acceptance. You may qualify for membership if you're able to prove that you meet the rigid financial guidelines. Some clubs only accept certain races of people, in addition to providing references from current members. These are just some of the many qualifications into restricted social clubs.

    Who of us has the authority and audacity to say who is worthy of the requirements of the country club of Jesus Christ? The Lord alone through His Spirit calls persons unto salvation? Mankind is the sinner and Jesus is the reconciler. Therefore, Jesus, the founder and sustainer of the church is the only one worthy to write the official rules of the church. I recall Jesus saying to this fact: *"Whosoever will, let them come."* Jesus came to claim those who are lost, those you are sick amongst us; those in need of salvation. Jesus came for the worst of the worst. Jesus came to set the captives free; those in the grave and those soon to be in the grave. Jesus came for those who were rejected and despised. Jesus came for the man wreaking of alcohol and wanting to come to the church for relief. Jesus came for the woman who just had survival sex (sex for money to meet a financial need) and is now in church praising God with tears in her eyes. Jesus came for the little boy who was molested by a grown man and is now living an alternate sexual lifestyle. This same little boy who wants to praise and worship God in the church, but has been rejected by the church; from the leaders to the worshippers, we have rejected the least of them. The Christian church is not a social country club that requires extensive qualifications for membership. Jesus says the only requirement for salvation is confession and belief (Romans 10:9).

Scriptures have something to say about salvation.

- Isaiah 53:6-We all, like sheep, have gone astray, each of us has turned to his own way; and the Lord has laid on him the iniquity of us all.
- Romans 5:12- Just as through the disobedience of the one man the many were made sinners, so also through the obedience of the one man the many will be made righteous.
- Romans 3:23, 24- For all have sinned and fall short of the glory of God, being justified freely by His grace through the redemption that is in Christ Jesus.
- John 1:12- To all who received him, to those who believed in his name, he gave the right to become children of God.
- 1 Peter 2:24- He himself bore our sins in his body on the tree, so that we might die to sins and live for righteousness; by his wounds you have been healed.

The fact is every believer was once an enemy of God. It does not matter what our sins were, we confessed our sins before the throne of grace and God forgave us and Jesus saved us. Paul said in Romans 10:9 *"That if you confess with your mouth the Lord Jesus and believe in your heart that God has raised Him from the dead, you will be saved."* Paul does not say all who have sinned will be forgiven if you repent and accept Christ, accept gays!

Paul speaks on the issue of past sins and grace in 1 Corinthians 6:11 *"And that is what some of you were. But you were washed, you were sanctified, you were justified in the name of the Lord Jesus Christ and by the Spirit of our God."* Paul is talking about all of our past sins that included sexual immoralities. God will look past those sins if we confess them. So why do some church leaders and congregations feel as if the once rejected now have the right to reject. No, let them come as they are, said Jesus. Let the gays and everyone else into the church as congregants. It is not our job, nor do we have the right to refuse a soul the opportunity to come home. God has taken it upon Himself to save, not us. None of us has the ability to personally save anyone.

Only the Word of God and the Holy Spirit can save. Our job, as my father in the ministry put it so well, he said, speaking of ministers: "We are in sales, not management." In other words, we preach, teach and live the Word of God as a living example of what God can do; God saves.

Could the body of Christ be responsible for gays forming their own church with their own doctrine, maybe? Why do the gay community who confesses belief in the triune God feels that it's necessary to start their own branch of Christ's church? Don't we have enough churches that are empty? Perhaps gays feel that since so much controversy has and is continuing about allowing them to worship in today's Christian church; they just decided the heck with us and so they started their own places of worship. Maybe, just maybe the leaders of today's Black churches should take some responsibility for not evangelizing all the lost! I hope the Christian community doesn't decide next to ostracize those Christians who are still committing infidelity and pre-marital sex. After all, if we did this, who would qualify to enter the church and who would qualify to preach to them?

So we the body of Christ dare not judge who can and who cannot enter into the house of prayer. There is no better place for sinners to come into other than the house of prayer. Let them come; all of them and sit under the power of the Holy Spirit and His Word. Under this type of power, when God says so, sinners and saints alike will be changed.

So that I am clear on this point. I'm for all people and all sins coming to the church for redemption and salvation. Remember, some of us sat in the church unsaved for a long time before we gave our life to Christ, so the church must be patient and let God move in a person's life. Moreover, let's be real; many of us shouting, and praising, singing and dancing, are still sinning. Many of us are shacking up and not married. Many of us are still drinking and smoking. Many of us are still lying and stealing. My point is better expressed through Scripture: *"Let he without sin cast the first stone."*

The church is a spiritual hospital where sinners come to find salvation and love. Remember Jesus said *"Come unto me all you who are weary and heavy laden and I will give you rest."* We the church must present ourselves in a humble, non-judgmental and accepting manner that says to the lost and hurting, we understand, let us introduce you to the Doctor, He's in and waiting for you, you never need an appointment. Let the church do away with the country club mentality; after all, if this was truly the case, none of us would ever meet the qualifications for membership.

Jesus said to Peter: *"Upon this rock I will build my church and the gates of hell shall not prevail against it."* No, Peter was not the rock; Jesus was pertaining to Peter's statement of faith, believing that Jesus is the son of God. My Brothers and Sisters, whether you want to believe it or not, time is winding up. Ecclesiastes states that there's a time for everything. I truly pray that now is the time for many of us to get our acts together. We must begin to ask ourselves the tough questions that make us think about our effectiveness in the body of Christ. We must think about our relationships with each other and God. Is God pleased with the time He's given us? Are we truly further ahead now, than years ago? Have we become a closer group of people with God, ourselves and one another? Have we individually and collectively improved society at large by demonstrating Christianity? Have our families been strengthened by our leadership? Have we taken advantage of the opportunities won by former slaves and of our patriarchs and civil rights leaders? Have we, the once rejected and enslaved, the people once considered non human and unable to learn. The once downgraded and ridiculed of society, have now become the mighty hand that inflicts the views once inflicted upon us?

We need more than preaching and praying

I have heard some Pastor's say that Sunday worship is the dessert of the week, not the main meal. If you think about this statement, the average Black church service lasts about 2-3 hours; some only lasts one and a half hours. For many of us this is the only time we attend church.

We do not attend many or any of the other ministry programs. So Sunday worship is our only fellowship and growth opportunity with other believers during the week. I once heard someone say to me "Black folks know their Bible." I will not debate that point here, however I will make an observation. If Black people truly know the Word, why is it that we don't live the Word?

There is no way any of us will receive the meat of God's Word without sharing in God's Word together. If Black folks know their Word, why are so many of us strung out on drugs? Why have so many Black men abandoned their parental responsibilities, if we know our Word? Why are so many Black teenagers experimenting with homosexual practices? I hear Scriptures speaking to this point, *"Do not merely listen to the word, and so deceive yourselves. Do what it says,"* James 1:22. How are we to understand how we are to apply God's Word to our lives? This to me is the meat of ministry. The Black Christian church must begin to do more than preaching and praying only on Sunday mornings.

Our people are dying and going to hell because of a lack of knowledge. The church must teach believers how to live holy lives. This is the purpose of the Holy Spirit giving believers spiritual gifts, and the church must stop rejecting them. Rejecting spiritual gifts to me is the same as rejecting the Holy Spirit. If the church began to educate its members on holy living, perhaps we would be in a better situation than we are in today. If and when a church does offer various ministries that meet the needs of issues in the congregation and community, members will have to put down the remote control and come to church. All members of the body of Christ must take more initiative to educate and participate in educational ministries that seek to train and prepare Christians for living in a fallen world.

Have you my Brother been the best husband, father, uncle, friend, and person you can be? If not, why not? What's stopping you from changing your wrongs and living the rights? Pastors and church leaders, have we been as effective, loving, caring, unified and humble to all who wish to enter into the church? Do we truly represent the glory of the Lord in our lives? The question must be asked of us: when are we going to return to God and serve Him in spirit and in truth? What gives us the right to say who can enter into the house of prayer? What right do we have to deny others an opportunity to seek liberty and freedom? What right do we have to judge others by our standards?

Who gave us permission to pass judgment over the least of them? What happened to *"love never fails?"* Is the Black Christian church loving everyone and meeting people at their needs? I think not! So, until we learn to look at all people with the eyes of Christ and a heart of love and reconciliation, we must first *"Seek the kingdom of God and His righteousness."* The church has many dysfunctions created through the sinfulness of man. Let's begin to shed the flesh of sinfulness and replace it with the love of Christ. Then we can all say that *"Love never fails."*

What is the African-American Church? We are the African-American church, in all of our diversities, strengths, weaknesses, challenges, attributes, faith and sins. We fellowship in a church house, but remember that we are the church, not the building. We are God's chosen people' chosen to love, obey and serve Him. Unfortunately, we are a blessed people who have seemingly lost our way.

Chapter Three
Addictions

Addictions

The Diagnostic Statistical Manual for Mental Disorder-4 records substance abuse as:
"The essential feature of Substance Abuse is a maladaptive pattern of substance use manifested by recurrent and significant adverse consequences related to the repeated use of substances."

The Drug and Alcohol Services Information System (DASIS) reported the following for year 2002.

Smoked Cocaine vs. Non-Smoked Cocaine Admissions for 2002:

In 2002, 13 percent of the 1.9 million admissions for treatment reported primary cocaine abuse. Of these admissions, 73 percent reported smoking as the usual route of administration and 27 percent reported other routes. Among the non-smoked cocaine admissions, 72 percent reported inhalation as the usual route of administration, 14 percent reported injection, 10 percent reported taking cocaine orally, and the remaining 4 percent reported other routes. Smoked cocaine admissions were more likely to report daily use prior to admission compared to non-smoked cocaine admissions (42 vs. 29 percent). Among smoked cocaine admissions, 57 percent were Black, 34 percent were White, and 7 percent were Hispanic. Both smoked and non-smoked cocaine admissions had similar (25 percent) reporting use of cocaine one to six times in the past week.

Roughly 108,000 Blacks reported in treatment facilities for smoking crack cocaine in 2002. Blacks represented the largest percentage of admissions to enter into a treatment facility in 2002. This report does not acknowledge other drugs of choice, only cocaine. However, the report does stipulate that 30 percent of smoked cocaine admissions reported using no secondary substance of abuse. Furthermore, the report also states that forty-one percent of smoked cocaine admissions were female compared with 33 percent of non-smoked cocaine admissions.

As I review these numbers, I'm deeply troubled by them. Of all cocaine abusers in 2002 Blacks represented the majority of people needing professional treatment. Another staggering number from this report is the fact that the report stated that out of the 73 percent reported smoking cocaine, 43 percent were females, which clearly states that females in 2002 were the highest population of people strung out on crack-cocaine so much so, they needed the services of a medical detoxification center.

What is this report suggesting about the impact of crack-cocaine on women in society today? The report did not break down for us the race percentage of females on crack. You have to assume since 57 percent were Black, Black women had to make up a fair amount of the total needing professional treatment. Why is this important? The dysfunction of the Black family has escalated to Black women as well. Chapter six has more statistics of crime and drug addiction. However, when I analyze this horrible trend involving Black women's drug addiction and incarceration statistics that are about equal to Black men, it raises more than an eyebrow.

My Pain Killer

Not only do we have more Black men in prison than attending college; we also have this pervasive trend that glorifies many Black women as being as dysfunctional as Black men. I have to ask the question. Who's taking care of their children? Who's feeding and bathing and teaching and holding and nurturing our incarcerated Brothers and Sisters children? Why are illegal drugs the dysfunction of choice for so many Black folks? What happened to that inner strength Black folks could pull from when times got tough? That fact is; there are a lot more questions than answers. Unfortunately, every question comes with a human being attached to it. Every unanswered question is affecting some young Black child. Every newly created question finds the Black family in greater turmoil and despair.

Have life for our Black brothers and Sisters gotten so out of whack for them that they can no longer tolerate the responsibilities of living? It's another question, I know! The way I see it, the demands placed on each human being by the world are steadily increasing. The pressures of the family are greatly affected by governmental decisions, rules, policies, interests and sins. In addition, the pressure placed on society to be more productive; reach higher and higher heights; make more money; have more stuff; hold more titles; be more innovative; be more giving of your time; and be number one, is sending a tsunami effect across the bow of each member of society and especially the struggling members of society.

As you analyze these facts, you must take into consideration that many of us are in economic recession due to unemployment, underemployment, layoffs, job cancellations, employment fraud; theft in office; loss of health and welfare benefits; product marketing aimed specifically at financially struggling Blacks, Latinos, Whites, Asians, and others. Rich companies are targeting Blacks and other races living in poverty situations with their ads for alcohol, cigarettes, pornography, gambling, automobiles and other target social ills. In addition to all of this, you must add in the mix church dysfunction, increased mental and emotional illnesses, financial stress, health care issues and personal selfishness. Add all this up in a mixing bowl, add one pint of low self-esteem, two cups of negative attitudes and toss gently. What you've created is a recipe for disaster!

The world with all of its weapons continues its attack on the spiritually weak. Remember, these attacks are not from bricks and mortar and dirt; but from other human beings. So what you end up with is a mixing pot of "I can't take this any more." We find the spiritually weakened Brother and Sister attempting to meet their needs anyway they can. And when all of their attempts fail, and the emotional, psychological, relational, behavioral and spiritual resources have all seem to abandon them, they turn to a way out of the pain, out of the degradation, the suffering, their responsibilities, their shame, and their sins. And they turn to drugs, alcohol, sex and a few other devices used to soften the impact of failure!

First it starts out as casual for some; others fall into it with their whole body, yet others fight the urge and temptation to give in to its devises. But after one too many trips to its web of seduction, they soon find themselves motivated by the next opportunity to dull their pain. Each time they take a sip, or another hit, or another syringe, or another john, another puff, play another number, or another snort, they find that the impact is not the same as it was the last time. They then find themselves indulging in greater amounts and increase visits to their "pain killer", just to dull the realities of disappointment, hurt, fear and a host of pains. Next thing they know they find themselves thinking only about how they can dull their pain again, how they can get some more, what they can do to obtain it again.

Some of us find ourselves driving down the street after a hard days work, and find a young beautiful lady (and some are not so young, and not so beautiful) pacing the sidewalk, You stop at the red light, and here this beautiful, but strange acting lady comes up to your car and offer anything she has for your money. And you know what? Some of us say OK. This struggling lady gives you the best time of your life, because she's trying to please you, so you'll please her with honoring her price, and even perhaps a tip. She does this not because she enjoys it at first, but because she's lost control over her infatuation with the pain killer of her choice. I want you to know that this lady can be any Brother as well. As both will steal and rob from family members, husband's, wives, children, bosses, church and who ever else they can get stuff from and turn it into money for their next pain killer. They'll go so far to even steal and assault others until they get caught by the police.

If you were to take a look into a medical detoxification unit, you will be blown away by who you'll find inside. No, its not just the destitute of society you'll find in there; but you'll also find a Pastor or two in there, you'll also find the banker, the accountant, the investment broker, the police officer, the lawyer, the school teacher; the athlete, the physician, the therapist, and yes you'll find someone that looks like you and someone who looks like me too. We're all in there; we're all strung out on something that has taken control of our minds, our bodies, and our spirits. We've giving the pain killer control over us, because we could not maintain our own control. We needed help! We needed someone to say to us, it's going to be alright; more so, we needed someone to do more than pray, but physically help us!

These strung out Brothers and Sisters are asking us the question, where were you? I was calling your name and you did not come and help me! When I really needed you, you were no where to be found, I called your name, I called your name, I called you and you did not answer me. You saw me on the street corner and you just drove past me and shook your head at me. I knocked on your door, because I read the sign above the door that said *"come unto me all ye who are weary and heavy laden and I will give you rest,"* but there were chains on the doors and bars on the windows. I reached out to you, but you said I needed a case number, and now look at me, look at what I've become. I'm a junkie! I'm a hoe to my pain killer of choice.

There are so many people hurting from one pain or another. Each year more and more and more teenagers and adults enter into medical detoxification hospitals, only to go back out into the streets and get high again. The turmoil of living life for your next pain killer is no life worth living. I'm sure this is the sentiment of many people, not just Black folks, but all people addicted to "Pain killers." This is how I see the primary motivator for addiction. We are all trying to meet our human needs and the needs of our families, and it's hard. I know all to well myself. Just because I'm writing this book and it may seem as it I have it all going on for me right now, that's not my story. No, I'm not strung out and never have been, but I understand what it feels like to try to make ends meet and can't. I'm writing this book because God's heart is heavy. God does not like to see us in so much pain. But His hands are tied. Yes, I said that. You see, God will not do all He can do for any of us until we first acknowledge Him. All the pain, all the suffering, all the despair, it's not for Him, it's for Satan. If we don't have a connection with Christ, we are suffering for the god we do serve and his name is Satan and he's the creator of sin and evil.

Many of us are struggling with some sort of vice or habit. Masturbation, cigarettes, lying, stealing, sleeping around, laziness, procrastination, perfectionism, and control, these are just some of the many habits that engulf us. All of them start off small and grow until we have lost control, and now what started off small is a mountain in our life, a habit; an addiction. These areas don't get the same fame as drugs and alcohol, but nonetheless they can be an addiction.

The Impact of Addiction

You only have to look around you to see the impact addictions have on our families. Many of us have at least one member of our family that is struggling with some sort of addiction. But we don't talk about it, we don't deal with the issues effectively, we attempt to resolve this person's problems, but then we leave them to their own devices. We walk away from them, instead of showing them a tough, caring and relentless love that says to them, *"I am by brother's keeper."*

Women, please stop trying to be like the men. Society does not need you to attempt to meet men at every level. You've got to be smart enough to know what is right and what is not. We don't need you out there in the streets trying to screw as many men and ladies; as men are with ladies and men. We don't need you drinking as much as men do or snorting or smoking or shooting as much as men are. There are some things you don't need to do. The competition between men and women has gotten out of control. If we lose our women to the same destructions that have been taking our men, what will be left of the Black family. We are already in a state of crisis. So where will we be if you decide that you can't take life anymore; like so many of our men have. What about the children?

51

Children are being born today addicted because their mother is addicted. Addicted mothers are having get high sex; unprotected get high sex for their next hit. And thus, children are being born addicted and must be detoxified from the chemical of addiction. In addition, these children are being born with mental retardation, pervasive mental abnormalities, emotional, psychological and physical limitations and problems. These children's lives are starting out from a foundation of pain and abnormality. Many of these children will not be able to learn as well as other children. Many of these children may suffer from Attention Deficit Hyperactivity Disorder, Conduct disorder, Oppositional Defiant Disorder, various learning disabilities, Autism, Asperger Syndrome, emotional disorders, personality disorders, and many other possibilities associated with developmental difficulties. The following statistics represent a clear impact of drugs on the family.

The DASIS Report (Drug and Alcohol Services Information System) reported the following information in regards to adolescents and treatment admissions for 1992-2002.

- Between 1992-2002, the number of adolescent treatment admissions increased 65%, while all admissions increased 23%.
- Between 1992-2002, adolescent admissions reporting marijuana as the primary substance increased from 23-64%.
- In 2002, more than half (54%) of adolescent admissions were referred to treatment through the criminal justice system compared with 40% in 1992
- By 2002, the percentage of adolescent admissions who were White had decreased to 60%, while the percentage of adolescent admissions who were Black and Hispanic had increased 9(Blacks 19%, Hispanics 15%).
- Among Black admissions, the percentage using drugs before age 13 increased from 8% in 1999 to 11% in 2003

Youth Marijuana Admissions by Race and Ethnicity-The Dasis Report

- Marijuana was the primary substance of abuse for 47% of youth treatment admissions compared with 7% for all other ages
- The largest percentage of youth marijuana admissions was among Black youths.

Alcohol Dependence or Abuse: 2002, 2003, and 2004

- Among persons ages 12 or older, 7.6% (18.2 million) met the criteria for alcohol dependence or abuse in the past year
- Alcohol abuse or dependence was more prevalent among adults aged 18 or older who were never married (16.0%) than adults who were divorced or separated (10.0%), married (4.6%), and widowed (1.3%).
- Among persons aged 12 or older, males were more likely than females to have met the criteria for past year alcohol dependence or abuse

Serious Psychological Distress and Substance Use among Young Adult Males:

- An estimated 10.3% of males aged 18-25 (1.6 million) experienced serious psychological distress (SPD) during the past year.
- Males ages 18 to 25 with past year psychological distress were more likely than those without past pears psychological distress to have engaged in heavy alcohol use, binge alcohol use and illicit drug use in the past month.

These statistical briefs indicate to me one primary thing. Greater numbers of teenagers using illicit drugs and alcohol are not only growing, but growing to the point where professional intervention is needed. There is a growing problem within our young adults that is not being addressed. I strongly believe the primary problem with many of our youths today is psychological distress caused by serious disruption within the family unit. The DASIS report, reported an estimated 1.6 million males ages 18-25 have reported a psychological distress. These numbers will not and do not accurately reflect the Black culture. The reason I say this, is because we're not so quick to seek professional intervention for a host of reasons. I believe we have a host of Blacks, adult men, women and teenage boys and girls in society not effectively addressing medical and psychological issues of health.

It is known that we as a human race don't effectively address our hurts and pains in positive ways. If the family unit is in tact and operating according to God's rules, I believe many of the psychological distresses in society would decrease. When we hurt, many of us will turn to worldly ways of easing our pain. And many of us are walking around today with serious undiagnosed and untreated mental and emotional dysfunctions. Black people don't easily trust the medical community. And because of this we don't quickly seek out assistance from them when we know something isn't right. I read one study that indicated that 70 percent of Blacks responding to the survey did not believe that depression was a serious condition. And those who did believe that depression was a serious condition would seek prayer and the church for assistance in addition to medication. But what happens when the Black church don't believe depression is a serious condition either?

As a professional Christian mental health practitioner, I am appalled by the amount of denial existing within both the Black community and within the Christian Black church that mental and emotional health is not a serious problem. There are many Black people today, both young and mature who are attempting to silence the voices of mental health by drinking and doing illicit drugs. This is not the answer, alcohol and drugs will only create additional problems. Mental health is real, and those of you who refuse to acknowledge this truth is living in a bubble called a lie, and this lie has kept you bound and chained and have led you to alcohol, drugs, sex and other addictions.

Some risk factors for mental illness in African Americans as presented by SAMHSA.

> African Americans make up abut 40% of the homeless population
> Nearly half of all prisoners in state, federal and almost 40% of juveniles in legal custody are African American
> African American children and youth constitute about 45% of children in public foster care and more than half of all children waiting to be adopted
> African Americans of all ages are more likely to be victims of serious violent crime than are non-Hispanic Whites. One study reported that over 25% of African American youth exposed to violence met diagnostic criteria for Posttraumatic Stress Disorder (PTSD).

I also found this statistic to be very alarming from the same report:

> While non-Hispanic whites are nearly twice as likely as African Americans to commit suicide, suicide rates among young black men are as high as those of young white men. Moreover, from 1980-1995, the suicide rate among African Americans ages 10-14 increased 233%, compared to 120% of comparable non-Hispanic whites.

Do you still believe mental illness is not serious? It's so serious, it's killing us and we refuse to acknowledge its existence. Here's another statistic from the *National Survey on Drug use and Health (SAMHSA)*.

> In 2004, 5.7 million youths aged 12-17 (22.5%) received treatment or counseling fro emotional or behavioral problems in the year prior to the interview. This is higher than the estimates for 2003 (19.3%) and 2003 (20.6%)

Let me now present you with data from 2004 as reported by SAMHSA:

> - An estimated 22.5 million persons aged 12 or older in 2004 were classified with substance dependence or abuse in the past year.
> - Of the 22.5 million, youths age 12-17 represented 60.5%
> - Young adults age 18-25 represented 39.2% of the 22.5million
> - And 24.3% age 26 or older were depended on or abused illicit drugs in 2004.
> - In 2004 males age 12 and over were twice as likely to be substance dependent or abusive as females.
> - In 2004 an estimated 1,867,500 Blacks were considered substance dependent or abusive.

We have to remember that we only make up about 14% of the nation's population, but yet we comprise high percentages in areas such as drug use and addictions. We are a strung out society on marijuana, crack cocaine, and a host of other drugs and alcohol. The overall issue is this; addictions are not normal. Addictions are a primary way of saying "I have lost control." Abuse of alcohol, drugs and other addictive agents are a clear sign that something is wrong. In mental health, it is known that addictive behaviors are a mask for underlying stress, pain and disorder. As a people, we cannot continue to drink away our problems; we can't continue to smoke away or snort away or sex away our problems. Addictive behaviors only lead to greater pain, misery, grief and depression. We as a race of God's children are in pain, and I believe a large percentage of this pain is caused by the serious disunity in the African American family, starting with the African American male.

Sexual Addiction

According to the National Association of Sexual Addiction Problems, it is estimated that 6-8% of Americans are sex addicts. This percentage equates roughly from 16-21.5 million men and women. I read another statistic that claimed that there were 8% of men addicted to sex and 3% of women. Roughly this number represents 28 million Americans. If you're waiting for me to suggest that we should get addictive to Christ instead of everything else, keep waiting. I do not believe we should be addicted to anything, including God. God does not want us addicted to Him; He wants us in perfect balance with Him. God is a God of order; thus to be addicted to Him is to be out of order, thus God wants us to be in a perfect relationship with Him, ourselves and others. It's because we are out of balance with God that we are attempting to meet our needs in ungodly ways; this is the source of our problem.

A client of mine wrote this prayer in response to conditions in her life, and I bless her for her strength and faith.

> *Lord bind up our child's broken heart.*
> *Our heart was broken and shattered by physical, emotional and sexual abuse at the hands of those who were charged with loving and caring for us.*
> *Lord our worth as your child was discounted and trampled on.*
> *Take us into your arms like Jesus did your children.*
> *Mend our shattered hearts with your porous bandage of love.*
> *So that our hearts may be protected and remain free to breathe love in and out.*
>
> *Barbara J. Winder*
> *5/23/06*

This prayer speaks volumes about the hurt, pain and abuse inflicted upon each other.

Homosexuality- An Addiction?

I don't have any statistics for you on Black homosexuality because the sources all seem to suggest different numbers. However, homosexuality is a real problem in the Black race. Some of you may believe that being gay is hereditary; well its not. Homosexuality is a choice. The dynamics of homosexuality can parallel that of any addiction, or loss of control. I'm pointing out this area, not to debate its origins, but to promote reconciliation. Some gays (male and female) have tested the waters of homosexuality as a result of the intense pain and disappointment affiliated with broken natural relationships. We, as a Black society of people have shunned those of us hurting as a result of unnatural (homosexuality) relationships. We are OK with the fact that pain and heartache is a reality of natural relationships, but we will not accept the fact that we are hurting from what we've done to each other, straight or gay!

I'm not advocating a homosexual lifestyle; however, I am advocating reconciliation from all sin. The Black church has shunned gays. Where are gays supposed to go to worship the Lord? Where are gays supposed to go to be healed of their sins? How are gays supposed to be convicted by the Holy Spirit if we don't allow them into the church house? The universal Christian church has said NO! to the healing of all manner of sickness and disease. It's seemingly Ok for Christians to drink and smoke and screw around; because God can forgive that! Right? Preachers, please stop with the claim that homosexuality is an abominable sin. I understand that. However, all sin is an abomination to God. Are we, the church stating that its OK to beat up our wives and girlfriends; engage in pre-marital sex, lie, and steal? We can be forgiving of those sins, right? My Bible tells me that homosexuality is not an unforgivable sin. So, as long as God is willing to forgive homosexuality, so am I. I say let the gays in the church, and let them become members. Give the Holy Spirit a chance to convict them of their sins, in the same way He's convicting many of the non-gays of theirs! The church does not have the right to choose what sins we'll forgive and what sins we won't. God has spoken and has given us a very clear understanding. Some of us sitting either in the pulpit or in the congregation are still doing some of the same things we did while we were supposedly in the world. But now we've become so holy that sin disgusts us. Get real! What we do in the dark will come out in the light. God has no respect of person when it comes to salvation, repentance and reconciliation. God is the liberator of all sin, not just the ones some of us only identify with.

Sexual addictions, or as the Bible calls them, habits; the victims, in many cases are not those who are far from us, but those who claim a family or close family allegiance to us. We're hurting one another; we're running away from the truth; we're exchanging truth for a lie. Addictions are just another lie that says to us that our pain killer of choice will help us. It won't, but it will create more problems than it will cure. We've got to get the word out that we are worth more than the negative statistics. We are worth more than bad press and media; we are worth more than addictions, drugs, alcohol, violence, rape, incest, homosexuality, and criminal activities. God did not make us to be junk, but when He made us He was pleased with His creation. It's about time we began to share that same attitude back to God, ourselves and each other. We are somebody, and somebody wants us. It's not too late; it's time to stop listening to Satan tell us what we can't do and how we can't reconcile; it's all a lie. While you yet have blood flowing in your veins, the time is right for a wonderful change; a glorious change; a change for righteousness.

My Brothers and Sisters, a change in the right direction is what God wants for us all. But I must warn you that a change in heart and mind does not only come to the person on the outside looking in, but change must come from the inside also. In order for change to be lasting with our Brothers and some Sisters, the Brother or Sister at home with the children must also have a change in heart and mind. It will be very difficult for positive and lasting change to take effect without a strong and supportive family foundation. We cannot blast our people seeking to do right, with every hurtful reminder of the past. We must forgive them as God forgives us. We must not badger, test, and place obstacles in the way. We must receive our loved ones in the spirit of reconciliation and newness, just as Christ receives us and forgives us when we constantly mess up. Our estranged family members need an opportunity to live for righteousness, and reconnect with children, wives and husbands, where possible. I understand that situations may have changed to the point where a separated or divorced husband or wife has remarried. In this case the former spouse still needs an opportunity to reunite with his/her children and create a supporting relationship with the children's father or mother.

I understand that trust can take time. I'm suggesting that we make the time to allow the process of reconnection to manifest. Let God's Holy Spirit have His will and way with our hearts and minds and re-unify ourselves with God, ourselves and each other. Rest, lean and depend on God for our strength, not addictions. Even in our lost of control (addiction) God can heal us of our addictions and the pains that led us to it. I must strongly encourage you to have patience and faith. It took you more than a few days to lose control and it may take you more than a few days to break it.

Control

2 Peter 2:19 *"While they promise them liberty, they themselves are the servants of corruption: for of whom a man is overcome, of the same is he brought in bondage."*

Addiction is a lost of control. Man is controlled by whatever master's him. The above Scripture reminds us that which we rely upon to sooth our pains is also that which enslaves us by its very nature. The problem has and continue to be the sinful choices we make in attempting to meet our needs.

"Verily, verily, I say unto you, Whosoever committeth sin is the servant of sin," John 8:32.
"Know ye not, that to whom ye yield yourselves to obey, his servants ye are to whom ye obey; whether of sin unto death, or of obedience unto righteousness? Romans 6:16

"And that they may recover themselves out of the snare of the devil, who are taken captive by him at his will," 2 Timothy 2:26.

Codependency is a serious problem in the Black family structure, a structure of struggle. Codependency as defined by the National Christian Counselors Association, "in its broadest sense, can be defined as an addiction to people, behaviors or things. Codependency is the fallacy of trying to control interior feelings by controlling people, things and events on the outside." Combine issues of Codependency with addiction issues and you have a real problem. Unfortunately, lots of Black women are supporting their black man out of fear of losing him, or abuse. Love is not a maladaptive control mechanism used to keep the support required of a dependent person in getting his needs met. In Codependency the dependent person uses controlling behaviors and attitudes to command support and adherence to his maladaptive thinking, behaviors, beliefs, habits, vices or addictions, from the codependent spouse or family.

The family out of fear and shame gives in to this person's demands in a protective mode to fulfill the needs and or desires of the dependent person. The interior family becomes enablers to the dependent person by giving in to that person's demands, instead of offering tough love and seeking help for the dependent person and the family. Clearly, there is a risk of personal harm in issues of Codependency. This risk of harm is one of the primary motivators that keep family members supporting inappropriate behaviors. The wife, or girlfriend and children will live in fear and retribution of harm by the dependent person, through their controlling measures. The wife, or girlfriend and even the children in the household will alter their normal sense of thinking and behavior to support the dysfunctional thinking and behaviors of the dependent person, thus creating a sense of Co-dependency for themselves, because they have lost the sense of normality and healthy thinking and behaviors within the family unit. This is the reason why so many women stay with their abuse husband or boyfriend.

I want all my Brothers and Sisters who are being held captive by one addiction or another to please come to believe that you can be set free.

"The Spirit of the Lord is upon me, because he hath anointed me to preach the gospel to the poor; he hath sent me to heal the brokenhearted, to preach deliverance to the captives, and recovering of sight to the blind, to set at liberty them that are bruised," Luke 4:18.

The purpose of this book is to encourage you with the truth. The Black family must be led by a strong Christian Black man. Black men whether you choose to love a Black female or another of God's beautiful race of people; that choice is yours, however, my point is that the Black man must be true to himself by being true to the God he serves. Who ever the Black man has made a family commitment with; it is his responsibility to see it through. So if you are one of the many Black men that have lost their way due to addictions or something else, the above Scripture is telling you that Jesus has come to set you free; and He's using this book to confront you with the truth of our sins and the joy found in His forgiveness through reconciliation.

Chapter Four
Christian Conflict Resolution
(Why do we argue so much?)

"What causes fights and quarrels among you? Don't they come from your desires that battle within you? You want something but don't get it. You kill and covet, but you cannot have what you want. You quarrel and fight. You don't have because you don't ask God," James 1:1-2

The world today is a world in constant conflict with itself and God. Nations can't get alone; nations war with one another over earthly riches, territories, principles, policies, and religion. Governments war within themselves. Local governments fight and argue believing what their fighting over is right and good. Races of people are in conflict with other races, men are in conflict with women, children are in conflict with children. And of course, that same spirit that separates all of us also separates all of our families because of conflict. We are a human race that cannot agree upon much of anything. Adam and Eve should have disagreed, but since they didn't, we're left to deal with the aftermath. Is it good to disagree? Is it good to always get your say so in? Are you always right? Why do we argue so much?

Scriptures reveal the answer to us in James 1:1, 2. We, the human race are a very selfish race of God's creation. If one was to study the animal kingdom, one would find a totally different kind of operational system. For example, animals usually don't kill or even attack their enemies unless it's for food, protection of territory, or threat to their families. Can we as a human race, or we as a Black race of humans, can we say that we only do things purely out of maintenance of life? If you'll refer to the prison statistics provided in chapter seven you'll find the support needed to answer this question with a resounding NO. We, the people who make up all of the various components of the Black or African American race of human beings are in a state of constant conflict.

Husband's disagree with their wives, wives disagree with their husband's, boyfriends disagree with their girlfriends, girlfriends disagree with their boyfriends, parents disagree with their children, children disagree with their parents, Pastor's disagree with Deacons,

Deacon's disagree with Pastor's, Pastor's disagree with other Pastor's, Grandmother disagrees with grandmother, grandfather disagrees with grandfather, and I personally don't agree with most things, and on and on and on. How in the world can we all be right, someone has got to be wrong? James informs us in Scripture that our disagreements come from within us. Disagreements are formulated out of a need or desire that goes unfulfilled.

Mankind has a need and desire to be fulfilled! Is this need or desire bad? I don't think it's an issue of good versus bad as it is an issue of right versus wrong. If man's heart, according to the Holy Bible, is filled with all manner of evils and Jesus reminds us what makes a man unclean is not what enters into his mouth, goes into the stomach and out of the body; but what makes a man unclean is what comes from his heart and out of his mouth. Mankind is born into sin and shaped in iniquity, but we don't have to sin, we can remain holy, but ultimately we don't choose holiness, we choose sin, thus we are sinful people at heart, according to the choices we make.

Isn't it the choices we make that throw us into disharmony with God, ourselves and one another? Refer back to the story of Adam and Eve in the book of Genesis. Eve and Adam ultimately made a choice to do what God had instructed Adam not to do. And because of the choice to disobey God's command, all mankind was punished, along with the Serpent and the earth. Eve and Adam sought to fulfill their own fleshly desires than be content with what God had already provided for them. So, is the issue of conflict an issue of personal selfishness? Yes! I believe it is, and then some. The term conflict as defined by Webster's means to be "incompatible; to be antagonistic; sharp disagreement, as of interest or ideas; emotional disturbance."

According to this definition of the term, Webster's is suggesting that humans may be incompatible with each other? Humans are in a constant state of sharp disagreement as of interest and or ideas; as individuals many of us don't share the same dispositions, not to mention that we are antagonistic towards one another. I do believe there is a significant amount of truth to Webster's definition of the term. The Bible in my theological understanding of it has stated this conclusion first. When you read the implications of Adam and Eve's disobedience in the Garden and the punishment placed upon them by God, you clearly begin to see how Webster's definition of the term 'conflict' supports Scriptural truths.

I'm suggesting that as far back as Adam and Eve's experience in the Garden, may well be the first indication that although God created perfection, out of disobedience towards God, man's heart was easily persuaded to evil and the fulfillment of his own selfish desires. God placed enmity between good and evil as a result of the fall of mankind. What causes fights and quarrels among us, mankind's need and desire to have more than God has already supplied. Mankind is in a constant state of dissatisfaction with what God has already abundantly provided. This would answer for me, the reason why so many rich people lie to protect what they have as they pursue even more. The rich keeps getting richer and the poor keeps getting poorer.

Why do nations and people war with one another, isn't it because of our selfish desire to have more than we have; which takes me back to the Black family. Why do we fight so much? Why is it that we cannot get along? Why is there so much competition in the Black family? Where does all the animosity come from? James already told us, it is our personal selfishness within us that seeks to be fulfilled. The fact is; this personal selfishness originates from the foundation of sin and evil. Paul gives us some insight into where selfishness and sin can lead us" in Romans 1:18-32, Paul writes:

"The wrath of God is being revealed from heaven against all the godlessness and wickedness of men who suppress the truth by their wickedness, since what may be known about God is plain to them, because God has made it plain to them. For since the creation of the world God's invisible qualities—his eternal power and divine nature—have been clearly seen, being understood from what has been made, so that men are without excuse. For although they knew God, they neither

glorified him as God nor gave thanks to him, but their thinking became futile and their foolish hearts were darkened. Although they claimed to be wise, they became fools and exchanged the glory of the immortal God for images made to look like mortal man and birds and animals and reptiles. Therefore God gave them over in the sinful desires of their hearts to sexual impurity for the degrading of their bodies with one another. They exchanged the truth of God for a lie, and worshipped and served created things rather than the Creator—who is forever praised. Amen. Because of this, God gave them over to shameful lusts. Even their women exchanged natural relations for unnatural ones. In the same way the men also abandoned natural relations with women and were inflamed with lust for one another. Men committed indecent acts with other men, and received in themselves the due penalty for their perversion. Furthermore, since they did not think it worthwhile to retain the knowledge of God, he gave them over to a depraved mind, to do what ought not to be done. They have become filled with every kind of wickedness, evil, greed and depravity. They are full of envy, murder, strife, deceit and malice. They are gossips, slanderers, God-haters, insolent, arrogant and boastful; they invent ways of doing evil; they disobey their parents; they are senseless, faithless, heartless, ruthless. Although they know God's righteous decree that those who do such things deserve death, they not only continue to do these very things but also approve of those who practice them."

This is Paul's discourse of God's wrath against mankind for their wickedness. I do not want to paint for you such a horrible and disgraceful picture of mankind that we feel it's too late to reconcile with God. That's not the picture I'm attempting to paint at all, but just the opposite. We as a people must know where we've come from, if we're ever going to get where we're going. In addition, we as a people must know what state we're in right now; if we're going to understand where it is we need to be. Thus far, I've wanted you to see where we've been and where we are today. We, the Black family must come to understand that we are more divided now than probably ever in our African American history. The cause of our division is clear, at least to me; we are divided because we have allowed our own selfish desires and needs to outweigh what God has intended for us. Just like Eve in the Garden and her desire to have more than God allowed her to have, we are no different today.

The Holy Bible teaches us to be content in all things. We are a very discontent race of people. We are blessed with stuff we never had before, and yet we're not satisfied. The love of money is still the root of all evil, and we have surely done our part to make others very rich, while we continue to struggle. We seek those things of quick satisfaction. We choose not to wait on the Lord; instead we choose to fulfill our hearts desires right now. Pushing drugs, prostitution and criminal activities of all kinds have landed us in the state that Paul spoke on. God has seemingly given us over to our fleshly desires, because we refuse to acknowledge Him and His righteousness. For us righteousness takes too long to get. We need righteousness now, that is, if it's going to put some green backs in our pocket. The Holy God of Israel is not a prostitute we can command; He is the Holy of Holly's; The Lord God almighty; He is the creator of all things created good and very good.

The first resolve in conflict resolution is to understand and identify yourself as a probable cause of conflict. The genesis of conflict resides in one's own heart. The heart holds your attitudes, beliefs, impulses, emotions, desires, mistrust and so much more; while your brain stores memories and sensory information. Your brain also is responsible for identification, interpretation, and the reactionary processes of what's going on around you as well as in you. So as Scripture indicates, what we allow in our hearts will eventually come out of us in words and deeds. So perhaps, we as a people have a lot of junk in our hearts that we need to get rid of. A lot of sinful feelings and attitudes, hatred, jealousy's, anger, etc. Within our families, we must come to understand that ultimately we must come to lean and depend on God for all of our needs. I have comprised a list identifying families' chief conflicts within my counseling ministry.

Families' Chief Conflicts:

- Marital selfishness
- Marital communications
- Marital mistrust
- Financial concerns
- Dad not spending enough time with the children
- Children's disobedience
- Parent children conflict
- Children performance issues
- The wrong crowd
- The church

Marital Selfishness

What exactly is marital selfishness? Selfishness by definition means being overly concerned about one's own interests over others. So as I look to apply this definition to marriage, I think of marital selfishness as one or both spouses being overly concerned about their own interests over the interests of their spouse. In Christian therapy circles, professionals seem to agree that the number one dysfunction in marital relationships is not communication, but selfishness; communication is often the second rated dysfunction. Do you remember what it was like when you first laid eyes on her/him? Do you remember all you attempted to do for her/him to impress them? Do you remember placing aside your interests for her/his interests? In fact, you were willing to be just about anything, and do just about anything to make her smile and win his/her heart.

When we apply the term "chivalry' to relationships, we imagine a knight in shinning armor coming to the rescue of the damsel in distress. This is the knight that places the need of his damsel over his own. During the courting phase of a relationship is when we often times find the Brother engaged in chivalry. The Bother during this phase is holding open the door for his lady; he's tucking the chair in under her at the table; he's inviting her to get ahead of him in the buffet line; he's allowing her to choose what movie they'll attend, all in hopes of snatching her up for his own. In marital relationships, we often hear of the honeymoon years, this is the point within the marriage where chivalry is still being exhibited by both spouses.

Then comes the "after honey moon phase." This term is used quite often to depict the point in the marital relationship where the true personalities of both spouses begin to break through the mask of chivalry. "The honeymoon's over," is often stated to acknowledge to spouses, family and friends, that reality has kicked in. During this phase of the relationship, chivalry begins to be replaced by one's own true temperament and personality. The "me factor" begins to dominate the once practiced "we factor." Thus spouses stop attempting to please each other and begin to place their own personal views, needs, opinions, likes, dislikes, and attitudes above the same for his/her spouse. This is what I call marital selfishness. The Bible tells us that the two shall become one flesh; this is the way it usually is in the beginning, but again, after the mask has been taken off by one or both spouse's, the spouses end up with someone they don't really know; or perhaps don't really care for.

Marital selfishness is extremely destructive and non-Scriptural in context. In marriage, each spouse's needs are fulfilled by the other spouse (chivalry), but in marital selfishness, the selfish spouse seeks to fulfill his/her own needs, thus usurping the marital covenant of becoming one flesh together and bypassing the fulfilling of the other spouses needs. Thus the unfulfilled spouse becomes dissatisfied with the other spouse because he or she has not met his/her needs. Not having our needs met is the cause of conflict. We are in conflict with the selfish spouse that has stopped caring for the unselfish spouse. When this occurs, the primary emotion expressed is unfulfillment leading toward anger.

Marital Communications

Marital communications is another mode of selfish expression. Do men and women communicate differently? Yes we do. Would a Black Frenchmen communicate the same way as a Brother from New Jersey? Probably not; although in both examples the person's skin is darkened, but darkened skin is not the primary factor in how we as a human race communicate to one another. I know many of you reading this will probably not agree with me, but that's OK. The bottom line to effective communications involves the process of sending a message, receiving a message and comprehending the original message. If this short process is completed successfully, effective communications have happened.

The problem with this theory is that Black folks within ourselves don't effectively communicate with one another. Most of the time, I don't comprehend what's being said to me by teenagers. On the other hand, many teenagers don't comprehend what I'm saying either. There are many barriers to effective communication. Here is a short list of some of them:

- Race
- Age
- Ethnicity
- Experiences
- Education
- Personality
- Temperament
- Emotions
- Gender
- Time
- Environment
- Personal health
- Generational nuances
- Technology
- Fads

Fashion
Learned Behaviors
Fear
Rebellion
Music and other Medias
Dishonesty
Motivations/Attitudes
Traumatic experiences
Mental/Emotional Health
Trust

At any given moment any one of the identified barriers can produce conflict in communications. There exist generational differences in various forms of communication. The age of the communicator must be considered, along with the educational level of the person, the environment the communications are taking place in. Also, the personality of the communicator, the physical and mental health of the communicator must be considered. Every Black person doesn't talk the same. We don't all speak Blackenese. Some of us speak very eloquently and use big words, as some of us may speak very loud and prefer to use simple everyday terminology.

So what's the difference in marriage? There are two totally separate individuals with different backgrounds, different experiences, different educational levels, different personalities and approaches to communications come together as one to disseminate and cultivate each other's style of communicating. The infusing of another person's life into their own creates a natural challenge for anyone, especially in marriage. Then we must consider sinful communications. Sinful communications in this context is where one or both spouses enter into a communication exchange with pre-conceived thoughts, questions, answers, emotions, attitudes and results. Effective communication must involve trust. Have you ever known a person to try to out talk you and talk over you? This style of communicating is ineffective because it comes with baggage attached to it. What I mean by that statement is this; let's say a wife who's in her second marriage is in communication exchange with her husband, and she asks her husband a question, but before he has time to respond, she expresses the answer. Then when the husband does get an opportunity to answer the question, the wife speaks louder than he does and with great aggression.

I have had a number of both women and men in my office who communicate this way. Often times, I come to find out that this type of communicator in past times was held back from expressing themselves, their opinions were not welcomed and their communication was always minimized. This type of person has decided that their no longer allowing others to control and limit what they can and cannot say. So, they communicate with hostility and great emotion, because they're going to be heard, no matter what. This is a good example of how past experiences effect the way we communicate today. In my example, the wife did not intend to present herself as being hostile or controlling in her communications, and she was not aware that she communicates in this fashion. This wife's style of articulating her words represents a serious communication conflict. Such a conflict will limit or shut down future attempts at communication thereby creating problems, or a different approach by her spouse in his attempts to communicate with her. Either way, the relationship cannot grow without each spouse effectively communicating to the other.

The most important aspect of communications does not come from the mouth, but from the ears. We so often forget that the most critical aspect of effective communications must involve the attentive and active listener. Here's what Scripture has to say about listening.

- James 1:19 "Wherefore, my beloved brethren, let every man be swift to hear, slow to speak, slow to wrath;"
- Proverbs 18:13 "He who answers before listening—that is his folly and his shame"
- Proverbs 29:20 "Do you see a man who speaks in haste? There is more hope for a fool than for him."
- Proverbs 13:13 "He who guards his lips guards his soul, but he who speaks rashly will come to ruin."

Scripture wants us to be effective listeners, more so than articulators. Usually what Scripture commands us to do, we do just the opposite. This is one primary reason God called me into the helping ministry. People do not know how to listen. Because of our selfish intent in communications, we only seek to enforce our beliefs without ever listening to the content of the message. To put this statement in another way, we often use language as a means of defense. It is the defensive measures in our communication styles that create conflict with others.

When we do verbalize our thoughts, Scripture has some commands for us to abide by:

> ➢ Psalm 19:14 "May the words of my mouth and the meditation of my heart be pleasing in your sight, O Lord, my Rock and my Redeemer.

Scripture wants everything we say to be pleasing and acceptable to God. What we say must be spoken with the intent to edify someone else by our words. If our verbiage does not have that intent, it is best not to speak.

> ➢ Proverbs 8:6-8 "Listen, for I have worthy things to say; I open my lips to speak what is right. My mouth speaks what is true, for my lips detest wickedness. All the words of my mouth are just; none of them is crooked or perverse."

Speak only those things that are beneficial to someone's ears.
Speak the truth in love.

> ➢ Ephesians 4:29 "Do not let any unwholesome talk come out of your mouths, but only what is helpful for building others up according to their needs, that it may benefit those who listen."

When you speak, don't let any sinful, degrading, obnoxious, hurtful and cutting words come out of your mouth, but only what is good for that person's needs, that what you say will be a blessing to those listening.

> ➢ Proverbs 15:1 "A gentle answer turns away wrath, but a harsh word stirs up anger."

Do not respond with the purpose of antagonizing someone else. But in emotional exchange, avoid harshness by responding with meekness and gentleness. So that anger is not the outcome of a distasteful communication exchange.

> ➢ Proverbs 10:19 "When words are many, sin is not absent, but he who holds his tongue is wise."

Don't talk too much! Many words are given with sinfulness present. But the wise communicator will seek to hold or delay his/her response as not to get trapped into sin.

- Proverbs 25:11, 12 "A word aptly spoken is like apples of god in settings of silver. Like an earring of gold or an ornament of fine gold is a wise man's rebuke to a listening ear."

Let our words be appropriate and in due season. Appropriate verbiage will bless the listener and not tear them down.

- Proverbs 15:4 "The tongue that brings healing is a tree of life, but a deceitful tongue crushes the spirit."

Let your words bring goodness, mercy and grace. Let your words provide wisdom, knowledge and direction. Righteous words bring life to an otherwise weltering vine. However, cruel words will crush the human spirit.

Lastly, we cannot forget about non-verbal communications. We often times don't respond to a verbal exchange. We do however respond to what someone is saying without verbally responding. Body language or non-verbal communications can be just as effective in sending a person's intent as verbalizing it. Below is a list of some of the ways in which people communicate non-verbally.

- Rolling eyes or starring
- Rolling neck or head
- Finger pointing or other gestures
- Pointing of one's feet or stomping or twitching
- About face-ignoring someone
- Poked out chest-a defensive stand
- Posturing-a defensive stand
- Coughing/sneezing
- Throat gurgles
- Facial gestures

In the content of the Black family, I remember clearly my mom giving me the sign. She would give me that look and I knew exactly what she was communicating. I also remember the sign she used when she was going to rip my hide apart. Familiarity with one another allows us to get to know each others non-verbal communication styles. I'm sure many of you have been the recipient of a Sister rolling her eyes and her neck at you, once or twice. And I'm sure you probably got the message she was sending you. A total effective plan of communications encompasses all the ways in which we as a people and we as a human race communicates. The problem in marriages is simply that spouses choose not to communicate and they also choose not to alter the ways in which they communicate.

With the joining of the two becoming one flesh, the two must remember that they're not alone anymore and thus they must alter the way in which they once communicated. The best way of communicating is by asking questions. Men don't ask questions, because we think we know everything. Woman asks men questions, just to see what we're going to say. Don't initiate argumentative communications. Conflict resides in the power of the tongue. I have already provided you with Biblical commandments and principles for effective communications. In addition, I'm going to add one more.

James 3:5 *"Likewise the tongue is a small part of the body, but it makes great boasts. Consider what a great forest is set on fire by a small spark."*

(Use your tongues wisely, you have the power to build up or tear down)

Advice giving is another area of communications conflict. The marital union is often complicated and thrown into conflict through the avenue of mother and father in-laws. Husbands express frustration because of their mother in-law's influence upon their marriage. Likewise, wives are also frustrated because of parent in-law's influence upon their marriage. Who should each spouse listen to? How about listening to one another! Why do parent in-laws feel as if they have to continue shielding and protecting their son/daughter. Scripture teaches us that a man should leave his father and mother and cling to his wife.

The man has entered into a new set of rules, totally different from the rules while he lived under his parent's roof. Adam refused to stand up to Eve and do what God instructed Him to do in the Garden of Eden. Men, don't make the same mistake. Each spouse must make a commitment to each other in every way. Spouses should listen and discuss matters themselves. If each spouse agrees to seek additional wisdom from their parents, that's fine. As long as they both agree, and they both take advice that's supported by Scriptures. In addition, during this time of advice seeking, please don't forget to first seek God's wisdom and direction. Remember, the primary source of immediate wisdom is found in the Holy Bible. If we begin to use Scriptural wisdom and less human advice, we'll find solutions for our answers and we'll enjoy less conflict.

Marital Mistrust

In unity separation does not exist. Unity means oneness, harmony, all parts working together in union. If this is the definition of unity, why do so many marital relationships have separation in oneness? How many husbands and wives; live in parents and others, have secret bank accounts. Why do so many spouses have their mail coming to their job, a safe-deposit box or to a family member's house instead of their own place of residence? Why do we have passwords on our cell phones and pagers? Just how many female cousins do we always have coming in from out of town? I'm sure you've heard this one: "These are not my thongs."

Marital mistrust is so prevalent in spouses today and it represents a very serious problem to the stability of the marriage, the family and society's well being. Marital mistrust is not only represented by spouses cheating on each other, but so many other ways we express mistrust in relationships. It used to be that infidelity was a man thing. We can no longer hold to those claims; women are just as guilty today as men are. Why do spouses cheat? In my experience one reason why spouses cheat is due to the fact that they are attracted to more that one man or woman (Lusts from the heart). The second reason why spouses cheat is because they feel unfulfilled by their spouse. The third reason why spouses cheat is due to outside influences upon the marriage and the fourth reason why spouses cheat is due to financial concerns. The ultimate reason why spouses cheat is sin and as mentioned, it is the internal desires of the heart that when allowed to fester and grow, the spouse responds to these inner compulsions and ultimately decides to act upon these desires within to sin, thus attempting to meet some perceived need or desire. Let's take a look at each of these reasons.

1. *The Heart of the Matter*

Reason One- Spouses cheat because they are attracted to more than one person. This statement is as old as Satan is. The lust of the eyes and the fulfilling of lust from the heart is the central theme in why spouses cheat. Of course, this explanation is made true by the simple fact that spouses are not truly committed to each other to begin with. Commitment is a serious problem in society and the Black family today. Because the government gives us so many loopholes and ways out of commitments, we are not held by the words we speak to God and each other. Another fault with commitment must be assumed by the church. The church has not taken a serious commitment towards the building up of the body of Christ. The church doesn't teach nor offer specific ministries on prevalent issues affecting today's congregations. Not to mention, there is no church discipline enforced in our churches. We can live anyway we want to and still call ourselves a Christian. As long as we pay our tithes and offerings, no one from the church will ask any questions. I hope you don't believe this! The church may not ask, but Jesus will!

Paul said in 2 Corinthians 10:5 *"We demolish arguments and every pretension that sets itself up against the knowledge of God, and we take captive every thought to make it obedient to Christ."*

Brothers and Sisters, we are not taking captive the thoughts that sets us up for destruction. We are giving in to every sinful thought that come our way. We must fight sinful temptations. When we say "I do," I stop. I say yes to commitment and turn away from destruction. We must remember that Satan wants to sift us like wheat. He wants to separate us from good and destroy us by the lust of our own flesh. It is not Scriptural to lay with everything that's not yours by commitment. Spouses if you cannot control your flesh, seek out a professional Christian therapist. The fact is, when we give in to our desires, those desires separate us from the love of God and one another. Remember, there is a cost for every evil and sinful thing we do, whether our spouse knows about it or not. God is an all seeing God and what so ever you do in darkness He'll bring to the light and you and I must answer for it. Not to mention, if you get caught, people lives will be altered forever. Is that momentary feeling really worth all the pain that comes with it? Commitment is the answer; we must first be in a true commitment with God before we can commit to anything else and have it be blessed.

If you don't think sin has its price, just refer to the statistics on STD's in chapter seven. The fact is, uncommitted sexual practices have a very high risk of acquiring a very aggressive STD or an STD that has no cure. Black people represent a crisis in the epidemic of Aids and also an increased rate of STD infections. Brothers you can wrap it up all you want to. The fact is HPV (Humanpapillomavirus) and HSV (Herpes Simples Virus) is not prevented by the use of a condom, but by direct contact with any infected part of the body. Trust is a component of commitment. The reason why our Black marriages and families 'are struggling is because we have substituted commitment for selfishness and because of this we're all paying for it. Allowing our sinful, selfish, greedy and self-satisfying desires to be fulfilled is a primary cause of conflict.

2. Unfulfilled Desires

Spouses cheat because they are still sinful in nature and many of them have done nothing to resist temptation. In discussing unfulfilled desires we have to discuss the sexual unfulfillment and the other unfulfillment areas. A spouse may be sexually unfulfilled because of problems stemming from marital miss-communications. Many couples miss the opportunities to talk to one another. Human emotions of shame, guilt, pride, fear, trust, jealousies, stress, and feelings of inferiority, false interpretations and past experiences all influence the dynamics of marital sexual communications. Many times spouses simply never communicate to their spouse their sexual likes, dislikes, fantasies, curiosities and experiences because of the emotions I described. The primary emotion experienced is fear. Spouses fear how they'll be viewed by their spouse for communicating their desires. Also, fear generated through former experiences of each spouse.

One report I read in a Christian journal claimed that 1 in 4 women in the Christian church have been sexually abused. If this is the case, unresolved fear would be the result of poor or restrained openness in communicating one's true sexual desires especially after a traumatic event such as rape or molestation. Post Traumatic Stress Disorder is an anxiety disorder that is characterized by the re-experiencing of an extremely traumatic event accompanied by symptoms of increased arousal and avoidance of stimuli associated with the trauma. According to the DSM-4, approximately 8% of the adult population experiences this type of anxiety disorder. In other spouses shyness may be the primary condition creating poor or restrained communications. Shyness deals with a maladaptive poor self-image and low self-esteem. Shyness is a condition that deals with issues of comfort and confidence. Shyness can be treated with Christian therapy, in addition to Post Traumatic Stress Disorder and poor communications skills.

3. Marital Influence

Married couples must be careful who they take advice from. I know that mom and dad, or your sister or brother, even your best friend, all have advice to give. But just because they have it to give, don't mean you should act on it. Single men and women always want to give spouses advice. I'm not suggesting that single people don't offer good

advice, only that their advice is skewed. Single living practices don't necessarily fit into marital practices, which represent a major problem in marriages already. Married people cannot live as if they are still single. Everything to a degree has changed, so must your thinking, behaviors and practices change to fit the coming together of the two to one flesh. When considering advice from anyone, ask yourself this one question. Does the advice I'm about to receive line up with the Word of God? This is the first question you must ask yourself prior to considering hearing what some advice givers want to tell you.
Let me make this a bit clearer; if someone wants to give you advice, the first thing you should do is ask them if the advice is from the Word of God.

This may surprise you, but everyone giving advice from the Word of God does not understand how to apply God's Word to your situation. So just because someone wants to quote Scriptures to you does not mean that what they are quoting is applicable to your particular situation. The Bible tells us that we are always to seek God's counsel prior to doing just about everything. In addition, the Word tells us to seek out Christian counselors, because there is safety in the multitude of counselors. Even Christians are sinners and will sometimes give wrong and misguided Scriptural advice. If a wife's mother advises her to use sex as a way of getting a new coat, I would not take that advice.

If a husband's father advices him to beat his wife to make her obedient to him, I would not take that advice. Spouses, if someone advises you to secretly open a separate checking account with your name on the account only; I would not take that advice. Good advice not only lines up with Scripture for your specific situation, but good advice must seek righteousness and holiness in its content. This is what the author meant when he said "there is safety in the multitude of counselors." If the advice being offered does not seek to promote and edify, then its bad advice. The Bible tells us that every word spoken must seek to edify and not tear down. Moreover, all advice must be given to the marital union and not a particular spouse. When you are united as one in marriage, stay united and connected in everything you do. Do not let good intentioned Christians or wolves wrapped in sheep clothing separate and bring disharmony to what God has joined together. Keeping unified in this matter will advance trust, harmony, unification and dependence upon each other. Advice givers are not the only influence on marriages; other people, media, situations, fashion, selfishness and the environment, all influence spouses in a marriage. Spouses must be careful who and what you allow to speak, act or influence you and your marriage. You must remember that this world hates what God has commanded and ordained, therefore the world hates marriage and have long ago set out to destroy it. You must not let anything influence you to do evil. Your body is holy and it is the temple of the Holy Spirit, therefore marriage is holy and it is a very respectful and honorable institution.

4. Financial Concerns

The love of money is still the root of all evil. I wish I could tell you that in my experience most spouses are in conflict over money because they feel as if they have too much of it, but I can't. Money woes provide wear and tear on the success of a marriage. Either spouse enter into marriage already having money woes or they soon develop money woes either due to irresponsible spending, improper budgeting, and imbalance in income to expenses or a lack of employment or underemployment. There are many Black families that still don't know how to balance their check book. Moreover, many of us still don't have a household budget. This is where the church can provide a ministry designed to help its members learn personal finance skills.

Of course the other issue is that we are irresponsible with the finances we do have. As Christians, we are to be good stewards of that which God has entrusted to us. In every area of life, we have responsibilities. Failure to acknowledge our responsibilities will quickly lead toward conflict. The issues of unemployment or underemployment are issues that create the most conflict within the marriage. The stress brought on by not having the financial resources you need to meet your basic financial responsibilities is the source of great conflict. Many arguments pursue because of financial strain. The mounting stress to meet marital and family obligations such as food on the table and clothes over your backs and a roof over your head is enough in today's world to lose your mind.

The continuous escalating costs to heat your home and cool your home and put gas in the car. Seemingly everywhere you turn; large companies are raising prices and gaining greater and greater wealth while the middle and poor classes of us are barely holding on. What about the cost of beef anymore. I think most Black folks eat primarily chicken and pork because it's somewhat affordable. But to eat many parts of the bull is just not affordable anymore. Jobs are struggling to stay in business and many cannot provide its employees with health care benefits. So the cost of maintaining your health goes up every year, and Black folks go less and less to the doctor, because we can't afford it, and don't even mention the cost of medicines!

All these concerns are enough to have spouses feuding with one another out of the stress and pressure to financially provide for the family. This type of conflict, if continuous, can lead to marital dissatisfaction. So much so, that one of the spouses may begin to look to another relationship where they believe could provide them with the financial means to live and sometimes to live very comfortably. In crisis, families are supposed to stick together and be strengthened by the experience, however today, many of us take the option out plan. After so much suffering (as we perceive it) and after the inability of our spouse to meet our needs, we begin to look elsewhere. We either have adulterous affairs or we have affairs that lead to the discontinuation of the marriage. This is a serious area of conflict.

I'm too Busy

'Surely you can understand all the responsibility I have to provide for this family' 'somebody has to work if we're going to be able to afford things.' Relationships are being stretched and pulled and twisted and tested by the need to meet the employment obligations, the school obligations, the extra curriculum events obligations, my personal hobby obligations, my church's obligations; my ministry obligations. In these United States of America, our capitalist society does not view the family as its greatest asset. If does however, view riches and power as its greatest asset. In order for this great nation of ours to continue to be the savior of the world; but not to it's own, it must mandate that we the people work harder, work faster, work more efficiently, work longer days, works holidays, work weekends, work, work, work.

Working all the time to meet everyone else's expectations is tough enough, but what about the family? When was the last time you spent quality time with your wife or husband, and oh, you did remember that you have children; didn't you? When are you going to throw that stupid palm pilot in the garbage, it's ruining our life!

Are you tired of people nagging you about how much time you spend distanced from your family? An area of relational conflict is due to the fact that the demands placed on us by so many are just impossible to meet. This is especially true if you have a personality that encourages you to always say yes when asked to take on something else. In our crazy, too busy kind of money making world, we must take time out to smell the roses while we're still alive. The fact is; money, houses, cars, boats, jewelry, or our status in the community will all eventually fade away. Family is that intricate part of us that sticks with you like a good bowl of grits. You can't count on employment positions today. You can't count on much of anything that the world has to offer; it's here today and gone tomorrow. What's really important is that group of people you see while quickly moving through the house on your way to the next commitment.

The most important commitment is the one you made when you said "I do." We must not remember what is really important. We must have a committed relationship with Christ, then with others as ourselves. Your spouse wants to spend time with you and you only, so keep your laptop at home. The kids miss those times when dad would go to the park and play baseball or volley ball. I even remember when daddy thought he had a jumper! Memories, is that all your life is about? Remember the memories of when you smiled and laughed with those who carry your last name. I'm not advocating anyone giving up their committed responsibilities, but I am advocating for balance. God wants us to be in balance with everything and everyone, including Him. Anytime we are out of balance with God, ourselves and each other, problems happen. Our stress increases, our anxiety increases, depression becomes a problem, and anger is turned way up; this is a primary cause of conflict. When do we have enough? When will we prioritize our lives? When will we restore that sense of priority to family? Success is not measured by how much money we have or how much stuff we can show off; but real success is finding and maintaining a sense of balance. A sense of balance means that you are meeting all of your obligations, those of professional, personal, and spiritual. In a state of balance you have joy and peace and your home is filled with laughter and love. Your relationship with your wife is good and you're enjoying one another. Your relationship with God and the church is rewarding and committed. All is well with the world. But when you are out of balance, you no longer experience the joys of life. Being in a state of imbalance leads to conflict, because conflict demands more of what you don't have; time. Conflict also suggests that the needs of your perfect world are not being met, nor are the needs of your commitment to God. You need a Christian time management plan to help you get back in balance and avoid conflict.

Disobedient Children

The number one type of call placed to the police station in the city I reside is, are "unruly charges." Single parents call the police station to file unruly charges on their teenager's. This is a primary area of conflict in the family. However there is another; disobedience towards authority. For those families that are intact (husband and wife), they are experiencing unruly and disrespectful children. Single parents are experiencing the same problem on a much larger scale, but single parents don't have the support of the missing parent to assist in raising and disciplining children.

Let's look at some of the cause of conflict in a two parent home. As previously mentioned, when a spouse or both spouses are overly committed to things outside the family, children are left to fend, mature, organize, develop, rule and exist in an environment without parental enforcement. Children, like a loving husband and wife, want and need the attention of both parents in order to properly develop their human personality. Without this nurturing, children become resentful, disobedient, rebellious and very angry. These outward expressions of emotions are a clear sign that something is wrong; thus this is a primary cause of conflict.

Sibling rivalry is another cause of disobedient children. The answer to sibling confrontations is addressed within the process called communication. All the children in the family must have a clear expectation of all ground rules. These ground rules must be effectively communicated and enforced equally and fairly. As children develop and age they are entitled to more liberties than younger siblings. Children must understand what the expectations are for duties at home, academic performance at school and so on. This information must be clearly stated and understood by each child, along with appropriate standards of disobedience. Parents don't be afraid to discipline your children. This is a primary reason why teenagers act the way they do today; this is because they have no fear of reprisal, because they never get chastised for wrong doing. Many children are without a healthy sense of reverent fear towards parents and authority, thus they do what they want to do because they have no respect (fear) for others rights. Children have not understood issues related to boundaries. Many parents today do not physically discipline their children and now they are paying the price for it. A lack of physical discipline is definitely a primary cause of current and future disobedient children leading toward grater and greater areas of conflict. Of course, I have to point out here that discipline of children can be most ineffective and difficult to administer without the foundation of masculinity in the home. OK, to be quite clear, for the most part, without a man around the home, children are more apt to manipulate single mothers (due to parent workload). The primary issues of discipline with children lye with parental inconsistencies, due to a lack of presence from dad.

What affects Parents, also affects the children. Parents and children alike demonstrate stress, frustration, impatience, fear, worry, grief, depression, anxiety and every other human emotion. Adults express these feelings slightly different than children do, but both are bothered by the stressors of life. With that said, often time's parents do not recognize their children's or teenager's emotional signs that signal something is bothering them. We must come to understand how our emotions are also cues to problems. Children and teenagers express emotional conflict as anger, misbehavior, bad attitudes, academic and social performance changes, mood swings and disassociation. The stressors of life that impact parents also impacts children, when we begin to notice that our children's behaviors are changing, take note of it, this is a warning sign that something may be wrong. Parents must deal with their children's emotional responses to family and parental stressors. Children are affected by marital conflict, financial conflict, sibling conflict, academic conflict, peer conflict, and other academic, family and social areas. Communication and reinforcement is the order of the day when it comes to addressing our children's emotional response to family conflict.

Parents must begin to engage their children and one another in continuous communications. I know Black folks don't engage in family roundtable discussions, but that must change. Parental hierarchy in itself is dysfunctional. Spouses don't effectively communicate with one another; spouses don't effectively communicate with their children; children don't effectively communicate with parents, each other and so on. Information sharing is very important to the family unit. Moreover, listening to one another in the family is probably more important for parents than always exercising parental authority in decision making. Not every piece of information should be disseminated to children, but a lot of what goes on within the family is appropriate for sharing and receiving feedback. If families started communicating more, issues that create conflict would lessen.

"Advice givers" are another area of family conflict. The marital union is often complicated and thrown into conflict through the avenue of advice giving in-laws. Husbands express frustration because of their mother in-law's influence upon their marriage. Like wise, wives are also frustrated because of parent in-law's influence upon their marriage. Who should each spouse listen to? How about listening to one another! Why do parent in-laws feel as if they have to continue shielding and protecting their son/daughter. Scripture teaches us that a man should leave his father and mother and cling to his wife.

The man has entered into a new set of rules, totally different from the rules while he lived under his parent's roof. Adam refused to stand up to Eve and do what God instructed Him to do in the Garden of Eden. Men, don't make the same mistake. Each spouse must make a commitment to each other in every way. Spouses should listen and discuss matters themselves. If each spouse agrees to seek additional wisdom from their parents, that's fine. As long as they both agree, and they both take advice that's supported by Scriptures. In addition, during this time of advice seeking, please don't forget to first seek God's wisdom and direction. Remember, the primary source of immediate wisdom is found in the Holy Bible. If we begin to use Scriptural wisdom and less human advice, we'll find solutions for our answers and we'll enjoy less conflict.

Parent-Child Conflict

Parenting used to be defined by Christian therapy principles as an 18 year process of letting go. However, this definition has now got to be altered. It's still a process of letting go, however the time frame has expanded. Some of our now 'grown up children' don't want to leave the nest. And some parents don't want their children to leave the nest. The natural development of children will come to the period in adolescence where children will begin to push their way into greater and greater independence. Children during adolescence are in the process of creating their own identity, establishing their own friendships, their own style, and their own way of doing things. Many times the ways children go about doing things is met with strong resistance by parents.

Children during the period of puberty are experiencing a great sense of awakening going on in their mind and bodies. This is the period of a teenager's life where they feel as if they know everything that was ever to be known by a human being. This is also a time of hormonal discharge. Relationships now become very important to teenagers, the way they dress and the way they keep their bodies clean are now very important to them. Teenagers are experiencing a new view of the same old world they were already living in. This is a very exciting time in adolescence and also a very scary time. Parenting during this phase of human development is met with a child that now has an opinion, and they are not afraid to use it either. But also this is a time of sincere bonding and hand holding and reassurance and mistake making and maturity and greater sense of responsibility. Young adults in this phase need support and encouragement for issues of the day and issues related to tomorrow. If parents do not recognize the opportunity they have to bond with their young adults instead of driving them as if they're driving cattle, these young adults will rebel and conflict will pursue.

Let me touch on some of the issues associated with single parenthood and children. I mentioned that in my city the police get a lot of calls from single parents asking how to file unruly charges. School age kids up to young adults are currently in a cycle of rebellion that I believe is primarily due to the fact that they do not have a stable, two-parent home in which to be nurtured from. I've already given you some statistics and their impact on children elsewhere. So let me reiterate some of that information. When families do not have a loving, God fearing and God following unified two parent family, there is a good chance that children will be dysfunctional. For the purpose of clarification, let me make this point clear. When I refer to a two parent family, you can be assured I am speaking of one man married to one woman as commanded by God. Any other earthly arrangement is the focus of great parental and family conflict that I am not going to cover at this time.

When a child grows up in a single parent home, that child misses out on half of the missing parent's nurturing. Parenting was never created to be administered by only one parent or two parents of the same sex. Disorder equates to dysfunction. When you think of what a man offers to his children, you must first think about what makes a man a man. A man must have a good understanding of his masculinity. Masculine by definition refers to the characteristics of being a man. I have heard mother's say to me, how can I teach a boy how to be a man? Women and mothers especially can do a lot of things, but some things she just can't do very well. Masculinity defines the primary differences between a male and a female. A very important component of masculinity is self-esteem. Male self-esteem is a by-product of understanding who God made men to be and how He made us to function. God made man to be perfect, thus this longing for true perfection must come through the introduction, modeling, understanding, and ultimately the commitment of a boy's life to God by his father.

Masculinity also refers to understanding Biblical headship. Scripture reveals to us that God made fathers to head their families. Masculinity does not speak only to the male body, but more about the male understanding of his role on earth. Masculinity speaks to how a man presents himself, how a man cares for him self, how a man protects himself, how a man provides for himself, how a man leads, how a man follows, how a man nurtures and care for his wife and family. Men may be masculine because of hormones, but a man must also understand that a masculine man is one that understands softness, and gentleness, sensitivity, peacefulness, conflict resolution, and helping others in their time of need. Masculinity means living the Word of God before your wife and family. Masculinity means leading your family in spiritual nurturing, praying with your family, discussing the Bible with your family, worshipping and praising God before your family and with your family. Masculinity means demonstrating to your children the impact of living for God everywhere you go. Masculinity means demonstrating to your boys how to treat a lady, and says to his daughters how to treat a man.

Masculinity is so much more that hormones and different bodies; masculinity is how God made men. Women don't have it and men don't have feminism, so such as we have, we each freely give for the nurturing of our sons and daughters. Do children go astray in healthy Christian families? Of course! But if you want to give your children the best chance at a healthy life, you must teach them as God has provided. Anything less and children will miss a great amount of learning and maturity. More so, children will miss a great piece of God and will be thrown into conflict. This conflict will be reflected in their attitudes, emotions, sense of responsibility, honesty, loyalty, dependence, intellect, in relational dynamics and in a host of negative behaviors such as drugs, alcohol, pre-marital sex, cursing, criminal activity, academic dysfunction, abuse, physical and verbal aggression and their inability to see God, among other things.

Performance Conflict

Performance conflicts envelop a host of all that has been mentioned thus far. Children do not meet the expectations of their parents in various areas of their lives. One reason for this not yet mentioned, is the conflict created by parents demanding unreasonable expectations from their children in areas parents did or did not perform well in in their youth. Parents tend to superimpose their dreams, desires, plans and aspirations upon their children without ever conferring with their children. If a parent is a physician, many times he or she expects the same out of their children. But what if one or all of the children have separate dreams, separate likes and interests opposite of their parents? This is the primary area of conflict in this matter. It isn't right for parents to live out their fantasies through their children, in addition to enforcing a higher standard of performance upon them. I'm not saying that parents should not expect, support and hold their children to their responsibilities; however, I am saying that your children may have their own dreams or desires that are in conflict with parents.

The Wrong Crowd

Every parent in the United States and especially in the African American communities is concerned with their children being influenced by the wrong person or crowd. I have heard many parental testimonies speak to the pain of confusion, incomprehension, hopelessness, concern and outrage as parent after parent told their heartbreaking story to me about their academically superior, quiet and yet introverted child that have now taken to drugs and alcohol for unknown reasons, sending the family into a state of conflict.

Why do kids get involved in drugs and alcohol? First, let's admit the truth of living in a fallen and evil world. Every person from pre-adolescence on is under the temptation to engage in drugs, alcohol, sex, or some other means of masking our needs and wants. Furthermore, some of us are not caught up in the wrong stuff because of our situations, but some of us, primarily adolescence, are coaxed into bad behaviors by an influential person or group.

Family stress, finances, academics, relationships, brokenness, low self-esteem, grief and depression, anxieties, dad and mom, ourselves, and more, are the culprits behind the attempts to resist doing wrong. At age 11 onward, many children and adults are increasingly under some kind of ongoing harmful stress that wears away at our ability to maintain control and balance in our lives. Every area of conflict mentioned thus far and every area covered in this book and then some, are all strong reasons why the human ability to maintain control comes crashing down like a title wave, drowning us in sorrow, despair, sadness, confusion, anger and the inability to maintain control. Thus after attempting to hold on, we eventually let go of our lifelines and we seek opportunities to evade the pain left behind from the wakes of dysfunction in our lives.

I hope you're not surprised that children are suffering with a lot of the same mental and emotional health issues as adults are. Always remember: what affects adults, affects children. The pressure for teenagers to outperform other classmates can take its toll on our youths. The pressure placed by coaches, parents and peers toward our youth to be the best in sports and other activities, are tremendous. We know that youths who participate in high school sports are not getting paid, but you couldn't prove that to many of them. To loss in a team sporting event is toward many of our youths equal to losing the Superbowl of football; the World Series of baseball; the Finals of basketball; or the Masters of golf championships. Today in high school sports the pressure to win is extreme, and when that goal is not obtained, the disappointment associated with losing equates to the impact of losing one's hopes and dreams.

Our youth suffers with issues related to grief, low self-view and often times, depression associated with losing. Our youths begin to question their abilities; they question whether they really have what it takes. In addition, everyone remembers a winner, but no one wants to associate with a loser. Thus the performance pressure associated with being a winner all the time brings some youth to the point of turning to drugs, alcohol, sex and other devices to help them cope with the pressure, the stress, the demand, the expectations associated with making a name. This same kind of stress is also associated with academics, employment, careers, marriage and other areas of life.

So, what about the other kind of person that is not caught up with any of the things mentioned thus far. What about that bright, bubbly extroverted youth or adult who sees the joy in life every minute of the day. Well, for the socialite, this person has a strong desire and need to be around people and be accepted. Sometimes, to be accepted means that you've got to do some initiation things to fit in. This is when you hear that cool brother or sister say to you, "just try it once" "you want to be accepted don't you?" The first rule of thumb here is that you must be OK with who you are. You do not need others to validate who you are and where you are in life. Remember it's very difficult for an imperfect person to validate another imperfect person. If you need validation, go to someone who understands validation; take it to Jesus.

In addition, also understand that not everyone in the world can live up to the expectations others place upon them and the expectations we sometimes place on ourselves. We have all sinned and fallen short of God's glory; therefore, we are not perfect and will not be perfect until Jesus comes back for us; that is, those of us who are believers. Everything that we do, we're to do it as if we're doing it for the Lord. This means that God expects us to give it our best; but when we've done that, we've done it; and there is nothing more we can do. So not every teenager will grow up to be a famous athlete or academician. Some will grow up never having their name in lights. But that's OK; the only book you don't want your name not to be in is the Lamb's Book of Life. As long as your name is in this book, you're alright. Keep on keeping on.

The Black Church

"One Faith; One Lord; One Baptism"

These are the words written by the Apostle Paul in his letter to the Ephesians. Paul wrote these words in regards to unity in the body of Christ. That's right, even then the church was involved in some things that needed to be taken care of, and it's no different today. However, today I believe the Black church is more divided, is more dysfunctional and is worldlier than ever before (my opinion only). Black Pastors do not collaborate with other churches. So many of our churches stand alone because its leaders are too selfish, untrustworthy, unbiblical, shortsighted and insecure in their ministries to ever expand and collaborate with other churches for the purpose of moving the gospel forward. There is just too much bickering going on between the officers of the church and the congregations of the church.

The point of ministry is to bring people to Christ. Jesus preached "The kingdom of God is at hand." Jesus preached salvation through reconciliation. The Black church and the Christian church as a whole is in a state of crisis. The United States once sent droves of missionaries to other nations of the world to evangelize them. Now these same nations are sending missionaries to us to evangelize us! Everyone else in the world can see that the once great Christian church in the U.S. has lost its savor and now these nations are trying to help us see Christ. How ironic is that! Not only are Black folks divided as a race of people, but this division in quite evident even in our churches. The Black church stands in need of a revival. We have grown too lazy for the gospel. We have become powerless, we have become weak, we have become overly tunnel vision focused in our vision and we have become too threatened by new ministers who exhibit a zeal for the Lord.

Many of our Pastors stay too long in their positions. There do come a time when the Pastor must sit down and allow someone else the opportunity to serve. Why are so many Black ministers starting their own churches? Because they can't serve God in the one they were in. There is only one Pastor in the Black church and he or she is the only minister receiving wages. Other people receiving wages are the musicians and the office staff. Why is it that the associate ministers receive nothing but more request for their time and talent? Where is the respect for all clergy that we once shared as a people? Associate ministers in some churches don't even get a chance to preach. Associate ministers are called upon to volunteer their time and skills to the church, but not be true to their calling.

Why do so many of our Black church Pastors feel threatened when a minister uses his/her zeal for the Lord? When a minister uses the gifts God has given him/her, especially the gifts of preaching, teaching and administration; when these gifts are used, the Pastor becomes threatened, and the result is conflict. An associates name cannot be mentioned more than the Pastor's name! If this happens, the associate is ostracized by the Pastor. When a little minister is not in the click with the big ministers, the little ministers get tossed out with the garbage. In other words, when the gifts of a minister (not a Pastor), are offered to the elite Pastors of the city, the minister is often refused because he/she is not a Pastor. Education also represents conflict to the Pastor. Some Pastor's don't want associate ministers who have more education than they do, or the same education. There can only be one chief in the Black church.

Many of our churches claim to be operated by a democratic, participative type government. I challenge the validity of this so called truth. The fact is: in the Black church, if the Senior Pastor does not agree with a new ministry or suggestion or activity, that item will get nowhere. It does not matter if the congregation wants the program or not, if the Pastor says no, its no. Why would the Pastor say no? Many times, a Pastor will say no, if it represents an unfamiliar area to him/her. Unfamiliar areas equate to discomfort and loss of control. And this is the primary reason for the dysfunction in today's Black church; control. A Black Pastor does not ever want to lose the reins of authority he/she has to govern the affairs of the church. Many of our Black churches should be growing, but they are not and the reason for this is that they are stagnant in their ministries, because there is conflict with the Pastor over ministerial views of the church and congregation, thus ministers, deacons and congregants leave the church and attend another where they believe they will have their needs addressed.

Black men especially, have historically exhibited issues of trust. A lack of trust can be viewed in Black men as far back as slavery. Black men have demonstrated issues of trust towards governments, the judicial system, the medical community, the educational communities, the social communities, the professional sporting communities, with God and with each other. Are the leaders of the Black church listening to the needs of their congregation; the community; the nation; God? Has the church lost its influence; it's stature in the world; it's ability to be holy? It's definitely has lost its ability to be the welfare system of the community. And so conflict is served as the 'special of the day'.

I hope that you have seen the pattern of dysfunction presented to you. Conflict has at the root of it, selfishness. Why do we argue and fight; because we don't get our way! What we want is more important than what others want; thus we have conflict.

Conflict as Opportunity

I've attempted to provide you an introduction to family conflict in the African American community. Not every subject mentioned will speak to your situation. But rest assured that every topic covered here and in the pages of other chapters, are real! These topics represent real issues in real Black people's lives. Conflict is an opportunity for Christians to demonstrate to those around them the characteristics of God through Christ Jesus. The world wants to know more about this man named Jesus. We will not admit this, but conflict brings upon pain and suffering, thus pain and suffering is where God really shows up and shows out. It is through our low points of life when we have lost control and have utilized all means to help ourselves, but have failed; this is when we want to see God, because we always knew in our hearts that He is the only one who could help us. So, Christians must demonstrate Christ in their lives by being a servant of Christ to others. We must demonstrate the love of God through Christ Jesus, whenever an opportunity is given to let His light shine. For many people struggling through life without Jesus, this could be the only opportunity to let them know that God still loves them.

Principles of Conflict Resolution

Proverbs 19:11
"A man's wisdom gives him patience; it is to his glory to overlook an offense."

Matthew 18:15-20
"If your brother sins against you, go and show him his fault, just between the two of you. If he listens to you, you have won your brother over. But if he will not listen, take one or two others along, so that every matter may be established by the testimony of two or three witnesses. If he refuses to listen to them, tell it to the church; and if he refuses to listen even to the church, treat him as you would a pagan or a tax collector. I tell you the truth, whatever you bind on earth will be bound in heaven, and whatever you loose on earth will be loosed in

heaven. Again, I tell you that if two of you on earth agree about anything you ask for, it will be done for you by my Father in heaven. For where two or three come together in my name, there am I with them."

Galatians 6:1-2
"Brothers, if someone is caught in a sin, you who are spiritual should restore him gently. But watch yourself, or you also may be tempted. Carry each other's burdens, and in this way you will fulfill the law of Christ."

Ephesians 4:29
"Do not let any unwholesome talk come out of your mouths, but only what is helpful for building others up according to their needs, that it may benefit those who listen."

2 Timothy 2:24-26
"And the Lord's servant must not quarrel; instead, he must be kind to everyone, able to teach, not resentful. Those who oppose him he must gently instruct, in the hope that God will grant them repentance leading them to a knowledge of the truth, and that they will come to their senses and escape from the trap of the devil, who has taken them captive to do his will."

James 4:1-2
"What causes fights and quarrels among you? Don't they come from your desires that battle within you? You want something but don't get it. You kill and covet, but you cannot have what you want. You quarrel and fight. You do not have, because you do not ask God."

Ephesians 4:32
"Be kind and compassionate to one another, forgiving each other, just as in Christ God forgave you."

Romans 12:18
"If it is possible, as far as it depends on you, live at peace with everyone."

1 Peter 4:8
"Above all, love each other deeply, because love covers a multitude of sins."

In this life we will experience conflict. The issue is not to dismiss all conflict, but to understand the dynamics of conflict, the levels of conflict, the genesis of conflict, conflict resolution and the opportunities in conflict to demonstrate God's righteousness in us. Very few people can agree upon any thing; especially me. Confrontation can be a very powerful tool to bring forth righteousness by confronting the truth about ourselves and those around us. *"As much as it depends on you, be at peace with everyone."* God is a God of peace, and not of human sinfulness. God wants every believer to demonstrate and be at peace with him/herself and everyone else. Peace is in your hand; you control peace. *"Blessed are the peacemakers, for they shall have peace."* But wanting peace and working toward peace remain two separate issues!

Chapter Five
The Father Connection
(The importance of fathers)

Before I get into this chapter, let me begin with a positive note. I want all husbands, live in fathers, step fathers, foster fathers, fathers of adopted children, single fathers and fathers attempting to do the right thing to please stand up and take your applause. Society and this book want to acknowledge you for doing the right thing. You hear almost daily, the ridicule, the jokes, the bad press and negative attitudes of society asking are there any good Black men? I want you to know as a single dad myself, good and descent Black men are still in the world today. Unfortunately, we have been overshadowed by many misguided Brothers, both young and mature, who have decided that being a man was something they did not want to participate in. We all understand that just because we have a bat and two balls, (which do not qualify us for the honor of being a man; it simply states our gender) males believe themselves to be men? So, on behalf of that part of society that acknowledges our struggles, our pains, our fortitude, our dedication, our commitment, our long suffering and love for our family, I want to personally thank you for hanging in there, and I want to encourage you to continue living right. And in your living right, please try to help another Brother that has fallen by the wayside. Brothers, this book was not written to you or about you; just the opposite, it is written to bring out the truth about the status of Black men in society today. This book is written to strongly encourage all Black men and God's children to step up to the plate and make a change for the good. This book was written to attempt to motivate Black men and women to come back to God, to come back to being husbands, and wives, fathers, mothers and families. I pray God's special blessings on each and every one who is filling the role of husband, father, and friend.

When you think of your father what thoughts or memories come to mind? Are you or were you one of the lucky children who had a live in father? Or were you one of the lucky ones who had a dysfunctional live in father? Or maybe you were one of the unlucky ones who had a father, but never saw or spoke with him? I can go on with the various scenarios. The point is; a father is a blessing and a disappearing entity within the African American family. When I think back on my own childhood with my father, I remember how fortunate I was to have both a mom and a dad living in the same house with my five brothers and me. My mom and dad have since gone on to be with the Lord, and I miss them both very, very much.

My Story

My dad was an alcoholic. My dad was abusive and highly argumentative towards my mom and other members in the family. My dad was tough on us boys, he demanded perfection and he taught us the value of hard work and earning your share. My dad was dysfunctional in every sense of the term. I grew up in a violent and dysfunctional family dynamic. But this was not always the case; my sibling order is second from the last. So my older brothers had an opportunity to enjoy my dad and our family in ways I did not. You see, I was reaching puberty when my dad began to meet all the criteria for alcohol addiction, prior to this time, I'm sure he would have met the criteria for alcohol abuse.

If you would have asked my mom, I'm pretty sure she would have definitely wanted to change history and live another way than how she lived being married to my dad. My dad was a boxer, a singer, a smooth brother, who went to work everyday. He supplied the financial resources for us to live and enjoy all the special days of the calendar. But it was still financially tough. I do not remember reaching for whole milk in the refrigerator, or name brand cold cereals or many of the foods I now take for granted. I remember my mother making mayonnaise, sugar, and mustard sandwiches to eat. No, I did not have a lot of things, but you know something; I had a dad. My dad was very intellectual after receiving a new life after alcoholism. My dad enjoyed with a great sense of passion the art of debate. If there was a subject to be discussed in the world, my dad knew everything there was to be known about it. He always taught my brothers and me to know something about everything, so you don't seem ignorant. As I have grown up, I now believe this view of my dad to be a good one.

"Fathers" The Missing Component in the African-American Family

Sunday's were always special at our house in the projects on Unwin road in Cleveland, Ohio. Sunday's was the family meal day. On Sunday's my mom would prepare a full course family meal. I still remember sitting at the table with my arm around my dinner plate, protecting and shielding my plate from my brothers. You see, all my brothers had a healthy appetite, and my mom was a superb cook, so if you wanted all of the foods on your plate, you had better protect them, because someone was always watching to see if you did not want to eat something on your plate. I remember my first bike. No, it wasn't a new bike from the store, it was a rebuilt bike made by my hands. In those days, living in the projects was a mechanic's heaven. No one in the projects could afford much of anything new, so if you wanted something, you usually had to build it. My dad would talk me through how to build a bike from various parts I found at the incinerator (the place where everyone disposed of their garbage). This is the same way me and my friends built go carts and other mobile toys to play with.

We were financially strapped. My family lived with the dysfunction of an alcoholic father; but none the less, we had one. I loved and now miss my father. I can say all kinds of bad things about my father, but that's not what I want you to know. I want you to know that not long ago, African American families stuck together. No family was, nor is ever perfect, least of all, a struggling family. But I can say with pride and a smile on my face that I had a complete family. I had both a mom and a dad under the same roof for the majority of my adolescence. In addition, I can say with pride, when people see me and my brothers together, "Hey! you guys all look alike." I'm proud to know that all of my brothers came from one mom and one dad and we all look alike. I did not have to deal with any of my brothers having a different mom or a different dad, like so many people today have to.

The day my dad past, was a very sad day for me. My older brothers always told me that I was my daddy's favorite. I did not agree with them, because my dad and I always fought. Isn't it strange to know that through all of life's up's and down's, hurts and pains; the one you fight with the most, is the very person who cares for you greatly, although they have difficulty expressing it. The very hour my dad's heart began to fail him, the nurse kept me advised of his condition, as I was the brother in charge of his care. The nurse said to me, when your dad's heart rate drops down to 30, he'll begin to go fast. So, when my dad's heart rate fell to 35, I assembled the family that was their and we entered his room. I grabbed my dad's cold and swollen hand. I watched him as the blood oozed from every orifice of his body, until his heart gave out as he gave up the ghost. At that very minute my family and I joined hands in prayer and I offered thanksgiving to God for the opportunity to be my dad's son and share in his life. Then I committed my dad's soul back to God. Just thinking of all this again, saddens me.

The dad factor in a child's life is very important. I'd rather have had a more loving and participative dad in my life, but I can say with pride, I had a dad. When I talk with people today, young and old, many of them share in the experiences of never having a dad around. I've talked with young adults who have never met their dads; some youths have met their dads but have not, cannot, and will not spend time with their dads, because he's in prison. Other youths have been taken advantaged of by their dads in all kinds of ways, and thus they have issues of grief and anger. Grown men and women share in the same issues as today's youths. Their dads never loved them, or their dads always promised to come and see them, but never did. The stories are endless and they go on and on, always, with tears in the eyes of the youth or adult telling me their story.

The Dad Factor

We're hurting today because of the dad factor. I do not want you to think that the absence of the father in the Black family is the only problem, it's not; but it is a very large one. Dads not only blanket the family with love and care. But dads provide needed attention to both girls and boys. Each gender of child has a special connection to their father. According to the website Fathers.com, let me share with you some of their information concerning dads in general.

According to 72.2% of the U.S. population, fatherlessness is the most critical family or social problem facing America.
(Source: National Center for Father, January, 1999)

- An estimated 24.7 million children (36.3%) live absent their biological father.
- The 1997 Gallup Youth Survey found the following among U.S. teen
    - 33% live away from their father
    - 43% of urban teens live away from their father
- 57.7% of all black children live in single parent homes. (Marital Status and Living Arrangements: March 1994).
- Black children living with mother only rose in 1995 to 51.2%. (Statistical Abstract of the U.S. 1997).

Reported Consequences

According to the National Center for Children 1996.

- Poverty in 1996 amongst young children living with unmarried mothers was five times as likely to be poor and ten times as likely to be extremely poor.
- Almost 75% of American children living in single parent families will experience poverty before they turn 11 years old. Only 20 percent of two parent families will do the same.

According to the U.S. Bureau of Census. Statistical Abstract of the U.S. 1994

- 67.5% of Black children living in single parent homes under age six lived in poverty
- 19.3% of Black children living in a two parent family under age six lived in poverty

According to the U.S. Department of Health and Human Services. Center for health survey on child health. Washington, D.C. 1993

- ➢ The fatherless are at a dramatically greater risk of drug and alcohol abuse
- ➢ Children growing up in a single parent household are at a significant risk for drug abuse as teenagers
- ➢ Unmarried mothers are less likely to obtain prenatal care and are more likely to birth a low birth weight baby.
- ➢ Children from single parent homes had more physical and mental health problems than children who lived in married homes. Additionally, boys in single parent homes were found with more illnesses than girls in single parent homes.
- ➢ Children in single parent homes are two to three times more likely than children in married homes to have emotional and behavioral problems.
- ➢ Three out of four teenage suicides occur in households where a parent is absent
- ➢ Children who lived with one parent had lower grade point averages and lower college aspirations, poor attendance records, and higher drop out rates than students who lived with both parents. Source-McLanahan, Sara and Gary Sandefur. Growing up with a Single Parent: Harvard University Press, 1994.
- ➢ Fatherless children are twice as likely to drop out of school.
- ➢ School children from divorced families are absent more, and more anxious and hostile, and withdrawn, and are less popular with their peers than those of intact families.

In addition:

- ➢ Children of single parent families are more likely to get into trouble with the judicial system
- ➢ Children in single parent families are more likely to be repeat juvenile offenders
- ➢ Children in single parent families are more likely to be chronic juvenile offenders

- Adolescent females between the ages of 15-19 years of age raised in a fatherless family are significantly more likely to engage in premarital sex.
- A survey taken found that 97% of girls said that having parents they could talk to could reduce teen pregnancy
- 93% said having loving parents reduced the risk of teen pregnancy.
- 76% said that their fathers were very or somewhat influential on their decision to have sex.
- Children in single parent families are more likely to get pregnant as teens.
(Source: U.S. Department of Health and Human Services)

A researched brief written by Child Trends.org stated the following:

Children benefit from positive relationships with their fathers.
- Warmth, closeness, and nurturance are important aspects of a healthy parent-child relationship regardless of whether the parent is a mother or father. But research also suggests that fathers contribute to their children's healthy development in ways that are unique from mothers. For example, in one study of young children's cognitive development, fathers promoted their child's intellectual development and social competence through physical play, whereas mothers promoted these skills through verbal expressions and teaching activities.

Fathers can positively influence their children's development by assuming a significant amount of the4 child care tasks.
- Several studies have found that when fathers spend more time on child care tasks, children benefit. For instance, in one study, preschool-age children whose fathers were responsible for 40 percent or more of the family's child care tasks had higher scores on assessments of cognitive development, had more of a sense of mastery over their environments, and exhibited more empathy than those children whose fathers were less involved.

Care by fathers may be particularly influential in the first year of life. In another study, children who were cared for by their father in their first year had higher scores on assessments of cognitive development than those children who were cared for in child care centers.

Fathers' involvement can affect children's social development, cognitive development, and academic achievement.

- Higher levels of father involvement in activities with their children, such as eating meals together, going on outings, and helping with homework, are associated with fewer behavior problems, higher levels of sociability, and a high level of school performance among children and adolescents.
- In two-parent families, when both fathers and mothers are involved in children's schooling, there is a higher likelihood that children in first through twelfth grades will get high grades and enjoy school, and a reduced likelihood that a child will repeat a grade.
- However, father involvement has been found to be a more important predictor than mother involvement of the likelihood of getting high grades. For children in first through twelfth grades living in single father families, high father involvement is associated with getting high grades and enjoying school, and a lower chance of suspension or expulsion from school.
- It should also be noted that the research indicated that the quality of fatherhood was the primary factor in children's stability and positive outcome factors.

Obie Clayton, Ronald B. Mincy and David Blankenhorn, in their book entitled "Black Fathers in Contemporary American Society Strengths, Weaknesses, and Strategies for Change," wrote three conclusions to the issue of Black fathers in America.

- Here is our first conclusion: steadily increasing the proportion over the next ten years of black children who are residing with their responsible, loving fathers is both necessary and possible. This reintegration of nurturing black fathers into the homes and therefore the lives of their children is the prime goal, the umbrella priority, under which all the others fit.

- This brings us to our second conclusion: Because marriage is a vital support for effective fatherhood, and because marriage on average provides the optimal environment for healthy child development, a major priority for black America and for the society as a whole should be to steadily increase the proportion of children growing up in two-biological-parent, married-couple homes.

- The three editors of this volume are themselves not entirely in agreement regarding the exact role of marriage in the renewal of black (and American) fatherhood. But we are agreed that marriage matters; that it is quite unlikely that we as a society will be able to turn the corner on father absence while simultaneously witnessing and permitting the further disintegration of marriage; and therefore, as a general rule, brining back the fathers and strengthening marriage are goals that stand best when they stand together.

- Our final conclusion: Contemporary U.S. father absence is less a black crisis than an American crisis, one that affects the entire society. Stemming primarily from broad societal trends, not subcultural, racial, or ethnic trends, the crisis of black fathers, thought urgent in its own right and deserving of special attention from policy makers, cannot be separated, analytically or prescriptively, from the broader crisis of U.S. fathers, which cuts across all lines of race and class. The fatherhood crisis we face in the United States is essentially societal, not racial (although it has racial aspects and implications). Neither is it a correlate of economic status (although it has clear economic dimensions). For this

reason, our response to the crisis must also be societal in nature. In the final analysis, fatherlessness is not a "them" problem. It's an "us" problem.
Source: American Values .org

There should not be a mystery by now concerning the importance of "Fathers" to the overall success of the family; not just the Black family but the family period. Without the proper functioning of the family, nothing else can develop. A strong family unit provides for the spiritual, emotional, psychological, behavioral, relational and intellectual development and functioning of the human person. A weak family cannot properly develop all the positive attributes obtained in a proper healthy family unit. Moreover, the family does not exist without first having a strong, unified and connected husband and wife. It is not enough just to have a father and mother living under the same roof, but the father and mother must first come together as husband and wife. Husband's and wives first must come together united and connected to God through Jesus Christ. If unity does not exist with God through Christ, proper unity will fail to exist between everyone. Christ is the unifier of mankind to the blessings of our heavenly Father. Jesus is the magnet that draws us into relationship with God the Father. Without a proper relationship through Christ, we can never obtain the full measure of both earthly and heavenly rewards.

A unified and connected husband and wife; father and mother, must have a spiritual connectedness with Christ. The individual must have confessed Christ, and is now living for Christ. The individual must join with another believer who shares the love and commitment to Christ. The two believers, if they are equally yoked in other areas of their lives, should be joined together as one. Once joined together as one, and living together to serve the "One," then come children. Any other process for the unification and procreation of man and woman will not be blessed. Only when we do things decent and in God's order will God bless us. Failure to follow His rules only results in dysfunction. Anytime we're out of God's order, we're in disorder. Disorder leads to dysfunction, and dysfunction leads to an array of problems from every aspect of life.

God did not ordain single parenthood. I truly believe that God blesses single parents, but it was not His original plan for the family.

Children Suffers Father's Sin

Exodus 20:5, 6 *"You shall not bow down to them or worship them; for I, the Lord your God, am a jealous God, punishing the children for the sin of the fathers to the third and fourth generation of those who hate me, but showing love to a thousand generations of those who love me and keep my commandments."*

It is my belief, that we are living in a time where our children are being punished by God because of the actions of their fathers and their fathers, father. The referenced Scripture in Exodus is referring to all the people of Israel that God set free from bondage in Egypt by pharaoh. God is instructing the Israelites (followers of God) not to worship worldly things (gods), because He is the one true and living God. God promises to punish the children of the parents who worshipped crack-cocaine, sex, drinking, gambling, lying, and stealing and so on. Moreover, the Scripture makes reference to God's judgment for sin (disobedience). God states that He is a jealous God and there shall be no other god's before Him. Could it be that God is punishing today's children because of the disobedience of fathers?

Have Black men turned away from God and worshipped worldly pleasures that have led him to the place he is today. Many of our Black men and now Black women are incarcerated, and of those incarcerated, three fourths of them are on their way to being addicted, or is already addicted to crack cocaine or marijuana. Father's who serve their own worldly desires over God's Will and their own parental responsibilities, have found not only themselves being punished but their children as well. Do your children deserve to be punished for your disobedience to God? Do your children deserve to be raised in a world that does not seek to honor, respect, and nurture or love them? Do your children deserve to endure the shame, ridicule, embarrassment and pain behind telling others their dad is in prison or strung out on one thing or another? What about your children's feelings? What sins have you or are you continually committing that has God's judgment against your children?

Have the Black man become so self-serving and selfish that no one and nothing is important to him but what he wants? No wonder we have so many angry Black women in the world today? No wonder we have so many Black people who's only out for themselves, most of us have endured enough emotional pain to last three life times, and many of us have not graduated high school yet. Is this fair to the children? Is this fair to your baby's mama? Is this fair to God? Instead of doing what's right, we are attracted to what feels good, looks good, taste good, and can get us 'moe money', 'moe money', 'moe money'! Just so we can turn around and mess that up too! Black men, we must be held accountable for our choices and actions. There is no place we can run to hide our talk and walk from God, even though we ran from our responsibilities to our woman and children.

How can the estranged Black man not feel some sense of guilt and shame? I personally don't want any of you to feel harmful shame, but feel righteous shame. Please let me explain the difference. Harmful shame leads one into depression and a worst disposition in life. I don't want you to feel this way, instead I want you to be compelled by the truth associated with your guilt and shame that would lead and motivate you to seek reconciliation with God, yourself, your baby mama's and your children. Good guilt leads toward conviction and conviction leads to righteousness. This is the place God wants all of us to be. Even though my words are tough, my love for you is tougher. I do not want to see estranged Black men hurt anymore unless it is necessary to move you through the process of righteous guilt and shame towards reconciliation.

Estranged Black men have got to attempt to right their wrongs with the mother of their children. Some Black women can be very tough; this is the truth, even if Black women don't agree with it. The reason why I'm not overly confronting Black women is because Black women do not hold the key to righteous leadership according to Scripture. God did not speak and give the commands to women and neither did He give women the role of leader. God did speak to the man and thus gave the man His commandments; therefore if we are to operate properly and in God's order, I must confront the men. The key to turning around a very violent and misguided youthful generation will never rest in the arms of government or law enforcement, but with these kids daddy! Father's are the answer, and just not any kind of father, but a God fearing, God loving and obedient father who loves the Lord.

Jeremiah 16:10-13 *"When you tell these people all this and they ask you, 'Why has the Lord decreed such a great disaster against us? What wrong have we done? What sin have we committed against the Lord our God?' Then say to them, 'It is because your fathers forsook me,' declares the Lord, 'and followed other gods and served and worshipped them. They forsook me and did not keep my law. But you have behaved more wickedly than your fathers. See how each of you is following the stubbornness of his evil heart instead of obeying me. So I will throw you out of this land into a land neither you nor your fathers have known, and there you will serve other gods day and night, for I will show you no favor.'*

African Americans origins lay in Africa, not in the United States. Africa was the land God gave us, but sin took us away from our land and placed us into a strange new land called America. We were outcasts in this land. We were mistreated and not considered human in this new land. But God took this new land called America and broke the chains of bondage that sin had shackled to our existence. God gave us liberty, freedom, a name, a purpose, a way out of degradation and humiliation. God made us somebody in the land called America. But years later we find ourselves once again struggling with shackles on our feet. Perhaps this punishment is self-inflicted or perhaps it is God trying to get our attention. Either way, African Americans have turned away from God and once again worshipped the world and not the world's creator. America is still our home, but now it is a home full of pain and turmoil on every hand. Why has life gotten to be so hard? It's simple; we have chosen to forsake God and His teachings for the pleasures of our hearts, minds and the world.

Why have so many of the Black youth of today gone astray? Many of today's youth have lost their minds because their fathers never taught them to love God. Father's have failed to demonstrate love for God, and neither has fathers taught their children about God, because they themselves do not know Him personally. Jeremiah in the above Scripture stated that the youth of today is worse than their parents. This is how the cycle of sin operates. Each generation of children who have forsaken God is worst than the generation before them. Each generation have chosen their weapons of destruction, whether drugs, alcohol, sex, or violence, each generation of youth born without the knowledge, love, and commitment to God, is worse off and more destructive and evil than the preceding generation. All of this evil and sin has and continue to occur because the fathers of our children have not stepped up to the plate and did the right thing.

Black families need and must have Father's who love the Lord and their families greater than they do their own desires and needs. Whether Black fathers are willing to admit this or not; estranged Black fathers are suffering. Many of you are suffering and don't know why. Many of you are still doing dumb stuff and don't have a clue why you're doing it. Many of you are sitting in jail cells playing your life over and over and over in your minds, trying to figure out just how things got so out of control. My Brothers, you made some bad choices. We all make bad choices, but when you realize it, you must agree within yourself that you need a course direction change. Airline pilots don't fly directly into bad weather if they can help it. Pilots read the signs on their radar, and by talking to the tower and by looking into the sky. Once they realize the storm may be too bumpy or dangerous, they take a course direction and fly another way around the storm.

This is what happened to many of you Brothers, you read the signs, you were given healthy advice, and many of you saw it coming right at you, but you failed to make a course direction change to safety. You navigated your way directly into the heart of the storms of life, until you found yourself in deep trouble with no other way to turn. When you finally realized where you were, it was too late. You were knee-deep in the heart of the storm and you found yourself lost in space, and you've been lost every sense. God asked me to throw out the life line to you. This is your wake up call; this is your call to arms. God is sending out the light from the light house. He's searching for you and He knows exactly where you are; don't you see His light? His light offers you safety, guidance, shelter from the storms and a new opportunity at life. See it? Don't you see His light?

The Heavenly Family: The Earthly Family

The heavenly family consists of God the Father, Jesus the Son, and the Holy Spirit. Our God is one God in three persons; three persons, but only one God. Our heavenly Father is the Godhead; Jesus His only Begotten Son represents God in human flesh. Jesus presents to all believers as our advocate. The Holy Spirit is the character of God. The Holy Spirit is every believer's comforter and guide. Each person in the Holy Trinity represents God and is God, although each person has specific duties within their relationship to each other. Each person in the Holy Trinity is perfect in every way. The trinity is perfectly aligned with one another and the Father as one. Jesus and the Holy Spirit subject themselves to the Father. In this way all things of the Holy Trinity works as God the Father wills it. This relationship between the person's of the Holy Trinity is resembled in the earthly relationship with man, woman and the family.

Jesus is subjective to the will of His Father. In this same manner, the wife and children is subjective to the commandments placed on the husband to the family by the triune God. The wife is a helper and supporter to her husband, just as the Holy Spirit functions as our helper and guide. God is perfect and thus He created us perfect until we fell to sin. God's perfection was given to mankind to immolate the perfection of Himself. Within this perfection, the husband, wife and children would have functioned perfectly as the triune God functions perfectly. Therefore, if we as a human race want to be blessed and live in harmony, unity and connectedness again, we must first come to be in harmony, unity and connectedness with the triune God through Jesus Christ. From this union, we can individually and collectively fulfill the roles God laid out for us. But this cannot and will not happen until our prodigal men; women and children return to God first.

We all want our children to succeed and be the best they can be. Dr. Tim Clinton in his booklet entitled "The Dad Factor," writes four primary factors in nurturing children.

"Fathers, bring them up in the nurture and admonition of the Lord."

This can be accomplished in four primary ways:

A. Through example. The foundation of effective fathering is a godly lifestyle lived out before your kids.
B. Through Instruction. Everyday you have influence in your son or daughter's life. What life instruction did you tech today? Parents have the God-given responsibility to teach the ways of the Lord (Dt. 6:6-9; Prov. 4). You are coach dad…they learn not only how to catch a ball, fish, or shoot hoops, but also how to manage anger, love, cope with failure and loss, how to be persistent and more.
C. Through Discipline. Kids need structure and boundaries. And they are notorious for pushing to see how far rules can be stretched. Healthy discipline provides a tremendous opportunity for learning. Discipline that teaches about how to face life opens the channels of communication between father and child. Good dads teach boundaries and lessons of self-control.
D. Through Love. Throughout your struggles as a father, don't forget to factor in the most important part of the equation—

love. What your child needs and wants isn't a trip to the Braves game—it's you. Heavy doses of you! That's because kids often spell love—Time. The gifts that come from love are many. Forgiveness, patience, kindness, truth, loyalty, and believing in one another are a few. Love does not allow jealousy, envy, pride, or selfishness (1 Corinthians 13).

Responsibility

"When I was a child, I talked like a child; I thought like a child, I reasoned like a child. When I became a man, I put childish ways behind me." (1 Corinthians 13:11)

Fleeing Responsibility

"But Jonah ran away from the Lord and headed for Tarshish. He went down to Joppa, where he found a ship bound for that port. After paying the fare, he went aboard and sailed for Tarshish to flee from the Lord." (Jonah 1:3)

Unfortunately many of our Brothers have decided to immolate the prophet Jonah. Jonah was called by God to go to Nineveh and preach against it, because of the city's wickedness, but Jonah ran away from what God called him to do. Jonah physically ran away from both the city and what God instructed him to do. But we all know the moral of this story, even if you've never read it before. You can't run from God, no matter how hard and how long you try. If God doesn't bring you to Himself here on earth, He'll catch you when you go up a little higher.

The question is why? Why have so many Brothers run from the responsibilities to their children, their families, to society and ultimately God? I know for a fact, that some Sisters make you want to run, and that's not a good thing for the Sisters. You see, if Brothers are going to move into their position in the family, the Sisters are going to have to get off of their negative attitudes. Sisters, you can't hope that your baby's daddy will step up to his responsibilities if you're nagging him, undermining him and degrading him in front of the children and other Sisters. If you're a Christian Sister, you're going to have to forgive him as God has and will forgive you. So I know it to be a fact that some Brothers have vacated their responsibilities because of a dysfunctional relationship with their baby's mama.

Another reason why Brothers are fleeing their responsibilities is due to the fact that their father's were dysfunctional towards them and thus when they grew up they reciprocated the same things toward their children. There is something in the study of theology called the "Sin cycle." Basically the sin cycle is a continuous cycle of repeated mistakes. Professionals understand how human beings learn, especially during our early years of development, from birth to about age six our personality (the totality of being human) is 85% developed. Therefore as expressed in another chapter, we learn by watching our parents and many others as they cross our developmental path. Each of these influencers has a parental responsibility to model before children righteous behaviors and attitudes. If our parents modeled a dysfunctional and sinful activity before us, the chances are pretty good that when we grow up we will model the same behaviors and attitudes, thus the cycle is repeated again.

Brothers, we hold power in our hands and in our tongues. The question we must ask ourselves is whether we're going to continue to express dysfunctional and sinful behaviors and attitudes or are we going to choose another pathway. The sin cycle can be broken, its all in the choices we make. We have the responsibility to stop the continuous cycle of sin and choose righteousness over sinfulness. Righteousness leads towards blessings and sinfulness leads us towards missed blessings and increased trouble and strife. The prophet Jonah fled from his responsibility. I understand that not everyone wants to be in charge. This is why on our jobs; some of us are floor supervisors, office supervisors. Some of us have climbed the management ladder and have taken on responsibilities of middle management and then some of us have been extremely blessed with being able to lead others from the executive level. But what about those workers who have done the same job for twenty or thirty years without complaining and without ever wanting to climb up the ladder.

The fact is as a human race, some of us are just fine being the worker bee and some of us are just fine as the queen bee. But, when it comes to our families, the dynamics are a little different. Roles and responsibilities have not been handed to us by a corporate boss, but by the Creator of heaven and earth. And yes, the Creator even left us with a corporate training manual, called the Bible. In this Holy book, God said to man; I have made you head over the woman and I have given you dominion over all the earth. In other words, God has given men a special role as leader, as supervisor over the wife, the family, and the earth. I know some of us did not ask Him for this special role, but nonetheless, we have it. And having it, means we must fulfill the requirements of the job. Men, we must reverse the trend of our culture.

In Black society today, a woman has become the leader in the family and moreover is now moving very quickly in the corporate world as well. I don't personally have a problem with a woman that has a well balanced life that includes and understand her role and responsibility within her family. The problem is that Black men have forced many women to become the head in their family because of the absence of the husband and father. Someone has got to lead the family, someone has got to head the family, and that someone today for the most part, is a woman and not a man. This is because men have decided that other areas of life are more important than the primary area of life, called the family. Just as the prophet Jonah fled his responsibilities, until he learned that he could not run from what God commanded him to do, and thus he finally got the message and became obedient to God's command and mission for his life.

In the Black family, God is saying to the Black man, you have fled from what I called you to do. I called you to leave your father and mother and take a wife. But instead you left your father and mother and slept with many women and left them with many babies. God is not pleased that we have shun His commandments, nor are our Black mothers pleased that they are single parents. This is not the order and direction for the family period. Of all cultures and races in the world, here in the U.S. statistics find Black families with the most divorces and least new marriages. In addition, Black folks are not getting married, but we are shacking up. I want you to know that shacking up is worst than getting married when it comes to social, educational, economic, emotional, psychological and spiritual indicators. And I understand why, God did not tell us to shack up, He said for us each to take our own wife.

How is the Black man to rule over his household if he is no where to be found. Where have all the Black men gone? This is the question being asked of from Black women. The fact is, we are everywhere, but in the family. We're in prisons of every kind, we're in bars and clubs of every kind, we're on the street corners of every neighborhood, we're outside the schools, colleges and university's selling drugs and hotdogs from the hot dog cart. We're in the drug rehab centers, half way houses; we're standing before judges and lying in cemeteries. There does not exist a shortage of the presence of Black men in society. However, if we're talking family, and we are, then there may be a problem; the problem is; if you haven't caught on yet; is simply this; the Black man has fled his responsibility to God, to his family and to society.

Running from the Truth

What is the difference between the truth and a lie? A lie leads you astray. A lie leads you further and further away from the truth. A lie is the serpent poisoning your mind to disobey God. A lie is the improper motivation for reaching a known destination by which the end result of the journey ends in despair and gross disappointment. A lie is the opposite of the truth. A lie is bondage, captivity and trickery. The truth on the other hand, is freedom *"you shall know the truth and the truth shall set you free."*

What lies have the Black man been living? I don't have enough time to exhaust every social implication of this question, however I will comment on several of them. How about the lie that states, with freedom you have the ability to do whatever you choose. Let's think about this, as I think this statement is a very powerful one. Our government has afforded every citizen of these United States of America the right to be free and to have freedom of choice. This right to have freedom has developed into state laws that give its citizens rights such as, the right to divorce. The facts are, if you want out of a marriage, you can get out. The facts are, if you do not want to pay child support; you don't have to. The facts are, if you don't want to work; you don't have to. The facts are, if you don't want to keep a pregnancy; you don't have to. Government and state laws allow for direct laws and loopholes of freedom that says to you and me, with freedom we have the ability to do whatever we choose. "If you'll make it; they'll use it." How true is that?

We make laws that give us the right to be just as lazy, just as irresponsible, just as corruptible and untrustworthy as we choose to be. "To every action, there is an equal and opposite reaction," I believe this is Newton's law of relativity. There is a law that grossly preceded Newton's law and I think it goes something like this: *"What so ever you sow, so also shall you reap."* And *"what ever you bind on earth will be bound in heaven; what ever you loose on earth will be loosed in heaven."* When I was a kid, we used to say "what goes around comes around," and "what you put out their, comes back to you."

"With freedom you have the ability to do what ever you choose." "Freedom is not the absence of responsibility, but it is the fulfillment of sacrifice." With freedom comes the inheritable right to fulfill and maintain the sacrifice that was given for the ability to be free. For example: the Reverend Dr. Martin Luther King, Jr. laid down his life in the struggles for freedom for all God's people. Dr. King and many others along with him and before him and some even after him have placed their own personal freedoms aside, so that you and I can enjoy the liberty to choose whatever it is we choose to do or not to do. We have a right to be heard as a free people within a free society because of people like Dr. King and others. We have the freedom to vote, which we do not take seriously. Even more than any of these personal rights as human beings living in the U. S. we have freedom to choose eternal life over eternal damnation, yet, by our living we have chosen eternal damnation over eternal life, these are the benefits that come with freedom.

When I think about someone's personal sacrifice, I think of Jesus Christ. For any of God's children to deny the truth that Jesus paid it all on the cross at Calvary, so you and I may be released from the bondage, the power, the penalty and the presence of disobedience; and enter into the power and presence of freedom, makes my head twirls. When we live a lie, it shields us from ever wanting to see and experience the truth. In truth there is responsibility. Another lie we believe and live is that freedom does not personally costs us anything. This is a bold face lie if I ever heard one, and I have heard one to two before. First and foremost, let me reiterate to you again, the cost that freedom placed on Jesus Christ, with freedom comes a sacrifice. The question I pose to you is**: "What sacrifice have you made for your freedom?** A better question is to ask is: **"What sacrifice have you given for the freedom of others?**

We as free men, living in a free country, with freedom of choice, what choices have we made to advance the cause of freedom to those younger than us and those who cannot articulate nor stand for their own rights to be free? What rights have we honored and protected of those babies still in their teenage mother's wounds, who are about to be aborted for the third time because of the awesome stupidity of it's mother to choose to spread her legs for the freedom to feel good without the freedom of responsibility! What is the cost of freedom? What does it cost a single mother who have the sole responsibility forced upon them to raise children without the leadership and support of their father! What is the cost of freedom?

What does it cost that 16 year old boy who's failing in school, strung out on dope and is now threatening to jump off the high school roof, all because he is so torn apart with pain because he feels as if he's unworthy to be loved, because his daddy abandoned him! What is the cost of freedom? What does it cost our children who have to explain to other children during the church's 'family fun day,' where's your daddy? Just to speak this reply; "I don't have a daddy", "I never knew my daddy"! What are the costs of shame, embarrassment and disappointment? What is the cost of freedom? So you still believe that freedom does not cost somebody something?

The costs of an individual's personal freedom may not be withheld to them, but what about the freedom withheld to our children and mothers who have to struggle, beg, borrow and steal; in shame, in degradation, in pain, in frustration, in weakness and in despair. What are the costs for our individual, selfish, freedoms that costs everyone else affected by our personal desires to take away everyone else's freedoms because we don't want to be a man and take responsibility for our personal freedoms. Is this what a strong Black man is supposed to be? Is this what our children will hear and read in history books? No wonder women have taken control of the Black family, after all, many of them didn't have a choice; their personal freedoms were taken away from them by others individual freedoms.

And to the ladies of these personal freedoms seeking Brothers, when will you wakeup and smell the coffee? You are just as much to blame for the destruction of the Black family as these men are. You don't have to spread your legs for every brother whispering a lie in your ear. Where is your personal pride and dignity? Using your head instead of your misguided ways may lend itself to less struggling as a single mother, if many of you only learn to develop a greater sense of respect for yourselves! You won't say no, because many of you are just like these brothers. The only difference is that you're the one who have to carry the baby. You must remember that both Adam and Eve was punished and not just Adam.

Freedom costs lives. Freedom cost the lives of husbands, fathers, wives, mothers, children and families. Freedom costs impacts our society and the world at large. Freedom impacts our souls. What does freedom cost you? What have you done to promote someone else's freedom? What personal sacrifice have you made for the cause of freedom? With freedom comes responsibility; are you truly free? Or are you still living in the web of a Lie? There is good news! As long as there's breath in your body and blood still flowing through your veins, freedom is calling; don't you hear it calling your name?

Galatians 5:13-15 *"You, my brothers, were called to be free. But do not use your freedom to indulge the sinful nature; rather, serve one another in love. The entire law is summed up in a single command; "Love your neighbor as yourself." If you keep on biting and devouring each other, watch out or you will be destroyed by each other."*

The apostle Paul informs us that we cannot run and hide from our responsibility. God's rules for living far exceed the rules of man's government. Even in God's rules for living, there are ways out of responsibility. We have the God given right to choose. The prophet Joshua said "Choose *you this day who you will serve; as for me and my house we will serve the Lord."* So God gives us freedom of choice. God Himself allows us to choose responsibility or irresponsibility. With freedom comes responsibility.

Divorce and its Impact

Divorce is one of the most significant altering life changes within the structure of both the family and society. With divorce comes what I'll call the "Loss syndrome." This loss syndrome is a host of emotional, psychological, behavioral, relational and spiritual dysfunctions. From the process of divorce comes the process of grief and depression. As a people called by God for relationship, we see the separation of the marital bond as a significant loss in our lives. At least we should view it in this way. The loss of marriage should be associated with the loss of life. Let me make this clear, I'm not suggesting everyone who gets divorced should run right out and kill themselves. That's not my meaning.

When we recite the marital covenant (contract), we promise to be together until death do we part. Therefore, when death is not the reason for the separation of the marital bond, we view this significant loss still in the context of a death.

Divorce means a loss of:

- Promise
- Commitment
- Love and affection
- Family and home
- Emotional support
- Financial stability
- Friends and acquaintance
- Stability
- Relationships
- Children
- Unity
- Identity
- Privacy
- Health
- Peace
- Future

When we divorce, we lose the ability to hold to the promise we made before God, our spouse and witnesses, to live together until death separates us. We view this inability to maintain our word as a great sense of loss. The Bible says this in regards to keeping promises in Numbers 30:2 *"If a man makes a vow to the Lord, or swears an oath to bind himself by some agreement, he shall not break his word; he shall do according to all that proceeds out of his mouth."* Scriptures require us to maintain all that we said we would do. Therefore, a Christian man and woman who do not honor their word to God should experience some sense of grief (loss).

The women I see in the counseling office going through marital disharmony often view divorce as a great sense of loss in love and affection. They often feel grief and depression over having to be involved in a new relationship with all the uncertainties a new relationship brings. Some women may even view themselves as unworthy to be physically loved again. Because of the great emotional expressiveness of many women, women are apt to frown upon the loss divorce brings in the area of familiar affection. You see in the "Old days," women were always considered to be more emotionally mature than men. Women had few problems with expressing their thoughts and feelings. At the same time, women thought more highly of their sexual expressions than men did. Women expressed a need in forming a bond, a trust, a commitment level with a man before any thoughts of sexual expression was ever considered. However, today this emotional protection of a woman's most private expression of affection has changed.

We are living in the "Just do it," generation. We are also living in a time where my needs are more important than your needs and I'm going to fulfill my needs, even if it violates a trust or bond. We are a tremendously selfish society that has very little concerns for others. This is definitely the case in marriages today. Some women still feel a great sense of loss over losing the love and affection due to divorce, while others view divorce as a credit card of freedom and liberty to express themselves freely without reservation or sense of morality.

When spouses of a divorce consider the impact of divorce upon the home, they must consider it as a great loss. The home was once viewed as a personal sanctuary, a kingdom, a piece of the rock. But with divorce comes the destruction of the temple that will not be rebuilt; at least not with the husband in it. Men view divorce as a financial nightmare. The laws of the land seemingly favor women when it comes to divorce. I believe this is because of the fact that the awarding of children is given primarily to the wife. Therefore, it is important in the judicial eyes for the children to have a stable, familiar place in which to continue to grow and develop. Well, this may be OK for the wife, but what about the husband who must now have to pay child support, spousal support, and may have to continue paying the house note and other financial obligations of the home, a home that he will no longer live in. In addition, the husband's liberties of his home have all been stripped away; thus he'll now have to find a new place to live and all of the expenses associated with a new residence.

Ladies, you want to know what really ticks an ex-husband off. Is when the ex-husband comes by the house he's still paying for but cannot live in, to pick up the children that he must now have permission to see, and find another man living in his house, running things and enjoying all the physical pleasures your body has to offer him; all on his dollar. Right or wrong, it's the truth. And don't let me even begin to mention the fact, that the two of you call yourselves Christians. I won't even go there. Christianity is thrown right out the window when it comes to divorce. If Christ was truly in it, we would not be divorced! If the wife in the divorce is not ordered child support, spousal support or any other financial support and support is perceived not to be enough, the wife becomes disenfranchised with the process and may choose to disallow the children's father to visit. Either way, grief and depression is the result of a marital loss.

Relationships are considered a loss. Both husband and wife who have developed inter-relationships over the years, find themselves having to pick and choose whose friends little Joe and Shaniqua will be. In divorce, we often ask, whether literally or through associations, what friends can we count on to be there for us. Who will testify for us, who can we lean and depend on, who will bring us comfort and who will watch the kids when I want to establish a new relationship? What about mother and father in-laws and brother and sister in-laws? All these people will have to be divided up between the two spouses feuding due to divorce. This dysfunctional process can be viewed by the proverbial 'pulling of straws' amongst friendships. This process will inevitably leave someone with out friends and many others with hurt feelings. This will mean that one or both spouses will have to find new friends, and don't forget in divorce you will fall out with some friends because of their allegiance. No matter what the reasons for divorce, divorce is viewed and experienced as a severe loss upon the stability of individuals, the family and society.

When the intention to divorce is publicly declared all rules of privacy and confidentiality is thrown out with last week's pickled pig feet. There are few secrets not being told by someone. Divorce is messy and hurtful and it leaves both spouses dejected. In divorce, what brought the two together will ultimately be replaced by its opposite. Love joins together; but hatred pulls apart. This is a part of marital grief. We move from a sincere, committed and passionate fiery love into a sincere, committed and passionate fiery hate. Love and hate are two of the strongest human emotions ever placed within the human personality. Whole cathedrals were built on the premise of love and also destroyed on the premise of hatred. In love, humans are capable of endless things out of a love commitment. On the opposite, hatred will also cause us to do the most deranged and loveless activities ever imagined. In divorce love is replaced with hatred, and thus it is these hurtful and spiteful feelings that initiate war zones of great casualties and costs, spurred on by the tactics of divorce attorneys. Nothing is considered sacred to the other spouse in their attempts to hurt, punish, damage and defame the other. If you did it, saw it, said it or wrote it, it's quite possible it will come out in the process called divorce. But the fact is we count it all a loss.

In all these losses brought on by divorce, why don't the children get a say so. Why don't we consider the children's sufferings? What is the impact of divorce on our children? In this chapter I mentioned some statistics on divorce and its impact on the children. Why is it when spouses get to the point of wanting to divorce, children become a casualty of war? Children are used as the weapon of choice for every lawyer, every husband and every wife. What about the children? Have anyone talked to the children and determined the impact of divorce on their psyche? What about the relationships with parents? What about the children's struggles with all of the emotions and feelings they're having and don't understand? What about the social, and financial strain placed on the children, because mom and dad has got to divert monies to pay high price lawyers to help us destroy what God said not to! Why are the children having problems in school? What about the children? Sorry kids, you'll get over it or you won't; this is a fact of life and you'll just have to deal with it! Count it all as a loss.

Well, it's not that simple. We cannot simply dismiss children's feelings in the process of divorce. What does the research say about the impact of divorce on kids? James C. Dobson, Ph.D. in his book *"Complete marriage and Family Home Reference Guide,"* writes: One landmark study revealed that 90% of children from divorced homes suffered from an acute sense of shock when the separation occurred, including profound grieving and irrational fears. 50% reported feeling rejected and abandoned, and indeed half of the fathers never came to see their children three years after the divorce. One-third of the boys and girls feared abandonment by the remaining parent, and 66% experienced yearning for the absent parent with an intensity that researchers described as overwhelming. Most significant, 37% of the children were even more unhappy and dissatisfied five years after the divorce then they had been at 18 months. In other words, time did not heal their wounds." Dr. Dobson offers this piece of advice: "The bottom line is that you are right to consider the welfare of your children in deciding whether or not to seek a divorce. As empty as the marital relationship continues to be for you, it is likely, from what I know of your circumstances, that your kids will fare better if you choose to stick it out." Please note Dr. Dobson's statistics are not separated by race.

Dr. James C. Melamed of the Oregon Mediation Center Incorporated wrote this brief on his internet site *to-agree.com*, he wrote in regards to the effects of divorce on children: "Boys and girls suffer; they just differ in how they suffer. Boys are more externally symptomatic than girls and act out their anger, frustration and hurt. They may get into trouble in school, fight more at home and with parents. Girls tend to internalize their distress. They may become depressed, suffer from headaches or stomach aches, and have changes in their eating and sleeping patterns."

Children suffer the same effects of divorce, but as stated they demonstrate these effects in different ways. It is no doubt that children not only may suffer serious short term emotional difficulties, but if not allowed to grieve properly, children may also suffer with anxiety issues later, in addition to depression, relationship difficulties, promiscuity issues, drug and alcohol issues, violence and crime issues, blame and guilt issues and issues of divided loyalties to parents, in addition to other symptoms. Please keep in mind that statistics tell us that the majority of divorces amongst African Americans lead to harsh financial consequences that many times leave a family in a state of poverty.

What about your health and peace of mind while you're going through divorce?

Here are the five stages of grief as presented by Dr. Kubler-Ross.

1. Denial and Isolation-(Refusal to accept what has happened)
2. Anger-(Anger at self and others, and at some point the anger is pointed towards God)
3. Bargaining-(The attempt to persuade or strike a deal with God)
4. Depression- (The point of deep sorrow, despair and detachment)
5. Acceptance-(Accepting reality and the truth)

Below represents a normal pattern of response to grief as prescribed by The National Christian Counselors Association.

1. Shock
2. Guilt
3. Hostility/anger
4. Restless activity
5. Things that were important lose importance
6. Letting go of emotions
7. Depression and loneliness

8. Panic and questions of survival
9. Beginning stages of revived hope
10. Surviving and rebuilding

Grief in teenagers and children usually follow along the same principles as for adults, however, because of a teenager's level of comprehension and response to grief, teens respond to grief slightly different. Dr. John D. Canine of Maximum Living Associates describes the following states of grief for teenagers.

Every child's grief is unique to his or her circumstances and situation. However, some grief responses can be considered "norms." As in adults, these normal responses can be defined as stages:

- Shock- that child's first reaction to death is generally a lack of sensation which leads to withdrawal.
- Alarm-Children look to adults for safety and security. When someone dies, their world becomes less safe. This feeling is intensified by feelings of vulnerability, separation anxiety, depression, immobilization, systems of Post Traumatic Stress Disorder and somatic illnesses.
- Disbelief- The conscious or unconscious defense a child uses to avoid, prevent, or reduce anxiety. The child attempts to forget or reject reality.
- Yearning-Yearning is another term used for regression. As a child begins to accept loss and return to a sense of normality, the child will sometimes enter into a stage of regression, where as a younger child will return to bed wetting, suck a thumb, cry for a bottle. An older child regressive behavior should not be an alarm but an indicator that the child needs special attention while working through the process of grief.
- Searching- Adults and children will at times compulsive search for reminders of a loved one in an attempt to reconnect with them. We may attempt to communicate with someone, day dream, wear clothing of the deceased.

- Disorganization-Grief is hard work. To try to understand emotions like sadness, guilt, shame and anger is extremely demanding on a child. Grief takes energy, thus attempting to meet the needs of grief throws children into disorganization in every order of their life.
- Resolution- Or another term for resolution is perseverance. This is the child at the end of the grief process. A whole healthy person emerges from grief ready to live and enjoy life again.

The authors are using death to mark the process of grief. But grief is the result of any kind of loss. Long term grief is associated with the inability to properly grieve any loss. Thus death and grief are interrelated components.

The divorce process will often times include not only marital grief due to the loss of the marriage and family, but also the emotional roller coaster ride that can lead many of us into situational of reactive depression. Reactive depression is a form of depression exacerbated by the way we react to a situation, thus the name reactive depression. Reactive depression is not a long-term depression. Reactive depression can best be resolved by changing the way we respond to a situation, like divorce. Often times, our thinking process is disruptive and maladaptive. Therefore, a proper thinking process and controlled emotions, will allow us to better adapt to a major change or situation. Below describes the basics characteristics of depression for both adults and children.

- Feelings of sadness
- Irritable/moodiness
- Diminished interest or pleasure in routine activities
- Weight loss or gain
- Altered sleeping patterns
- Sluggishness
- Feelings of fatigue or loss of energy
- Feelings of worthlessness

- Increased feelings of guilt
- Difficulty in concentrating
- Indecisiveness
- Suicidal ideations
- Body aches and pains
- Somatic illnesses
- Crying

In many cases of reactive depression, once a person begin to change their thinking patterns from a downward thinking pattern to a upward thinking pattern and begin to address the issues facing them, they will find that their depressive moods will also change. In addition, having a good support structure is very important to the process of divorce, grief and depression. Reactive depression can be very serious and should not be taken lightly.

Whenever depression is mentioned, one must also analyze the thought patterns of a grieving or depressed person's thoughts of suicide. Divorce is a traumatic life changing event that must be treated with compassion, sensitivity, support and dignity. The American Association of Suicidology offers the following warning signs of suicide.

Signs of suicide

- Hopelessness
- Rage, uncontrolled anger, seeking revenge
- Acting reckless or engaging in risky activities, seemingly without thinking
- Feeling trapped-like there's no way out
- Increased alcohol or drug use
- Withdrawing from friends, family and society
- Anxiety, agitation, unable to sleep or sleeping all the time
- Dramatic mood changes
- No reason for living; no sense of purpose in life

Here is an easy mnemonic to remember these warning signs: IS PATH WARM?

I	Ideation
S	Substance Abuse
P	Purposelessness
A	Anxiety
T	Trapped
H	Hopelessness
W	Withdrawal
A	Anger
R	Recklessness
M	Mood Changes

Here are some things you can do to assist someone contemplating suicide.

- Be direct. Talk openly and matter-of-factly about suicide.
- Be willing to listen. Allow expressions of feelings. Accept the feelings.
- Be non-judgmental. Don't debate whether suicide is right or wrong. Don't lecture on the value of life.
- Get involved. Become available. Show interest and support.
- Don't dare him or her to do it.
- Don't act shocked. This will put distance between you.
- Don't be sworn to secrecy. Seek support.
- Offer hope that alternatives are available.
- Take action. Remove means, such as guns or stockpiled pills.
- Get help from persons or agencies specializing in crisis intervention and suicide.

According to *the American Association of Suicidology* suicide was the third leading cause of death among African American youth, after homicides and accidents from 1995-2000. For African American youth, the rate of male suicides was 6.6 times higher than that of females for the same time period.

There is little doubt in this professional's mind that marital and family disharmony is a major factor in the destruction of peace! Worldly trouble and strife does not produce peace, but rather robs people of an opportunity to know peace, and peace cannot be obtained living by worldly means. Peace comes from knowing and following God's commandments found in the Holy Bible. In today's world men and woman of all ages, racial and cultural diversity live their entire lives seeking a sense of peace that's always out of their reach, this is because they are not willing to meet the requirements for obtaining peace; the world can only offer confusion and in Jesus and His Word is peace; God is not the author of confusion.

Laziness and Mediocrity

It has been suggested by some that some Black folks have ceased to desire excellence. Of course you can apply most statements written in this book to other cultures and races as well, but my focus is on us. I have to agree with this observation that some of us have stopped desiring and working toward a sense of excellence in our work ethic and overall sense of duty and responsibility. Some of us have willingly accepted mediocrity as a lifestyle. Mediocrity in its context is not laziness, but being content with the best you can do at that time. Mediocrity also means inferior. It is this aspect of the word that I want to focus on. Have Black folks become so comfortable in our lives that we no longer need to dream or set higher expectations for ourselves? God bless the fast food restaurants, without them many of us would never have employment opportunities and opportunities to learn valuable skills.

However, unless you have aspirations of becoming a manager or franchise owner, some of us should not be content with that type of job as a career choice. I personally spent nearly thirty years of my life in professional food service, and I understand the values learned in the fast food environment. However, I did not want to stay in that position for the rest of my life. I know that I'm picking on fast food restaurants, but you can apply the example to any mediocre lifestyle. When you drive and walk through the Black neighborhoods, the only businesses you'll find are not owned by us. Black folks spend billions of dollars a year in the American economy, yet we own very little. What happened to the aspirations of owning your own? We are a blessed group of people, we have more education now than ever in history, yet many of us refuse to take advantage of it. Many of us would never consider working at a fast food restaurant because there's not enough money in it for some of us.

You know; the 'some of us' that are still living with our mother; the some of us that can't seem to pass the proficiency tests in high school; the some of us that don't have to pay any bills or take on any financial responsibility, but you think that getting a mediocre job is above you. Get real! My Brothers, do you think selling crack and weed and smoking on cigars is the best way for you to meet your financial ambitions in life? If you said yes, you must be high! There must be more Brothers taking advantage of opportunities that we did not so long ago had. I understand that college is not for everyone. Perhaps a trade school or business school would interest you? Any career choice is better than what many of us are doing right now. Jail is not a career choice, nor is pushing drugs or making babies and not taking care of them.

Many of you Brothers have got to see that what you're doing is not because there are no good paying jobs out there, or that the man is keeping you down, you are keeping you down, because you have chosen to be lazy and not accept responsibility for your actions, thus, you lack motivation, drive and good decision making abilities. Why choose fast money, expensive cars and fat butt women, when many of us can't sign our own name or complete an employment application? Many of you Brothers don't even have a high school diploma and what's really sad about this truth, is that many of you Brothers don't care that you never finished high school. The fact still remains: many of you lazy brothers believe that you can make it in life off the sweat and backs of some lady with a low self-view of herself. Let me be the first one to tell you brothers: your stuff is not that good! When you get a little older and begin to see your belly sticking further out and your stuff pushing further in, then you'll understand; she'll need more than what you can provide.

Does living a lazy life make some of you Brothers feel a great sense of pride in yourselves? This is not why countless numbers of Blacks died. So many others before us gave their very lives so that we can move up from a position of mediocrity into excellence. However, many of us may never get to the point of being in excellence, but we're not lazy and we're not mediocre either. The Bible tells us that if we don't work, we don't eat. Many of you Brothers have so many skills and things that you're really good at, but refuse to explore your talents. You need not be afraid of what your homies say about you, you must make the choice to move out of this dysfunctional lifestyle and into a real future with hope and promises for you. We as Black people once used to hold up our fist and say "Black power." We must get back to that unified spirit of excellence, believing that through Christ we can do anything but fail.

We must return and regain those days where we believed in ourselves. We believed in obedience and righteousness and family. We believed in mutual respect for one another. We believed that "It takes a village to raise a child," we believed in reaching out and reaching down to help someone else. We believed in protecting our children and our communities, we believed in providing for others who could not provide for themselves, we believed in helping another family out when sickness was upon them, we believed in educating our children and ourselves, we believed! We believed, we believed! My Brothers, God, myself and lots others, still believe; and we still believe in you. My Brothers, life is winding up and the Black family is spiraling downhill into the abyss of nothingness. We need you; all of you; young, old, whatever; we're still hoping and praying that many of you will see the error of your ways and make the course correction. If none of this applies to you, then I'm not referring to you. But if it does, the question has been posed.

Manhood

Without a father, how is a young boy to learn how to be a man? When most of us think about manhood, we think in terms of the outer man and not the inner man. When I think of the outer man, I think of a man being masculine, strong, durable, and aggressive, not easily moved, protector, provider, handy, leader, free of fear, attentive to his wife and children. And when I think of the inner man, I think of a man being emotionally strong, intelligent, kind, generous, prideful, protective of his emotional weaknesses and driven. Even in identifying just some of my personal views of the characteristics of a man, I must make mention, that I'm describing what is seen and known from a worldly point of view. But even in this worldly view, many of today's men have fallen short; the worldly view in fact is the measuring rod for how society judges one other.

What is a man? One description of this process of childhood into adulthood can be termed the "Coming of age." The coming of age is a young person's formal transition from adolescence into adulthood. The age at which this transition takes place varies amongst societies. Many cultures retain ceremonies to confirm the coming of age, and thus significant benefits become available with this life transition. Another term to describe this stage of life is called the "Age of accountability." This is the age at which a child is old enough to understand the moral consequences of his or her actions and can be held accountable for sins. It is also called the "Age of reason." Though it does not correspond to a particular age for every person, due to differences in personal and psychological maturation, it is sometimes set down arbitrarily as 12 or, in the Catholic Church, 7. A child who has passed by the age of accountability is said to know the difference between right and wrong and to be capable of obeying the moral laws of God. Those persons, due to disabled mental or emotional development may never reach a sufficient level of abstract reason, and are therefore covered by grace for life and are sometimes known as "the innocents." In Christian traditions which practice Believer's Baptism (Baptism by voluntary decision, as opposed to baptism in early infancy), the ritual can be carried out after the age of accountability; on the grounds that children do not understand what the ritual means. Full membership in the Church, if not bestowed at birth, often must wait until the age of accountability and frequently is granted after a period of preparation known as catechesis (Wikipedia, the free encyclopedia).

Whether we term manhood by the 'coming of age' or the 'age of accountability,' or simply that point in a boys life when he has developed full sexual function, the primary importance of manhood lye's with his moral awareness. Fathers must teach their son's values, morals, intellect, social skills, obedience, and a host of human developmental skills. In addition to these necessary developmental skills, fathers must articulate and demonstrate holiness. All human beings travel through the stages of development, however not all of us travel through stages of morality. You cannot be human and not at some point ask "is this all there is."? Human beings long to develop a nurturing relationship with the God. Unfortunately, many of us are polytheistic (serving many gods) in our choice for God instead of being monotheistic (serving only God) in our relationship with the triune God. *"Train up a child in the way he should go, when he is older is will not depart from it."* Scriptures teaches parents to train our children in holiness. If we demonstrate anything else, children will learn that which is taught and modeled before them. Therefore, fathers must model manhood after the God-man Jesus. Boys must learn to be men by immolating Jesus and His characteristics of manhood.

If you were to study Jesus, you will find that Jesus was a man who was decisive and direct in His confrontations with sin and evil (John 9:14). Jesus was firm and forthright regarding His position on various situations (Mark 2:10). When confronted with differences and conflict, Jesus was honest and direct (Luke 22:48). Jesus also demonstrated courage and resolve, He had an earthly task to complete and He did not let anyone or anything stop Him from completing that task. Jesus was brave in the midst of sufferings (John 19ff). Jesus was a man of great humility (Matthew 20:28). According to A.P. Andelin (1972) in *Man of Steel and Velvet*, Jesus is described in this way:

> "Never did He lose sight of His responsibility to complete "the work He was sent to do." He maintained His devotion to it until the end when He said, "It is finished..." He had the moral courage to introduce ideals and standards which were in conflict with popular teachings of His day. He dedicated His life to the service and salvation of others, lifting people to higher plane of thought and living. He was indeed a builder of society for His day and for all eternity...His character was spotless...He was eager and enthusiastic about life...He had humility...and with this humility there was a self-dignity which commanded respect."

If men are to teach young men to become men, men must change the dysfunctional model of training now being offered. A true man is one that takes on the characteristics of Jesus. Do you ever recall reading about Jesus in the Bible, and the Bible stated that Jesus grabbed his crotch? Or that Jesus wore His pants down below His butt crack? Have you ever read that Jesus was a man because He had a penis? Or that Jesus stood on the dirt corners of town selling crack? You get the picture? I have mentioned several times in this book how infants and children primarily learn. We learn by watching others around us. This is called 'modeling'. As parents and human beings we are in a constant cycle of watchful learning or modeling. Modeling is simply the act of someone presenting information to us in a host of environments. Therefore, how are our children to learn good and wholesome things, if there are not Jesus men around to model them before them? Jesus gives all men a wonderful example of how to be a man and yet not sin. Jesus demonstrated to all men how to be a strong man, a courage's man, an intellectual man, a craftsman, a rebel for the truth, a sensitive and compassionate man, a devoted man, a man on a mission, a loving and nurturing man. Jesus demonstrated in His life what it means to be a man of God. I do understand however, that there is a qualifier that must be met if a man is to immolate the life of Christ and "Be a man of God." The qualifier is that you must 'be a man of God'; it's not good enough to know of God or Christ, but to personally have a personalized, committed and enduring relationship with Christ; this is the first step to learning how to 'become a man of God'.

When I think about a Jesus kind of man, I think also about the kind of Jesus man that will admit when he's wrong. This is one area of Jesus' life where He never had to demonstrate. Jesus was a perfect man, and thus He never sinned. Having never sinned, He never had to apologize for anything He did. But you and I today will never reach the level of man Jesus was, so you and I, who always fall short of God's glory, must admit to God, ourselves and one another our shortcomings if we're to grow into a Jesus kind of man. You and I must admit the truth of our mistakes. None of us have done everything right. None of us have achieved excellence of life awards. We've made mistakes along this winding road called life. But it's not too late to own up to our faults. We must understand that Jesus was and will be the only perfect man. Our goal is to strive for perfection, knowing that while we wear flesh we will never reach it. But it is a goal. Stop kicking yourselves Brothers; God wants you to return back to Him; and in returning back to Him, you also return back to the family. Your children need you. The Black family needs you. Society needs you. You're not helping anyone by sitting in prison or smoking dope on the street corner. Take that first step into a brave and exiting world knowing you'll never have to take another step alone.

Chapter Six
"Let My People Go"
(Breaking free from a mind of bondage)

"Do not conform any longer to the pattern of this world, but be transformed by the renewing of your mind, then you will be able to test and approve what God's will is-his good, pleasing and perfect will" (Romans 12:2).

Mind over Matter

Black men in America were once enslaved with chains on their wrists and shackles on their feet. The Black man and woman often cringed by the pains and sounds of brutality, as each of them suffered and witnessed beatings and whippings by their slave masters. Black children often witnessed their parents degraded before them, after all, Blacks were not considered to be human. The Black man was simply a tool by which the oppressor could accomplish his goals. The Black man was simply a platform by which he could reach higher status in the community. The Black man was considered a piece of moveable property by which the oppressor could gain greater wealth and stature and comfort in his life; his children's lives and within a society that only sought to withhold all sense of purpose and meaning to life in the mind of the oppressed Black.

The Black man was considered less than dung. Dung that worked the cotton fields under extreme physical, environmental and human intolerance. Dung that cooked the meals inside the kitchens of one's master, cleaned the houses of their oppressor, delivered and raised the babies of those who looked upon them as only property, only to be raped and molested and used for the will of the oppressed. Black females were obviously good enough to rape and molest, but not good enough to take to dinner! Yet, in the minds of the oppressed Blacks was an uncanny sense of intelligence. An intelligence that soon understood that out of oppression would one day come deliverance. Deliverance meant in the mind of the oppressed Black, that there was that one thing that was greater than all the oppressors put together.

Blacks held a strong sense of belief in a divine power that once created the skies and the land, and also created everything that flown in the sky or swam in the seas. That same power that gave life and sustained life, would one day hear the cries, the screams, the pains and desires of an oppressed people that was stripped of all sense of dignity and humanity. I believe in the minds of oppressed Blacks was a sense of patience, perseverance, stamina, intelligence; a sense of longing, hope, resilience and desire for that divine power that had not become new to them in this new oppressed land, but a power that was well known and worshipped in the lands of their birth.

Black men, women and children held on to a sense of freedom, not in the physical sense of bondage, but in the deeper sense of the meaning, a meaning that flowed like rivers of living water out of their bellies. A hope and belief in the minds and hearts of the oppressed was perhaps these words engrained in their souls: *"The Spirit of the Lord is upon me, because he hath anointed me to preach the gospel to the poor, he hath sent me to heal the brokenhearted, to preach deliverance to the captives, and recovering of sight to the blind, to set at liberty them that are bruised,"* (Luke 4:18). These heroes of the African American race demonstrated hope and faith in a liberating gospel that they had just come to hear within the English context. It was these heroes that demonstrated to all men today what perseverance and long suffering meant in the human experience. I believe these heroes became minister's of Christ's gospel message (Luke 4:18). A message of hope that each of these brave heroes demonstrated to each other in their own unique ways. Out of troubled waters comes stillness and from stillness comes peace.

Our enslaved African brothers and sisters indeed were imprisoned within a new society, a society that viewed them as only a commodity to be captured, sold and purchased. But, I declare to all reading these words; our enslaved brothers and sisters were demoralized in body, but never in their spirit. It is the spirit that leads one's mind and heart to endure difficult days and suffer through difficult ways of life; and never can a determined spirit be captured by mankind. Man can enslave another's body but one's mind and heart cannot be physically enslaved, only spiritually broken. However, these heroes did not allow themselves to be spiritually broken, only strengthened by the experience.

These Black heroes were strong and free within their minds, heart's and spirit's. It is this same liberating spirit that only comes from God. God's spirit allowed these brave and determined souls to persevere through some of the most known injustice the world has come to experience. Liberation means to be "Released from slavery; enemy occupation" (Webster's New World Dictionary). Just as our Black forefathers and mothers broke free from the yokes of bondage that worked to keep them enslaved in their body, these slave master's soon understood that they could not enslave one's hope and faith, that one day their bodies would be just as free as their minds, heart's and spirit's.

Black people have a rich history in America of exercising strength, stamina, perseverance, knowledge and faith. Black people have long come to understand that we have a heritage of overcoming insurmountable odds. Not in and of our own strength, but because of our faith in the God of liberation. Men of sin do not understand the wisdom of faith. Only by faith can Blacks and all God's people, come to understand that *"No weapon formed against me shall prosper; I'm more than a conqueror in Christ Jesus."*

Choosing Our Weapons of Warfare

"Do not conform any longer to the pattern of this world, but be transformed by the renewing of your mind" (Romans 12:2A-NIV)

In today's times Black men have seemingly chosen different weapons of warfare. Today Black men seemingly no longer wage war with the enemies of God (unbelievers) through prayer and faith and hope and a sense of longing for acceptance of who we are; as God saw fit to make us, no! Instead we have seemingly become the enemy. We have created a paradigm shift that replaces yesteryears physical enslavement with cognitive and spiritual enslavement.

"The weapons we fight with are not the weapons of the world. On the contrary, they have divine power to demolish strongholds. We demolish arguments and every pretension that sets itself up against the knowledge of God, and we take captive every thought to make it obedient to Christ" (2 Corinthians 10:4-5 NIV).

According to the U.S. Census Bureau, Census 2000 "We the People: Blacks in the United States." (The following is a highlight of some of the statistics from this report)

- The Black population in 2000 consisted of 36,213,467 or 12.9% of the U.S. population.
- While 27% of the U.S. population 15 and older had never been married, the corresponding percentage of Blacks was **41%**. 36% of Blacks were married, compared with 54% of the total population.
- **Blacks were more likely than the total population to be separated, widowed, or divorced.** Five percent of Blacks were separated; 7 percent were widowed; and 11 percent were divorced.
- **32% of Black households were maintained by married couple families**, compared with 53 of all households. **The proportion of households that were family households maintained by Black women with no husband present nearly 3 times the corresponding proportion for all households.** Less than 6% of both total households and Black households were family households maintained by men with no wife present.
- **The majority of Black households wee family households.** However, 30.5% of households were led by a woman, compared to only 5.7% led by a man.
- Overall, Black women had higher educational attainment levels than Black men. About 15% of Black women had earned at least a bachelor's degree, higher than the 13% of black men.
- A higher proportion of Black women than Black men were in managerial and professional occupations. In 2000, a higher

proportion of Black women (30%) than Black men (20%) were in management, professional, and related occupations.

When I look at the aforementioned statistics from 2000 (six years ago), I notice that many Blacks are choosing not to get married. However we're having sex, we're just not getting married and owning up to the responsibilities of the family. I also notice that only 36% of Blacks are married as of the 2000 Census. What really disturbed me was the fact that Blacks are more likely than the total population to be separated, widowed, or divorced. On top of this news is the report that our overall households are predominately led by a woman instead of a man.

When I look at these numbers analytically, a see the numbers reflecting a very real problematic view of marriage in the Black family. These numbers share the fact that Blacks do have families; however they are led by women, not men. Moreover, it's my belief based on my experience in the counseling office and my continuing studies that young people (as statistically stated) do not view marriage positively. And I believe they have a valid point when they analyze the benefits and consequences of marriage. If I saw someone seriously burned by improperly setting fire to a charcoal grill, which would be enough to alarm me to the consequences of improperly lighting the grill. The consequences could be interpreted to be so harsh that perhaps I would never attempt to light a grill.

Well, let's take that illustration to the view of marriage and young people, when young people view the effects of dysfunctional marriages all around them, at home, with friend's parents, relatives and even the pastor at church. And all they see is confusion, pain, disappointment, physical, mental, and psychological pain, not to mention male dominance, drug and alcohol addictions, laziness, financial stress and overall family disharmony; that view is enough for many of our young people to say marriage is not for me. Please let's not forget the major problem with infidelity in both the husband and wife. Why would you want to get burned by marriage; it's better to have some of the benefits of marriage without the commitment?

Black spouses must do a better job unifying oneness in marriage. Marriage is not to be taken lightly! Many of our Black married families do not possess the necessary information needed to understand the specific roles, rights and responsibilities within marriage. Many of our married couples never sought the Lord's direction for them and their marital lives. This is where pre-marital counseling comes in, and I do not mean the few sessions with the pastor to discuss superficial marital relations. I'm not going to get real heavy right now in this subject, because I address it in another chapter. But it is very important that we meet the qualifications for marriage by being tested and qualified to be equally yoked together. Pre-marital counseling must teach each person what their roles are in the marriage according to Scriptures. In this program of pre-marital counseling, areas such as parenting, sex, arguing, roles, rights, responsibilities, leadership, spiritual education, obedience, finance, step children, birth control, families and so much more must be discussed.

I believe when we begin to look to Scriptures and the Holy Spirit for our training in marriage, instead of our girlfriend who's been divorced three times now, or the brother who's never been married and sleeps with anything with a hole in it. We must be careful who as married people, we listen to. All advice is not good advice, unless that advice is found in the Holy Scriptures. Then and only then will our young people see the true meaning of marriage and desire it. This takes me to the point why Black couples suffer greatly with divorce and separation. When we do not do things God's way; we're asking for failure. We divorce because of the selfishness in our hearts. We argue and fight, we cheat, we abuse, we lie, and we perpetrate and use each other for our own selfish needs and wants. We as humans don't like having to share anything or have us told what, when and how to do something. But I got news for you, the reason why Black folks marriages are in the toilet is because we want to do things our way and to hell with what Scriptures say, that's our problem! So because we've attempted to do things without God, we're suffering the consequences of our own desire to live God free.

Brothers, it can't all be the sister's fault. Many of our sister's are just like we are, they're seeking and doing and using us the same as many of us are using them. So, if the brother's are dishonest and the sister's are dishonest, whose fault is it that so many of our families are headed by single mothers with children? Why is it that so many of our marriages end in divorce? Why is it that so many of our young people are experiencing so many social ills (drugs, violence, incarceration, etc.)? Now lets take a look at the role reversal of women taken the leadership role in society because so many men have decided that drugs and so many other social ills are more important than the family. As proved by the statistics above, women are moving on and upward. Since there is so much friction between men and women today, both men and women have decided, according to statistics, to do things on their own. We as a Black society have decided that we don't need each other to accomplish the goals and needs we have. That's a bold face lie!

That's a lie that Satan has implanted in many of our hearts and minds to keep us apart from God, ourselves and each other. We and all God's people were created for relationship with Him and then each other. We need each other, we must be with each other, and we cannot make it in this life alone. If any of you are pet owners, you know that you cannot leave a pet alone too long, because they will die of loneliness. We, much like an abandoned pet, have been left alone by those who promised to take care of us, by those promised to be there for us. By those who said they love us, by those who said we can count on them. Well, I want to tell you the only thing we as a people can count on is Jesus Christ.

What has happened to the Black family? It has not been that long ago that we were still being considered property. Many of our Black men who we once praised for their character, for their conscious, for their integrity to their families, their race and their God, we once praised Black men for standing up for what was right; not what was acceptable, but what was right! Black women and children could count on their husband and father to provide for their needs. Black men held a deep sense of conviction to their family and to their community.

Black African men of yesteryears brought with them from the mother-land the working proverb that states "It takes a village to raise a child." This type of community responsibility believed that the elders of the community were very special to them. The elders of the African community were sought out for their wisdom, their faith, leadership and guidance. Children within this society demonstrated respect, honor, and love for their parents and grandparents, and others in the community. In this African society, families and villages celebrated various milestones as a community. They laughed as a community, they buried their dead and cried as a community and they protected their community as one family.

Many of today's Black men have succumbed to the evils of living in a fallen world. Many of today's Black men have chosen to run and hide from a world that has sought to quiet his roar. Have the evils of the world finally defeated the great Black people? Marijuana, PCP, crack-cocaine, heroine, cocaine, methamphetamines, wine, and liquor have now become many of the Black man's gods. Many of us have chosen to tuck our tail in and run; But what about the children? What about that mother who suffered with a painful labor to deliver your baby (babies). Did I hear someone on T.V. say "You are the father." What are they to do now that you've decided to become a coward?

Has the Black freedom fighter of injustice now become the oppressor of his own race? When a person looks at various statistics of the African American family, I'm sure they can't help but raise an eyebrow. When one looks into the prison system and see such a large population of Black inmates (men and women). When one looks inside the juvenile justice system and again see so many multi-colored Black faces, it must raise an eyebrow. When one looks into the higher education system and asks the very astute question: "Where are the

Black people." When there are more Blacks in prison than attending college, someone have to raise an eyebrow. When one looks into the demographics of the family and notice how many single mother homes with children there are, it must raise an eyebrow. When one attends the annual father-son retreat at church and come to find out there's not enough fathers to have the retreat, then one must raise an eyebrow.

How about when one is driving down the street in a predominately Black neighborhood, and one wonders why so many young men are hanging out on the street corners? Unfortunately, many of our male youths are selling crack-cocaine, weed and more. And its not just males anymore selling death wrapped in a baggie, females are taking part in this most lucrative entrepreneurial venture as well. We're making fast money from faces that look like ours; this is a most lucrative business these days. Drug pushers understand the marketing trends of some Blacks. These pushers have analyzed marketing forecasts, demographic studies, selling strategies, positioning strategies within new markets, supply and demand strategies and security measures to protect their distribution and investments. If we only invested in life, instead of death, oh what a people we could be?

When we put Christ back on the throne, we will begin to come up out of the abyss of our self-inflicted hell. God is a God of reconciliation, that's why He sent His only begotten Son, Jesus Christ. It is because of God's love for all humanity that He sent Jesus to the cross at Calvary. God loved us so, that He wanted us back in a proper relationship with Him. Likewise, God does not want His people separated by sin. He wants us to renounce our evil ways and reconcile our hearts and minds with Him and each other. I want to tell all of you reading this; you are living a lie if you think you can make it in this world alone. You are slowly killing yourself and all those around you who are influenced by your sin. God's calling you back to Him through Christ. After you've reconciled with God, you must reconcile with your baby's mama's or baby's daddy's. We have your children out here in society and they're telling us that they want a family, they're longing for a relationship with their estranged daddy; Daddy please come home; Mommy please come home! Men you are more than sperm donors, Ladies you are more than incubators; you are created in the likeness and image of God Himself.

Black men and now Black women have realized the demoralizing implications associated with addictions; But at what costs? Who needs a high school diploma? Who want a college degree? You say what! Learn a trade? Man you must be crazy! With all this money out here on the streets, who needs the white man's dreams? I'm sure this brief interchange has happened between you and someone who looks like you before. Well, let's look at this. How many people do you know of, both in your immediate family and those outside your immediate family, that has either done illegal drugs, addicted to illegal drugs, have attended rehab from illegal drugs, or have been in trouble with the law because of illegal drugs?

If you're honest with yourself, you too will reach the same conclusions many others have. Too many Black folks have a serious problem with drugs and alcohol. Read the latest statistics related to addictions and incarcerations.

According to the "Sourcebook of criminal justice statistics online, 2004":

Of the 10,021,050 total offenses charged by the judicial system, Blacks represented 2,714.041 of the total offenses charged. This number equates to 27.1% of the total offenses charged by the judicial system in 2004. There are many identified areas within this report; however, I will mention only a few.

Out of 2,714,041 Charged Offenses in 2004, Blacks was charged with the following number of offenses:

- Aggravated Assault (104,587)
- Larceny-Theft (243,724)
- Violent Crimes (157,810)

- Property Crimes (339,451)
- Other Assaults (290,977)
- **Drug Abuse Violations (410,552 or .33% of all drug abuse charges for 2004)**
- Driving under the Influence (91,862)
- Disorderly Conduct (163,493)
- Drunkenness (51,870)
- Liquor Laws (44,504)

Please keep in mind that Blacks represent only about 14% of the total population in the United States according to some analysis.

Let me share with you from the same resource (Sourcebook of criminal justice statistics online-2004) the number of Blacks arrested under the age of 18 years old.

Of the 1,594,166 total arrests in 2004, Blacks represented 447,294 arrests, or 28.1% of the total arrests. Of this number here is a highlight of some of the more repetitive arrests.

- Aggravated Assault (17,059)
- Larceny-Theft (64,605)
- **Violent Crimes (30,416 or 46% of the total violent crimes)**
- Property Crimes (93,033)
- Other Assaults (67,269)
- **Drug Abuse Violations (37,808 or 27.2% of the total drug abuse violations)**
- **Disorderly Conduct (56,601)**
- **Prostitution (689 or 52.7% of the total)**
- **Murder and Manslaughter (528 or 49.7% of the total crimes)**
- **Robbery (11,776 or 63.5%)**
- **Forcible Rape (1,053 or 34.7%)**
- **Motor Vehicle Theft (11,267 or 40.2%)**
- **Gambling (1,068 or 86.5% of the total)**

(Emphasis mine)

According to the Bureau of Justice Statistics "Substance Dependence, Abuse, and Treatment of Jail Inmates, 2002" reported the following:

Of all jailed inmates in the year 2002, 68% were dependent on drugs or already abusing drugs.

Of the Blacks jailed:

- 40.4% were determined to be drug dependent
- 23.7% were determined to be abusing drugs

The total numbers of jailed Blacks abusing or dependent upon drugs were 64.1%.

Of the 64.1% of Blacks jailed:

- 66.1% were 24 years of age or younger

The gender of those jailed in 2002:

- 67.9% jailed were male
- 69.2% jailed were female

Of all inmates, the following represents the drug of choice used prior to incarceration:

- Marijuana-75.7%
- Cocaine or Crack-48.1%
- Heroin/Opiates-20.7%
- Depressants-21.6%
- Stimulants-27.8%
- Hallucinogens-32.4
- Inhalants-12.7%

According to US Census data there is approximately four times the amount of Whites living in the U.S. than Blacks. Yet, as we look at

some of the aforementioned statistics above, you'll see that Blacks are disproportionately represented in areas where we should not be. Why in 2004 were Blacks one third of all drug related arrests (410,552)? Why do we feel the need to be so high! What is it that we're running away from? What is it in life that is so difficult to take that we must mask our pain by getting high? What happened to the strength and perseverance of the Black man? What has gone wrong?
I do not proclaim to have all the answers; that's not why I wrote this book. I wrote this book to bring awareness and hope to those of us that believe we're no longer important, we're not needed, and we're not valued. We must believe that Black families need all their members, especially the Black man.

When I look at the numbers above, I gain a greater understanding to the principle of 'cause and effect'. 'Cause' a large percentage of Black people are dealing with pre-addiction and full blown addictions which has led us to stealing, assaulting and outright acting foolish (disorderly conduct), our young people are attempting to beat some of us at our own game. When we look at the above statistics on Blacks under the age of 18 years, we can clearly see that our young people is modeling the same behaviors and attitudes of those of us who are supposed to teach and demonstrate positive, moral characters. But this would be a very difficult task to do when parents and a large portion of the Black population are themselves addicted to one thing or another. When we the people responsible for raising children (all of us) are too busy trying to make all the money our hands can get a hold of; and still not be satisfied. Then how is it that the mature Black person is supposed to teach morality, responsibility and righteous living to others, when many of us don't believe in the God of our salvation and His only begotten son Jesus Christ our savior and redeemer. How is it that we've turned away from the focus of our freedom? Not just freedom from physical enslavement, but freedom from all bondage. How dare parents blame others for the problems of their children? Children are only immolating what parents have already demonstrated to them by their behaviors, and by their verbal, emotional, and spiritual teachings. Children learn by watching others, therefore every person who comes in contact with a child has a parental responsibility to demonstrate Holy living before that child.

So instead of demonstrating Holy living as the primary form of non-verbal instructions, we tell our children it's OK to act like me by exhibiting or modeling dysfunctional behaviors, well it's not. When that brother is first told that his woman (girlfriend only) is pregnant and he's the father, that brother decides the relationship is over. So many times this same type of brother goes from woman to woman loving up on her until she gets pregnant and then he's gone. The sister is left to fend for herself. So young men and women now grow up and add to the previously mentioned statistics. Why? As a Christian mental health counselor, I believe many of our children are exhibiting anger over being abandoned by their father. If you're saying to yourself, what about the sisters who abandon their children, it's not always brothers. That's true, however over 90% of single families are taken care of by the mother.

God bless the brother who takes care of his own; my hat is off to you. But the focus here is on the 90% of brothers who have not stepped up to the plate. Our children are stealing and robbing whoever they can. Their raping girls, murdering people, their unable to get along with others (disorderly conduct), their using and abusing drugs and prostituting their bodies. Is this what parents are proud of? Is this what the absent Black husband and father is proud of? Is the Black man expressing his joy with friends after hearing that his son or daughter made 'America's Most Wanted,' while shooting a game of pool, in prison. Do we say "That's my boy." Or look my daughter has scored another John (Trick), "I'm so proud of her, she's really working hard."

The fact is: the strung out father cares only about his next fix and damn his parental responsibilities. And that's just what's happening in our society today. Our family is damned. We are struggling to exist. The Black family is on the verge of a total melt down. Black men are too busy doing and selling drugs, and making babies from foolish, low self-esteem sisters who's just as dysfunctional as some of the brothers their sleeping with. Many brothers and now sisters are stealing anything they can get their hands on to feed their drug needs. Our youths are having relational difficulties in the home and fighting with mom and other siblings. Many of our youths are also exhibiting relational difficulties in school. Many Black youths and adults alike are attempting to find purpose and meaning to their lives. Thus, they attempt to meet their emotional, relational, and spiritual needs through ways that create more problems and greater pain.

Pain, that's the four letter word that describes the Black family today. We are in pain, and our way of muffling the pain is wrapped up in sinful desires, actions, behaviors and thinking. No one wants to hurt, but young Black men don't know how to express their emotions. Young Black men were never taught that it's healthy to talk about your feelings. They feel ashamed to tell someone their hurting. As I speak to youths in my practice, I often times find that a major indicator of emotional or behavioral problems stem from a sense of unidentified pain in the youth due to a lack of relationship with their father.

These youths tell me, many times while crying, how they long for a relationship with their dads. And because they did not get a healthy relationship with their father, they exhibit signs of depression and a lack of human emotions for the feelings and rights of others. Many times, both young men and women are aggressive in their body language, their verbal speech and their overall personality that has been altered to protect an already sensitive and devastated heart. These and many other symptoms are characteristics of a deeper problem. Our children are lonely and are in need of a healthy relationship with mom and dad, however they do not know how to express it, and moreover, many of them are afraid to express it. To open up and share your feelings with someone is dangerous. We live in a society that shuns honesty and realism, yet we're quick to promote pain.

Many Black men were raised not to share their weaknesses. To share your inner most feelings is a sign of weakness. It is my belief that fathers taught their sons to deal internally with their pains, fears, shortcomings and weaknesses by bottling them up, instead of releasing them in a healthy way. This to me sounds like how our slave fathers dealt with their issues. I understand that it was not possible to exhibit human emotions like pain. This was neither acceptable nor desired behaviors. After all, the slave master could care less if your emotional, physical, relational, behavioral and spiritual needs were being met, we were slaves! Black men had to be strong in every area of like, or die!

As time went by, this parenting style was maintained. So we now have brothers and sisters afraid to say to someone, "I'm hurting." It is true that we don't have to articulate it; we view the results of it everyday on the news and in the newspapers. We view it's devastations in our homes and in our neighborhoods. When people don't understand what their needs are and how to meet those needs in an acceptable way, we'll often go with what ever works to fulfill that need, and many times it ends up creating more needs than fulfilling the initial need.

Therapeutically, when humankind fails to understand their God given needs and how God intended for us to meet those needs, the results are always problematic. We are all born in sin and shaped in inequity. Therefore, when we fail to understand that God is the same God yesterday, today and forever more, and He wants to meet our needs, but we must first acknowledge Him above everything else. Then we understand that the first step in meeting our needs is through an intimate relationship with Christ.

Black female youths suffer with issues of self-esteem and a low self-view of themselves. Many times they seek a relational attachment to a young or older man who simply tells them nice things about themselves (true or not) and is willing to spend time with them. When this young or older brother does this, the Black youth in many cases gives in to the males request for sex. Statistics are now recording young Black girl's age 12-13 years old, experiencing sex for the first time. Some of these girls may not have even started puberty (their first period), but that does not stop them in having sex, oral, anal, and vaginal sex. Statistics state that more and more of our young girls and teens are paying for time and attention with a male through the vehicle of their bodies.

Black male youths suffer with issues of aggression, hostility, control. These issues are all issues involved in masking of their true feelings. Black male youths force girls to have sex with them and will use control and aggression as a means to get what they want. And many times, just as their dad did, they deny responsibility when the girl says she's pregnant, and the cycle continues again.

R.E.S.P.E.C.T.

"Train a child in the way he should go, and when he is old he will not turn from it," (Proverbs 22:6).

Webster's New World Dictionary defines the term respect as "To feel or show honor or esteem for; to show consideration for." I wonder how many abandoned children along with their mothers believe their abandoned husband, boyfriend or baby daddy, deserves to receive respect. If Webster's define the word respect as "To feel,' well, I guess that identifies the first problem. As previously touched upon, many of our Black women and their children have placed their deep emotions (feelings) behind a 10 inch steel door with motion sensors; previously named the heart. All people respond to pain the same way in the beginning stages. However, many of us end up in a protect mode. You only have to suffer a broken heart once to understand what I'm referring to. When we are deeply hurt relationally, we tell ourselves (our self talk) that we're never going to put ourselves in the position of getting so hurt again.

When we allow ourselves to fully let our guard down and trust, we're acknowledging that we're also allowing a very real possibility of being hurt. Thus, when we are deeply hurt the first time, we begin to think differently about our relationships. We don't allow our hearts to get to deeply involved. Neither do we truly love without conditions.

When we are hurt deeply in a relationship, and this relationship can be a relationship between a parent, a spouse, a sibling, a friend, etc., the point is, when we are open, honest and true to ourselves and others, we set ourselves up to be taken advantage of; this is a well known fact. Thus, what we are saying (many times without speaking words), to that special person we freely give our emotional well-being to, is simply this: "Please do not break by heart."

When we love without conditions, we are saying to that special person, "I trust you with my heart." This is the purest sense of love here on earth that I can think of. Our society today is a society full of emotional grief (heart pain). Many of us that have lived beyond adolescence have already been hurt multiply times, by multiple people. One problem with this point of view is the problem of how we love. As babies, then children and on to our adolescence stages of development, one primary way we learn is through environmental learning or another word for this is called "Modeling."

Our parents model behaviors, attitudes, emotions, personalities and response stimulus before us. In other words, as our overall personalities (everything that makes us humans) are forming, birth to about age 6 or 7. We watch and learn and thus repeat what's been modeled before us by everyone who comes in contact with us. With this premise in mind, when we think about how we individually model love for one another in its various arenas, we are repeating what we've previously learned through environmental learning or modeling. Thus, one primary problem with how we initially love can be blamed on faulty environmental learning or modeling. Think about how you watched your mom and dad interact with each other and family and friends. How did dad demonstrate love towards mom? How did mom respond to conflict with dad? How were you disciplined as a child? Was their a difference in discipline styles between mom and dad?

As you analyze the differences between mom and dad, sisters and brothers, you invariably begin to understand how we can become products of our environments. Every child has the opportunity to witness all the imperfections of those responsible for their nurturing. The Bible refers to this style of learning as the "Sin cycle." Environmental learning will continue with each generation of parenting. That's not the problem; the problem is how we parent and what we as parents are modeling before our children. The question the Bible asks, that can be applied throughout the New Testament church is this: *"Choose ye this day whom you will serve."* In other words, as adults we don't have to continue to make the same mistakes our parents made when raising us. We either learn healthy parenting through the word of God and other God fearing role models, thus choosing to nurture our children in a righteous environment where they can learn righteous living characteristics, or we choose to continue producing children raised in unholy, maladaptive environments.

Just because dad demonstrated his love for mom by drinking and beating her, does not mean that I have to choose the same pattern of parenting when I have children. It also does not mean that just because my dad may have slept around on my mother and called my mother every name but sweetheart, does not mean that I have to repeat the same treatment to my wife. God has inherently given us the ability to understand that there is a primary difference called right and wrong. We must choose which way we are going to parent.

A second primary way of demonstrating love is by the process of attempting to understand and meet our needs. Often times, we as human beings are attempting to meet what we have determined to be a need for us, and thus we attempt to meet this need in unholy ways, which leads us to even greater distress. We love out of our need. All humans have the same basic needs of life. Food, water, shelter, security, etc., these are the basic needs to sustain life. I contend with you that the need for human relationships and love is a basic necessity of life. God created Adam for relationship. God created every creature with a partner (a mate), and thus, God realized that Adam was alone and created woman for relationship with man (Adam). God created relationships. The first relationship belongs to God. (The greatest commandment-*"Love the Lord your God with all your heart and with all your soul and with all your mind and with all your strength"* Mark 12:29-31).

If we are deficient in first loving God as He wants to be loved; then how are we to demonstrate love to others, not knowing how they want to be loved. God instructs us how to love Him. Jesus said if you love Him you'll keep His commandments. If we are to demonstrate true love, them we must be in relationship first with God through His son Jesus Christ. Then, we are to learn how to love God by reading and doing what His word says to do. Then, and only then are we equipped to understand what love is, what God intended love to be and how to demonstrate it with each other. If you ask 10 youths the question, what is love? You'll get 10 different answers, because none of them understands the greatest gift one can ever give to another; love. *"For God so loved the world that He gave His only begotten son. That whosoever believes in Him will not perish, but have everlasting life"* John 3:16.

Our need to express love comes from our need to have relationships with one another. Man did not write the rules for relationships. If you're a married couple, God has already given you the rules and order for your marriage. So don't even think of creating your own standards, that is, unless you like dysfunction. Parents, God has already given you rules on how to raise your children. Oh, and by the way men, that means you. The operative word here is "Parents." A child must have both parents actively in their lives if that child is to have the best chances at a proper development. Remember I said that this is the primary reason why our youth is so angry today, the dad factor. Children, God has spoken to you too! God has even giving us directions on how to love our neighbors.

So if the parenting and relationship book has already been written, why are their so many books in the book stores on parenting and relationships? It's simple; we have not picked up the Bible and read it. Neither have we done what it said to do. We have chosen to disobey

God and shun His gospel message. This is the primary reason why Black folks and all God's peoples are suffering. You don't have to have a PhD in child psychology to understand that a child is rebellious because he's not getting what he believes he should have. You don't need a PhD in relationship counseling to understand why married couples aren't getting along; they're not following Scriptural principles for the marriage. God understands the needs of His creation; therefore, He also understands what happens when we attempt to meet our needs in ways He did not prescribe. If you want to be blessed; do what Scriptures says; if not, don't!

So again, the question is asked how do a child show respectful feelings for an abandoned dad? How do I as a child respect my dad who left my mother and me?

"Honor your father and your mother, as the Lord your God has commanded you, so that you may live long and that it may go well with you in the land the Lord you God is giving you" (Deuteronomy 5:16).

Scriptures command children to give honor (respect) to a dad who has disrespected them. A bastard child society calls them. This child grows up the best way he and his mother can. Let's say that this child grew up in a loving household with all the finery of life. Do you think this child ever thinks of his dad? Do you think this child has forgotten what his dad did to him and his mother? Many Black children like this example are experiencing this very scenario. Children are growing up without their dads and no matter how good a life they have, the fact is: there is a great black hole in the minds and hearts of our Black children.

Many children hope that one day they'll have an opportunity to face their dad and tell them… Many children want to ask the question why? These children grow up not fully understanding how to commit their hearts to someone, because their dad never committed his heart to them. Many children grow up with issues of detachment. These kids don't know how or even want to create close relationships with others. Many of these children grow up to abuse drugs and alcohol and become users of women and often times; they find themselves with a history in the judicial system. Some of these kids grow up to murder, rape, steal and abuse. Many of these kids grow up with issues of anger, rage, hostility and a sense of disrespect for others and life in general. This is what we see on the outside of the hurting Black youth. However, if one would spend some time with one of these youths, you'll come to find out that their not as brash as they seem.

What these youths demonstrate on the outside is simply a mask to protect their insides (their heart). You see, their young innocent hearts were abused and tossed to the side by someone that probably looked just like an older them. So as these youths matured they quickly learned that they did not like the feelings that were coming from their heart. After all, the answers they were seeking was not available to them, so they protected themselves by masking their true feelings of guilt, shame, confusion, pain, disappointment, a sense of longing, a sense that something is missing, which led to anger, depression, a low self-view of themselves, issues with self-esteem, rejection, abnormal thinking and negative reactionary conduct in society at large. This is a primary belief in the structure of gangs.

If you were to study the dynamics of youth gangs in America, you'll find out that many of the youths participating in gangs, are youths without fathers. These youths feel a sense of brotherly affection from fellow gang members. Gangs offer youths a sense of family, purpose, protection and emotional brotherhood that some youths did not get at home. So gang members perform duties to prove their sense of loyalty to the gang, this sense of loyalty stems from misplaced loyalty from an abandoned or unproductive dad. Gang members feel a sense of security, knowing that if they're in trouble, other gang members will stand beside them.

Gangs feed and clothe and shelter gang members as well as provide them with a means of income. Gangs play basketball together, go to movies together. In addition to supplying the gang the foundation for its existence, which is drugs and other illegal activities. New gang members believe that having to participate in the illegal component of gangs is a small price to pay for the sense of relationship they get from the gang. What gang members really get from gangs is misplaced emotional attachment and loyalty. All the things a youth need from the dynamics of gang involvement can be found in a nurturing relationship with his father.

Drugs and STD's

Why have so many of our young Black men and women turned to drugs? As you look back at the statistics, one area sticks out, drugs. Nearly 70% of youths arrested in 2002 were already using or abusing drugs. The sad reality of this number is nearly equally represented by males and females. Marijuana and crack is the primary drugs of choice with 67.9% of youth arrests comprising of males and 69.2% comprising of females, and lets not forget that of all arrests in 2002 for youths, Black females represented nearly 53%, what happened? It is a known fact that marijuana gives you a feeling of euphoria. So when things are not going your way and you're feeling stressed out and need to relax. People smoke weed in its many forms. Weed is laced today with all sorts of additional chemicals that greatly intensifies the effects of smoking weed and also increases the risks.

Smoking weed can be a gateway to using more potent drugs. Crack cocaine is very different than smoking weed. Crack cocaine is so powerful to the brain that using it one time can create an addiction to the drug. The side effects of using crack cocaine are greatly pronounced as the risk of addiction is very high. Both of these drugs cause a lack of inhibitions. It is the euphoric effects of these drugs and the lack of inhibitions that create the risk factor for unprotected sex. Many youths are addicted and thus use sex as a means to obtain greater and greater amounts of these illegal drugs. When you talk about Sexually transmitted diseases, you must mention the fact that there are four incurable sexually transmitted diseases.

They are:

> HIV/AIDS
> Herpes Simplex one and two
> Human Papilloma Virus
> Hepatitis

*Note: According to the CDC Blacks in 2004 accounted for 52% of Aids cases. Of the overall 40,331 cases, ethnic people comprised a total of 75.2% of Aids cases, while whites during the same year comprised of 24.8% of Aids cases. The cumulative estimated number of Aids cases through year 2004 looks like this:

> Whites-375,155 cases of Aids
> Blacks, non Hispanic- **379,278** cases of Aids
> Hispanic-177,164 cases of Aids
> Asian/Pacific Islander-7,317 cases of Aids
> American Indian/Alaska Native-3,084 cases of Aids

Using condoms does not protect us from every sexually transmitted disease, especially herpes and the human papilloma virus. A person who is infected and is in an active stage of these diseases can infect another person simply by coming in contact with a person's flesh. African American youth represent the fasted growing population of new HIV/AIDS cases in America today. Yet, we're still prostituting our body and buying and selling death to people who look like us. It's again my opinion that the majority of these sinful behaviors is due to our need to mask our true feelings, which is left wanting.

Sex does not fulfill the need of true love. True love has nothing to do with having sex. Jesus so loved the world, but He didn't have sex with anyone to prove it. Because He knew better than anyone that love and sex is two entirely different components of the human experience. Jesus also knew that when you take love or sex out of context with Scriptures, what you end up with is greater pain than what you started with. You see, God intended sex for marriage only! So in that context God blesses it. Likewise, when we take what God intended for good and use it sinfully (evil), we set ourselves up for the righteous judgment of God and thus sexually transmitted diseases is a by-product of sin and thus we inflict ourselves with these diseases through the decisions and behaviors we exhibit. And let me say, yes, oral and anal sex is sex. Both oral and anal sex is conduits for sexually transmitted diseases. Sex does not satisfy the need for true relationship, it's only a mask that hides the true needs of the individual.

A Closer Look at Incurable Sexually Transmitted Diseases (STD's)

According to the American Social Health Association the Human Papillomavirus (HPV) has over 100 different viral types. This is a virus that is most commonly known to cause warts on the hands and feet. Other types of infections affect the genital tract. Genital HPV types are sexually transmitted and cause external genital warts or cause cell changes on the cervix that increases a woman's risk for cervical cancer. There are high risk types of HPV, two of the most common identified types are 16 and 18. These two identified types place women at risk for developing cervical cancer. There are 13 or more types of HPV that are associated with cervical cancer. Types 6 and 11 are the most common types found in genital warts. The primary mode of testing for HPV in women is done through a Pap test.
(ASHA brochure).

Human Immunodeficiency Virus/Acquired Immunodeficiency Syndrome (HIV/AIDS) is a non-curable sexually transmitted disease. HIV is the virus that causes AIDS. There are two primary ways of contracting the disease. You can get HIV by having any kind of sex, whether it is vaginal, anal or oral sex. You can also get HIV by sharing needles to shoot drugs, pierce body parts, some tattooing, and contact with HIV infected blood. Latex condoms have been proven as an effective barrier to the transmission of the HIV virus. However, when drugs are introduced into the mix, the behaviors become more risky toward protecting one during sex. The effects of drugs can strip a person of their common sense and cause them to engage in risky, unsafe sexual practices. In addition, the sharing of needles and other drug paraphernalia increases the risk of transmission of the HIV virus. It is common sense that doing drugs and having sex can be an explosive, life threatening and life altering event.

Herpes Simplex Virus (HSV) is a sexually transmitted disease of two types. Herpes simplex virus-1 prefers to live above the waist. It's identified by fever blisters of cold sores that people get around the lips, mouth, and nose. Herpes simplex virus-2 prefers to live below the waist. Below the waist the virus produces sores on the genitals that sometimes resemble cold sores. HSV spreads from person to person through direct contact with vulnerable skin cells such as the soft skin of the vagina, anus, scrotum, penis and the mucous membranes such as in the mouth. As with other STD's latex condoms is a recommended barrier to the spread of STD's, however, even condoms are not 100% effective in STD's transmission, as some STD's can be transmitted if while using a condom.

The Emotional Effects of Sex

Before a person thinks of having any kind of sexual encounter, they should be thinking how their relationship with their partner will be effected, questions of pregnancy, disease, worry, regret and other emotions should be expressed and questions asked and answered prior to engaging in any sexual relationship. The primary question many of us stopped asking is "How will my relationship with God be effected"? Of course, God will forgive us of our sins! This is the excuse we always come up with, but how many times are we going to play that card? Remember Scriptures teaches us that it is out of our love for God that we obey His commandments. So then the question must be asked: "Just how much do I love the Lord"?

Many people in today's society rush into having sexual experiences. Statistics tell us that the age group of children experimenting with sex is occurring at earlier and earlier ages. Many young people feel that sex is the "In thing," after all, everyone's doing it. Sex is a powerful, emotional, psychological and spiritual issue that must be addressed prior to engaging in. First, sex was not meant to be the "In thing," unless you were married. Sex outside of this God ordained order will be met with curses. Just take another look at the aforementioned STD's above.

The emotional side effects of usurping God's intention for sex includes problematic relationships whereas a person who engages in sex too early or outside of its intention, may experience the inability to form close and enduring relationships. A staple in marriages must include respect, honesty, trust, open communication, dedication, stability, safety, understanding, an emotional bonding, unity, synergy, love, duty, and the marital covenant between two people that states their intention to spend the remainder of their lives together, in health and in sickness; for richer or poorer. Sex in a marital union was meant to be an expression of joy and unity, as well as procreation. Sex involves the giving of one's entire being and personality. It's an expression of one's commitment to their spouse, but ultimately it's an expression of obedience to the covenant between man and God. Scriptures record in the book of Genesis 2:24 *"Therefore shall a man leave his father and his mother, and shall cleave unto his wife: and they shall become one flesh."*

The Scriptures speak to the fact that a man willingly accepts the responsibility and desire to leave the care of his parents and become responsible for another (his wife). The joining of man and woman in sex is a literal joining of two bodies as the man enters the woman's wound. This is the act of vaginal sex. This act literally joins two bodies as one. If you think about this further, a man and a woman not only joins together in the act of sex, but also chemically. A man and the woman both secrets sperm and this sperm is made up of the individual characteristics of each person's physical, emotional, behavioral, psychological and spiritual makeup. This is what the Bible is referring to when it states "The two shall become one flesh." Sex is not simply the act of two people of the opposite sex getting their grove on. No, it's so much more than that. Because it's seen by many youth and mature Black men and women today as merely a mechanical act, the curse of usurping God's intention for sex is and have been placed upon us.

What emotional or spiritual bonding is to be shared by engaging in sex with a whore? Young men and women; middle age men and women; old men and women; everybody's having some form of sex outside the confines of marriage. I contend that just as I was once a whore, so are many of the black population today. Pastors are whoring with the congregation, deacons are whoring with the deaconess; and three fourths of the couples sitting in the various congregations are whoring around with one another, because none of them are married. We're a society of whoremongers, as Scriptures reveal to us to Ephesians 5:5 *"For this ye know, that no whoremonger, nor unclean person, nor covetous man, who is an idolater, hath any inheritance in the kingdom of Christ and of God."* Moreover, Hebrews 13:4 states: *"Marriage is honourable in all, and the bed undefiled: but whoremongers and adulterers God will judge."*

Many of us, old and young have fallen into the trap of Satan by lusting after the flesh. Solomon gives us brother's some wisdom in Proverbs 23:26-35, as Solomon instructs the men on the value of truth. He states in verse 27, 28: *"For a whore is a deep ditch; and a strange woman is a narrow pit. She also lieth in wait as for a prey, and increaseth the transgressors among men."* In other words, Solomon is saying to us that sex outside of marriage is way to get your self lost. If you think about a deep ditch, a deep ditch is often unseen until you stumble across it and fall into it. You never intended to be trapped by it. Inside the ditch may house all matter of unclean and harmful things. The fact is, you're stuck and AAA Motor Club can't help you, and now you're kicking yourself and calling yourself all kinds of names because you're angry at yourself for allowing yourself to be stranded and caught up in something you could not see. Sex outside of marriage is a very luring trap just waiting for you and me to taste of her forbidden fruit. Remember my brothers; everything that looks good or feels good is not good. For every decision we make, there is a consequence. The reality is that what Solomon is saying in the above Scriptures applies to both men and women. Women, "everything that swings isn't good to ride on."

My brothers and sisters, sin begat sin, and the wages of sin is still death. Haven't we all endured too much suffering? Why do we feel the need to help Satan do his job? Sometimes I think we're trying to put Satan out of business by taking over the business. Why do we sell death to ourselves? Why do we rob and steal from ourselves? Why do we curse and abuse ourselves? Why do we pimp and prostitute ourselves? Why do we rape and murder ourselves? Why are so many of us in prison? Why are we not in college? Why we are not married? Why do we step on people who look like us? Why do we rob and steal from the Church? Why, why, why… We once were a people that would literally harm another human being to protect our families. Now, it's the family we've got to be concerned about! And for God's sake, stop blaming White people! A Black person today is the primary reason why a Black person is enslaved, because Black people have turned from being slaves to being the slave masters.

When an unmarried female thinks about whether or not she wants to have sex with a brother, I would seriously hope she thinks about her self-value. I would hope she asks herself questions similar to these:

- Am I giving up too much to be with this brother?
- Why do I have to give up so much?
- What about my relationship with God?
- What about my sense of morality?
- Do I have more respect for myself than that?
- What about my soul's salvation?

My sisters, simply speaking, you give up the cookies way to soon! It used to be that a brother (saved or not) had to really win you over before you would even allow us to kiss you. But now, you're thinking of letting us stick our hands in the cookie jar even before you discover what we're all about! It used to be said that men only think of sex, well, that's not the case anymore. We've become so sexually stimulated in sin that dads are molesting their babies, and it does not matter whether the baby is a boy or girl. We're date raping our girlfriends and friends with drugs that allows a perpetrator to have their will. Blood brothers are sleeping with their sisters; husbands (what few there are) are sleeping around on their wives; wives are sleeping around on their husbands; sons is having sex with the male basketball coach; and girls have just lost their minds by having sex with other girls and acting more like a player than men! Instead of this known fact being appalling to us, it turns us on. Black folks are seemingly more attracted to sin now than ever before (in my opinion). I heard a Deacon friend of mine say: "You can get sex when you can't get something to eat."

Black folks have fallen deep into the trap of sexual sins of all kinds; we have increased the emotional stress and dysfunctions associated with our sins. We are a more depressed people than ever in history; we are an angrier group of people than in past times; we are a more violent group of people than ever in our African American history, our churches are more split and dysfunctional now than in past times, and thus we as a people have lost the desire to be a righteous family of God. I wonder how all the former slaves would think about what's going on with us today. Just think about their struggle for freedom and human recognition; just to have us end up enslaving ourselves by our sinful thinking, beliefs and behaviors.

Curable STD's and Their Impact

Chlamydia

Let me start out by giving you some overall numbers, taken from the *Center for Disease Control* website concerning Chlamydia infections.

> In 2004 there were 929,462 Chlamydia infections reported to the Center for Disease Control (CDC). This number represents an increase of infections reported by 5.9% in 2003. The numbers of reported Chlamydia infections were more than two

and one half times the number of reported cases of gonorrhea in 2004.
- From 1987 through 2004, the rates of reported Chlamydia infections increased from 50.5 per 100,000 population to 319.6 cases per 100,000 population.
- In 2004, the overall rate of reported Chlamydia infection among women in the U.S. (485.0 cases per 100.000 females) was over 3 times higher than the rate among men (147.1 cases per 100,000 males). The lower rates among men suggest that many of the sex partners of women with Chlamydia are not diagnosed or reported. From 2000 through 2004, the Chlamydia infection rate in men increased by 47.7% (from 99.6 to 147.1 cased per 100.000 males) compared with a 22.4% increase in women over this period (from 396.3 to 485.0 cases per 100,000 females).
- Among women, the highest age-specific rates of reported Chlamydia in 2004 were among 15-19 year olds (2,761.5 per 100,000 females) and 20-24 year olds (2,630.7 per 100,000 females). Age specific rates among men, while substantially lower than the rates in women, where highest in the 20-24 year olds range.
- **In 2004, the rate of Chlamydia among African-American females in the U.S. was: more than 7 and a half time higher than the rate among white females** (1,722.3 and 226.6 per 100,000, respectively). **The Chlamydia rate among African American males was 11 times higher than that among white males** (645.2 and 57.3 per 100,000, respectively). **Since 2000 - 2004, these men have been characterized by high rates of HIV co-infection and high-risk sexual behaviors.**

Syphilis

Let me also share with you some syphilis numbers, also taken from the CDC website.

- In 2004 P&S syphilis cases reported to CEC increased to 7,980 from 7,177 in 2003, an increase of 12.2%

- The rate of P&S syphilis between 2003-2004 increased 11.9% among men (from 4.2 cases to 4.7 per 100,000 men).
- The male to female rate ratio for P&S syphilis has risen steadily since 1996 when it was suggesting an increase in syphilis among men who have sex with men.
- Between 2003-2004, the male to female rate ratio for P&S syphilis decreased in whites but increased among African Americans (from 27.-3.3) and among Hispanics (from 6.1-7.9).
- **In 2004, syphilis rates increased from men and women in almost all racial and ethnic groups.** African Americans accounted for 41% of cases of P&S syphilis in 2004 and 39.2% in 2003. During 2003-2004, the rate of P&S syphilis increased 16.9% among African Americans, reflecting a 22.2% increase in the number of cases among men 9from 2,005-2,450) and a 1% increase among women (from 805-813).
- **In 2004, the rate of P&S syphilis reported among African Americans was 6 times greater than the rate among non-Hispanic whites and 5 times greater in 2003, and reflects an increase in syphilis among African Americans for the first times in over a decade.**
- The incidence of P&S syphilis was highest among women aged 20-24 years and among men aged 35-39 years.

What type of emotional effects would you suffer with if your case was identified in the aforementioned statistics? Please keep in mind that Blacks only represent a total of approximately 14-16% of the U.S. population. However, when it comes to devastating statistics we seem to be near, if not at the top of many indicators. I don't know about you; but, I don't want to feel proud of attracting or spreading HIV/Aids, Chlamydia, and Syphilis or be known for beating up, raping, robbing, selling dope or any of other identified societal woes.

If we examine the numbers above they tell us that when it comes to syphilis, the problematic group of Blacks is the 20-24 years olds and the 35-39 years olds. When it comes to Chlamydia females between the ages of 15-19 and 20-24 are the problematic age groups, while men

20-24 years of age are the problematic age group. According to this information, our teenagers are not practicing safe sex. Let me clarify what I mean when I say "Safe Sex." Safe sex (just in case you haven't read it before) is "NO SEX." If you're not married, you have no right, or privileges to neither stick anyone with anything, nor be stuck by anyone! Oral sex is still sex, so this means no oral sex of any kind until you're married! Oh, and anal sex is sex, and no you cannot have any until you're married! All other acts of sexuality must fall within the qualifications of marriage only. As I mentioned before, the above sexually transmitted diseases is the outcome of not following God's order and purpose for sexual intimacy. I'm sorry, but sex isn't free, it cost. I know many of you reading this believe that I'm just another preacher spilling out religious jargon; you're right! However, look again at the statistics and tell me that your life and health is worth a little time in sexual bliss?

Sex involves a covenant relationship with God through Jesus Christ first; then a covenant with God in marriage. If you want sex that bad, go and get married. It is my interpretation of Scripture that God has allowed those of us whose loins are on fire with passion to get married, rather than burn in desire which leads us to sin. Paul states in 1 Corinthians 7:9 *"But if they cannot contain, let them marry: for it is better to marry than to burn."* Paul goes further to say in 1 Timothy 5:14 *"I will therefore that the younger women marry, bear children, guide the house, give non occasion to the adversary to speak reproachfully."* This word reproach (according to Nelson's New Illustrated Bible Dictionary) means to scorn, rebuke, or shame.

So what the Apostle Paul is teaching us is that it is better for us to get married than to allow Satan and our own sinful desires to consume us and give us a bad reputation. Further more, Scripture has a two fold meaning when using the term burn. The Scriptural term burn is used figuratively (According to Nelson's New Illustrated Bible Dictionary), as in emotions and literally as in a physical burning. With this information in mind, when we again look at the above referenced Scriptures, we find out that Paul is saying to us to marry instead of letting our emotional desire for sexual intimacy get the best of us (burn), also Paul is saying that its better to marry than sin and burn in eternal damnation (literally). Both ways, there is a consequence attached to usurping God's will for sex and perhaps the reason why Black folks are at the top of some social indicators is clear, we have usurped God in multiple areas of our lives. Individually and collectively, we as a group of God's created have within us the ability and opportunity to change our destination; it's simply a matter of our heart's mind over sin's matter.

Chapter Seven
"And the Two Shall Become One Flesh"

In the Beginning

"In the beginning God created the Heaven and the earth" Genesis 1:1. *"And God said, Let us make man in our image, after our likeness...,"* Genesis 1:26 A

"And the Lord God said, it is not good that the man should be alone; I will make him an help meet for him. But for Adam there was not found an help meet for him. And the Lord God caused a deep sleep to fall upon Adam, and he slept: and he took one of his ribs, and closed up the flesh instead thereof; And the rib, which the Lord God had taken from man, made he a woman, and brought her unto the man. And Adam said, This is now bone of my bones, and flesh of my flesh: she shall be called Woman, because she was taken out of Man. Therefore shall a man leave his father and his mother, and shall cleave unto his wife; and they shall be one flesh. And they were both naked, the man and his wife, and were not ashamed. And God saw every thing that he had made, and, behold, it was very good."
Genesis 1:1; 1:26 A; 2:18; 2:20 B-25;1:31, Holy Bible KJV.

God created all things that were created. God created every living thing after its kind but man. When God created Adam (man), God Himself realized that He created Adam alone and thus Adam did not have another after his kind. Thus God created Eve (woman) out of Adam and brought her to Adam. God created mankind for a personal relationship with Him and then each other. God saw everything He had created and said *"Behold it is very good."* God was very pleased with their creation (God the Father, Jesus the Son and the Holy Spirit). God gave instructions to <u>Adam</u> on how he was to govern himself.

Our Sovereign God created mankind out of His personal desire for fellowship with us. God created mankind for a personal relationship with Him. In the Garden, God walked with mankind, thus God was not distant, but He associated with mankind in a very personal way. The Bible proclaims in Genesis 2:25 *"And they were both naked, the man and his wife, and were not ashamed."* God created "Relationship."

When we think of the term relationship, we must think in terms of a connection; a connection made by blood or marriage. Lets first look at how we, mankind, is connected to God and each other by Blood.

Oh! the Blood

When we study the human definition of the term blood, we see that Webster's define the term as: "The essence of life; parental heritage; lineage; and kinship." When we think of the human relationship, we must associate a blood line in conjunction with our family of origin, someone born into our family by the blood of immediate family members. However, someone must be the originator of the blood line. From the original blood flowed a lineage of human connections. Although, the original blood has been introduced by other blood lines, the fact still remains that genetically, the originators blood must be present in order for the blood line to continue. Without the original blood, an identifiable connection will be lost, hence the term blood line. My daughter cannot be my direct descendent without my blood running through her veins, hence the term paternity.

My family blood lines have incorporated within them elements of African, Irish, and Indian blood lines. From the various blood lines flow identity, personality, health, psychological abilities, skills and talents, characteristics and temperaments; which are those God given characteristics of our personality. Within me is a melting pot of ethnicity, and influence. Have you ever heard someone say to you that you act just like your father, mother or relative? There is a connection to each provider of the blood line, but ultimately, we choose how to demonstrate these blood lines characteristics through our thinking, our emotions, and behaviors, relational and spiritual factors. We hold a stronger bond to others who share with us similar blood lines. We call members of our social groups "Family."

Families are usually composed of what we term our "Immediate Family," and then there are our relatives. Relatives stem from a blood lineage centered within the primary or immediate family. Our grandfathers and grandmothers represent the blood lineage to our father or mother, therefore grandparents hold a position of esteem within the family of origin. Then we have cousins. Our aunts and uncles represent another level of blood lineage to the primary family of origin. Aunts and uncles are sisters and brothers of our mother and fathers; therefore they hold a considerable position of esteem in our family of origin. Then there are cousins who could represent multiple levels of blood lineage. Cousins stem directly from the children of those represented in the primary family of origin. Cousins are categorized through the relational dynamics of the family blood lines. In addition, cousins are also intertwined into a family through the coming together of two in marriage.

Any one person not connected to the family through a blood line or by marriage is not considered within the primary or secondary levels of a family unit. Families do accept members into their family dynamics through relational connections. We often call people of this category our "Play" brothers or sisters. We also incorporate many friendships, associations, academic, professional and other social connections to comprise the dynamics of our families. The human race is a race that seeks various relationships with other humans to fulfill the various psychological, emotional, behavioral, relational and spiritual components of our lives. The fact is, without the proper fulfillment of the various components and dynamics of human relationships or connections; we will feel deprived of our basic needs for survival. The lack of these connections often times results in grief and depression, often brought on by loneliness, detachment, feelings of low self-worth and wholeness.

Theologically, when we look at the term blood, we see this term used in the Holy Scriptures to represent both a spiritual connection, and a blood connection, a death connection and a life connection. The spiritual connection is not associated with the genesis of Adam and Eve's direct blood line, but of the triune God to Adam and Eve. If we're going to talk spiritually, we must first then come to understand who God is. God is the creator and sustainer of the universe who has provided humankind with a revelation of Himself through the natural world and through His son Jesus Christ. The Bible does not seek to prove the existence of God; it simply affirms His existence by declaring *"In the beginning..."* (Genesis 1:1). God has revealed Himself through the physical universe (Ps. 19:1; Rom. 1:19-20). By observing the universe, one can find positive indications of God's existence. Creation reveals the results of a universal mind that devised a master plan and executed it. It makes more sense to accept the idea of God as Creator of the universe than to assume that our orderly universe came into existence apart from a divine being.

The greatest revelation of God, however, comes through the Bible. Through the inspired written record, both existence of God and the nature of God are revealed in and through Jesus Christ. Jesus stated, *"He that has seen me, has seen the Father"* (John 14:9). Although the full revelation of God was in Jesus Christ, the human mind cannot fully understand God. One reason for this is that Scripture does not record all the actions and teachings of Jesus (John 21:25). Another reason is the limitation of the human mind. How can our finite minds understand the infinity of God? It is not possible.

Although we can not fully understand God, we still can know Him. We know Him through a personal relationship of faith and through a study of what the Bible teaches about His nature. God may be described in terms of attributes. An attribute is an inherent characteristic of a person or being. While we cannot describe God in a comprehensive way, we can learn about Him by examining His attributes as revealed in the Bible.

God is a Spirit- Jesus taught that "God is Spirit" (John 4:24). God has no body, no physical or measurable form. Thus, God is invisible. He became visible in human form in the person of Jesus Christ, but His essence is invisible.

God is Changeless- Progress and change may characterize some of His works, but God Himself remains unchanged (Heb. 1:12). He does not change; otherwise, He would not be perfect. Thus, what we know of God can be known with certainty. He is not different from one time to another.

God is All-Powerful- God's power is unlimited. He can do anything that is not inconsistent with His nature, character, and purpose (Gen. 17:1; 18:14). The only limitations on God's power are imposed by Himself (Gen. 18:25). "Impossible" is not in God's vocabulary. God creates and sustains all things; yet He never grows weary (Is. 40:27-31).

God is All-Knowing- God possesses all knowledge (Job 38:39; Rom. 11:33-36). Because God is everywhere at one and the same time, He knows everything simultaneously. That God has the poser to know the thoughts and motives of every heart is evident from many Scripture passages, notably Job 37:16; Psalm 147:5, and Hebrews 3:13.

God is Everywhere- God is not confined to any part of the universe but is present in all His power at every point in space and every moment in time (Ps. 139:7-12). Thus, God does not belong to any one nation or generation. He is the God of the whole earth (Gen. 18:25).

God is Eternal- Eternity refers to God's relation to time. Past, present, and future are known equally to Him (2 Pet. 3:8; Rev. 1:8). Time is like a parade that human beings see only a segment at a time. But God sees time in its entirety.

God is Holiness- The word "holy" comes from a root word that means "to separate." Thus, it refers to God as separated from or exalted above other things (Is. 6:1-3). Holiness refers to God's moral excellence. Being holy, God demands holiness in His own children. And what He demands, He supplies. Holiness is God's gift that we receive by faith through His Son, Jesus Christ (Eph. 4:24).

God is Righteousness- Righteousness as applied to God refers to His affirmation of what is right as opposed to what is wrong. The righteousness of God refers to His moral laws laid down to guide the conduct of humankind, as in the Ten Commandments. Righteousness also refers to God's administration of justice. He brings punishment upon the disobedient (Gen. 18:25; Deut. 24:4; Rom. 2:6-16). Finally, God's righteousness is redemptive. In the book or Romans the righteousness of God refers to God's declaring the believer to be in a state of righteousness as though he had never been unrighteousness (Rom. 1:16-17; 3:24-26). This is possible because of the sacrificial death of Jesus on our behalf.

God is Love- love is the essential, self-giving nature of God. God's love for humankind seeks to awaken a responsible love of people for God. Divine love runs like a golden thread through the entire Bible. Nature is eloquent with the skill, wisdom, and power of God. Only in the Bible, however, do we discover God giving Himself and all He possesses to His creatures, in order to win their response and to possess them for Himself. God loved and gave; He loved and sought—just as a shepherd seeks his sheep. God loved and suffered, providing His love by giving His all on the cross for the redemption of humanity. God, in His love, wills good for all His creatures (Gen. 1:31 Ps. 145:9; Mark 10:18).

God is Truth- All truth, whether natural, physical, or religious, is grounded in God. Thus, and seemingly inconsistent teaching between natural and physical sciences and God's revelation of Himself is more apparent than real. Truth is magnified in an absolute way through God's revelation.

God is Wisdom- God's wisdom is revealed in His doing the best thing, in the best way, at the best time, for the best purpose. Some people have knowledge, but little wisdom, while the most wise at times have little knowledge. But God is "the only wise God" (1 Tim. 1:17). In creation, history, human lives, redemption, and Christ, His divine wisdom is revealed. Human Beings, lacking wisdom, can claim God's wisdom simply by asking (1 kings 3:9; James 1:5). Believers' understanding of God continues to increase throughout their earthly pilgrimage. It will finally be complete in eternity when they stand in the presence of God.

So now that we have an understanding of who God is, we can begin to piece together the "Two becoming one flesh." Adam and Eve has a direct Spiritual blood connection to the creator. Adam was the first man of creation and thus Eve was the second human being of creation. God said to His Son Jesus and His Holy Spirit, *"Let us make man in our image, after our likeness,"* thus, God created human beings to have some of the characteristics of the triune God. If God is perfect and He is, then God made us perfect, prior to mankind exercising his will to choose unrighteousness over obedience. God made mankind to be similar to Himself, with similar characteristics, likes and dislikes. More importantly, God gave us His Spirit. Scriptures record that God *"Breathed into the nostrils the breath of life; and man become a living soul,"* Genesis 2:7.

"He is the Rock, his work is perfect: for all his ways are judgment: a God of truth and without iniquity, just and right is he," Deuteronomy 32:4.
"Be ye therefore perfect, even as your Father which is in heaven is perfect," Matthew 5:48.

God is perfect and when He created us, He was well pleased with His work. No one knows the mind of God, but God does reveal Himself to us through His word and direct revelation. From a theological study of the creation story, God created mankind for relationship with Himself. He created mankind to share similarities with Him, which is the reason why He created us with His Spirit, His characteristics and most of all He created mankind with the ability to choose. God created mankind with the ability of awareness. During this time of creation, God created only mankind with this primary characteristic of Himself. Mankind was and is indeed very special to God. Thus by the creation account, and as Scripture reveals to us: *"Let us make man in Our image, according to Our likeness"* (Genesis 1:26). We can clearly extract from God's actions, that He created us to be like

Him. God created us with a special connection and similarity to Him. God created mankind to be aware (a will). God created mankind to have dominion over all other living things including the earth. Mankind's characteristics are so much like God's that He considers us a sort of first fruits (The best of the best).

Mankind is special to God. God wants mankind to love Him as He loves us. Scriptures reveal Jesus teaching of the greatest commandment: *"Thou shalt love the Lord thy God with all thy heart, and with all thy soul, and with all thy mind."* Thus Jesus instructs us on the next greatest commandment: *"And the second is like unto it, Thou shalt love thy neighbour as thyself,"* Matthew 22:37-40. God wants us to love Him as He loves us and then He wants us to demonstrate this same type of agape love to others. God is saying to us that He wants us to be in a special connected relationship with Him, as He is with us; then, He wants us to immolate that same agape relationship to one another. This is a very special understanding of Scriptures and how God intended mankind to treat one another in relationship to Him and each other.

Thus, we can extract from this brief theological study that God created mankind to be in perfect unity (relationship) with Him and each other. There is a Spiritual blood tie to God as creator; as our heavenly father; as daddy God. Therefore, since God created us, and set the rules by which we are to be unified to Him and one another; we have little choice but to follow the diagram that daddy God has already given us, if we're to have success in relationships. The problem is that we have usurped God and His diagram for relationships. We are not in a unified, connected relationship with God, therefore, how can we be in a healthy, unified, connected relationship with ourselves and each other. If you'll refer back to the statistics you'll clearly see that we're neither in a proper relationship with God nor anyone else for the most part.

Chaos is a by-product of disorder. The Black family is in a state of chaos. We are not in order with God, who has set the order for living a blessed life on earth. The Black family is in disorder because we are out of relationship, first with God. And because we are out of relationship with God, we cannot live in proper relationship with God, ourselves or anyone else. "Out of disorder comes dysfunction." It is my professional opinion, as statistics has supported, that the Black family is in a crisis state of spiritual disorder resulting in both human and spiritual dysfunction. God created man with three parts to immolate the completeness of Himself. God is a triune God (trichometist being), and therefore He made us also with three elements of existence. Man is body, spirit and soul (trichometist beings). God created mankind to be in perfect unity or relationship even within our human bodies, our spirit and our soul, to parallel His perfection.

If we're not in a proper relationship with God (as God has designed it according to His Word), then the rest of our relationships are improper as well. I'll use the term balance here to suggest that we are out of relationship with God and ourselves, as God has made us. Mankind is out of equilibrium (a state of balance). We are out of balance with God, our self and each other. In counseling, when a person has been thrown out of equilibrium or balance, they are in a state of crisis and stand in need of assistance in returning to at least the state of where they were prior to entering into the state of crisis. The Black family is out of equilibrium with God and thus we are in crisis and need to at minimum, return to the point where we were prior to entering into the crisis. Let me make this clear. The reason why we are out of balance with God and each other is because we have vacated a righteous relationship with God the creator. God wants us to do all things "decent and in order." Unfortunately many Black people are overly engrossed with doing things their way; thus, mankind's way only leads to greater separation with God and greater human disappointment. Black folks have sought to fulfill our needs outside the proper relationship with God, hence the term imbalance.

Once God had established the human relationship through the creation of Adam, God realized that He had made all things to be in relationship with its own except Adam. Therefore, God put Adam to sleep and out of Adam He made Eve (Woman), thus Scripture states:

"And brought her unto the man," Genesis 2:22b. *"And Adam said, This is now bone of my bones, and flesh of my flesh: she shall be called woman, because she was taken out of Man,"* Genesis 2:23.

"She was taken out of man."

"But for Adam there was not found an help meet for him." Genesis 2:20. *"And the Lord God said, It is not good that the man should be alone: I will make him an help meet for him,"* Genesis 2:18. God said, it is not good that I have made everything with a mate, but for Adam there is not a mate (Paraphrasing Scripture). God took it upon Himself to provide Adam with an help meet, because God said is was not good, therefore, God made the situation good. Adam needed companionship with another human being, after all, God created every other living thing with its own. Thus, God established the second level of relationships.

God had already established the relationship with Himself and Adam. And now we see that God then created the relationship with Adam and Eve. The creation of this second level of relationship was to fulfill the needs of Adam (Man). God created man with a helpmeet. Let's take a closer look at what this term implies. Nelson's Bible dictionary defines this term: "King James Version word for helper, companion, or mate, used by God to describe Eve before she was created as Adam's spouse (Gen. 2:18; helper comparable to him, NKJV; helper suitable for him, NIV). From this definition we can assert that woman (Eve) was created from Adam (Man) and brought to Him by God, as a helper, a companion, a mate, and a wife for Adam.

Now we find that not only did God create man to be in perfect relationship with Himself, but He also created woman to be in a perfect relationship with Himself and with man. Ultimately, everything that God created must answer to the authority of God the creator. Now we can clearly say that both Adam and Eve must devote their loyalty and obedience to God first, then to one another as supported by the "Greatest Commandments" Matthew 22:37-40. Scriptures goes on to state in Genesis 2:24 *"Therefore shall a man leave his father and his mother, and shall cleave unto his wife: and they shall be one flesh."*

Scripture is teaching us that because God gave us a free will spirit that allows us the ability to choose; <u>men</u>, when the time is right, we must choose to be involved in a unified relationship with a helper (wife). Prior to this, the Scripture suggest that while we are yet in our youth, we are still under the parental care and authority of our parents. At this point in our life we are ready to leave one family unit and establish a new one with a wife. We are at the point in our lives where we so choose to be involved in an intimate relationship (emotionally) with a woman. We then make a conscious choice and admit to ourselves that we are ready to leave the nurture and watch care of our parents. We are saying to ourselves, brothers, we are ready to live life as an adult. And as an adult, we are choosing to engage in an intimate relationship with a woman. However, in our decision making, we must be careful of the information we receive from ourselves or others.

We must seek wise counseling in matters of marriage. We must first come to understand who we are? And who's we are? If we cannot clearly say to ourselves that we are a child of God by way of acceptance of His Son Jesus Christ, then we are unfit for Holy matrimony. Secondly, if we're not looking for Holy matrimony, but looking for some adult fun under the sheets only, then we're looking for the wrong thing. The reason why a man takes interests in a girl is because he likes her. This is called dating or courting a girl. Doing this period of establishing a surface level relationship, the brother and sister is getting to know all about each other. This period defines whether or not the couple mutually decides to raise the commitment to each other. I call this level of the relationship "A deeper commitment." In this level of the relationship the couple decides that they will not see any others and they pre-commit to being with each other exclusively.

Doing this phase of the relationship, a deeper trust and dependence begins to develop. Expressions of daydreaming, heart palpitations and feelings of euphoria are experienced when the couple is with each other. Then comes the true commitment level, I call "Engagement." This is the level where the brother has decided that there is enough in common with the woman that he wants to claim her for his own. In doing so, he commits to her for the rest of his life by asking her hand in holy matrimony. He proceeds to lay claim to his commitment by placing a symbol of his commitment on her finger, called an engagement ring. Engagement is the time of love, joy, anxious anticipation of wedding jitters and the marriage consummation. Marriage is a lifetime commitment to connectedness between husband and wife as they come before the very presence of God who ordains it so.

"And the two shall become one flesh."

What does Scriptures refer to when it speaks of the "Two becoming one flesh?" A virgin, either man or woman, is a person who does not know each other. In other words, neither person has engaged in sexual practices. When a man and a woman come together in sexual unity there is a sharing of the two bodies with each other. Let's take a closer look at what I mean. Prior to a man and woman having intercourse, there is an excitement phase happening to both of their bodies. The man experiences the pre-ejaculatory semen from the tip of the penis. The woman's vagina swells and increases vaginal fluids in preparation for penetration. When a man's penis enters into a woman's vagina, the two of them share semen. When a man ejaculates, he releases more of this semen. Male semen contains approximately 200-500 million sperm, among many other things.

One of the primary ingredients of sperm is deoxyribonucleic acid (DNA). DNA contains the genetic instructions specifying the biological development of all cellular forms of life. DNA is often referred to as the molecule of heredity as it is responsible for the genetic propagation of most inherited traits. In humans, these traits can range from hair color to disease susceptibility. During cell division, DNA is replicated and can be transmitted to offspring during reproduction. Lineage studies can be done based on the facts that the mitochondrial DNA only comes from the mother, and the male 'Y 'chromosome only comes from the father. Every person's DNA, their genome, is inherited from both parents. The mother's mitochondrial DNA together with twenty-three chromosomes from each parent combine to form the genome of zygote; the fertilized egg.

Now, we can clearly see what the Bible means when it talks about the two becoming one flesh. During vaginal intercourse the man and woman share the foundational genetic existence of what they are individually with each other, thereby no longer being one unique person, but clearly becoming joined together chemically, emotionally, behaviorally, relationally, intellectually, and spiritually as one flesh. But this is not all that the Bible is referring to when it mentions the 'two becoming one flesh.'

Clearly, this day in age the Bible wants believers to be equally yoked to believers. This is a pre-requisite for Christian marriage. To be equally yoked is to be united as one with Christ and one with one another, both must be Christians. But, this is not enough; this is only the foundation for being equally yoked.

What about having some things in common? Scriptures tell us that Adam said to God when He brought Eve to her: *"This is now bone of my bones and flesh of my flesh."* Adam was clearly stating the fact that woman came from him (Man). Women are joined together with men for all humanity. No matter how we as men and women attempt to separate and divide us; we'll never be able to because without each other we'll cease to exist. We are unified; we are connected; we belong together. Unfortunately, we are engaged in a distant and turbulent form of relational expressions that continues to disconnect the Father's natural design for us to be harmoniously together.

Men and women choose to engage in mating rituals because there is something about the person they like. Being equally yoked also means having other things in common that two people can share. This sharing can come from areas of intelligence, such as reading, poetry, arts, drama, careers, education, etc. It may also involve areas of social enjoyment such as: bowling, movies, fishing, sports, opera, dancing, dining, boating, horseback riding, etc. Other areas of connectedness may include attitudinal expression. For example, I'm a peacemaker and I do not like to argue. I personally am not attracted to a person who is always confrontational and disagreeing. There must be a solid foundational agreement in which two people can stand and build upon in a lifetime relationship. This does not mean that two people are book ends, but it does mean that there must be common grounds in which to agree, thus establishing, maintaining and prospering unity. The rest of life is about balance with other likes and dislikes. Remember; a serious component of balance is "Respect," hence the term reverence.

When it comes to Christian denominations, I believe as a Christian counselor that a family should be unified in its worship practices. That's to say that if I attend a Baptist church and my fiancé is attending a Pentecostal church; I'm suggesting to her that we choose one church to attend. We should worship as a united and connected couple, thus a united and connected family; because family is all about being unified and connected, although we have differences.

The more families do things apart, the more opportunity for the enemy to bring separation and disharmony. The primary emotion that creates disharmony in relationships is selfishness. This emotion must be kept in check at all times. Selfishness suggests that we are no longer two people becoming one flesh, but one person staying one flesh. Selfishness is the reality of many marriages in American and the Christian church. Clearly, the focus has changed from unification to observation. At one point many of us were truly committed to the relationship, now we're on the outside of the relationship looking in by our own choice. Many of us have lost our sense of unity and perseverance to the relationship; as the focus has switched from 'us to me.'

Please, let me say this to the single Sisters. Puppy love does not involve a serious commitment, nor does it involve sex of any kind. If you're not ready for marriage, you're not ready for sex. If he wants the milk, but does not want the cow; tell that brother to keep stepping, because only serious handlers need apply. Brothers, the same thing go for you. I know you may say, "All preachers say stuff like that." Perhaps you should start listening. If the sisters ever wised up; many of you players would be in trouble. Sisters remember: "No ring; no thing."

What's Love got to do with it?

What is marital love? Love for Jesus Christ is the basis for love towards each other. It's not necessarily a physical love, but an emotional, spiritual love that goes beyond the shell of one's internal drives, but seeks the attachment to the inner-self; the person's heart. Marital love is a commitment to love in spite of one's rollercoaster feelings. This type of love seeks to serve and not be served. This type of love is trustworthy, full of honesty, dedication, perseverance, loyalty; Paul said it better than I can ever say:

1st Corinthians 13:4
"Love is patient, love is kind. It does not envy, it does not boast, it is not proud. It is not rude, it is not self-seeking, it is not easily angered, it keeps no record of wrongs. Love does not delight in evil but rejoices with the truth. It always protects, always trusts, always hopes, always perseveres. Love never fails."

Brothers, Jesus said: *"I did not come to be served; but to serve."* This is the essence of what love is. When or if you ever find this kind of love on earth, I hope you appreciate it, because this type of love is difficult to find. Not because it is difficult to live like this; but simply because we choose not to!

Love in the Bible begins with giving. Love is the giving of yourself for another; it is giving your time, your interest, your thoughts, your considerations, your money, your creativity, or even your very life. When one regularly gives himself to another, he deposits a "treasure" in that other person, and that is where his "heart will be also," This basic self-giving, self-initiated love is the love required in marriage, and it is the very love that will make any Christian marriage a success.

"Husbands love your wives and do not be cruel, severe or offensive to their feelings," Colossians 3:19.

Love is the essential component in a marital covenant. Love is the essential component in the family covenant. Love is the essential component in choosing one's career or sport activities and many other choices. However, marital love is a love worth dying for. Jesus died for our salvation. Jesus died out of love. Love is what the world needs now and forever, if Christians are to live a piece of heaven on earth. Love is that component that motivates us to do things we normally would never consider doing. It is this agape type of love that Jesus offers us an example of in Ephesians 5:25-28 *"Husbands, love your wives, just as Christ love the church and gave himself up for her to make her holy, cleansing her by the washing with water through the word, and to present her to himself as a radiant church without stain or wrinkle or any other blemish, but holy and blameless. In this same way, husbands ought to love their wives, as their own bodies. He who loves his wife loves himself."*

Christ redeemed all mankind with a sacrificial love. This is the agape type of love that looks past personal need to see and meet the needs of others. Christ says to the husband to love your wives and give yourself up for her to make her holy, by the cleansing of water and the Word. In other words, Christ is saying to husbands, that the way you demonstrate love to your wife is through a sacrificial love that looks past your personal needs. This agape type love expects the husband to blanket his wife through spiritual renewal (salvation) and by the guidance of Christ's Holy Word as the instruction book. Christ made mankind holy. To be holy is to be set apart for divine service, to have moral and ethical wholeness or perfection; freedom from moral evil; to be righteous. Therefore, Jesus is saying to the husband that the husband blankets his wife and ultimately his family with holiness. This blanketing parallels Jesus' blanketing of all believers. Jesus continues on to reference a person's body, as it is uncommon that a person would do harm to his own body, but instead would cherish our bodies, care for them, protect them, maintain them, develop and nurture them and feed them. Jesus is saying to the husband that he is to care for his wife as he would care for his own body. Jesus says that the husband must present his wife without defect, but perfect in every way.

I know what you're thinking Brothers; that's a lot to require of the husband? I understand, but please be encouraged. Remember that we can do all things through Christ that strengthens us (Philippians 4:13). Christ has shown us how we are to achieve these requirements; simply by following his commandments in Scripture. A great start to understanding love (once you know Jesus) is to study and practice 1 Corinthians 13 as it gives us instructions for charity (love). If you begin to follow these characteristics of love, you'll begin to understand what the traits are of unity, connectedness, and love.

Why did Jesus give the command for husbands first to love their wives and not to wives to love their husbands? This is a question of headship, and again, we now understand that Christ is the head of the church. Christ is the bridegroom and we (Christians) are the bride. Therefore, as God has commanded the husband to be the head over his wife (as a result of the garden), this means that just as God loved us before the foundations of the world ever existed; man, the symbol of God's headship must also demonstrate the responsibilities and qualities of God by initiating and sustaining love. In response to the love both verbalized and demonstrated to the wife, the wife in turn reciprocates love with an element of respect for her husband for what and how he has demonstrated his love to her. This process of demonstrating love is equated to how God loves us and demonstrated His loves towards us in word and deed.

Therefore husbands, you are responsible for speaking and demonstrating love. There is always a blessing for obedience, as well as punishment for disobedience. *"Husbands in the same way, be considerate of your wife and treat her with respect as the weaker sex and as heirs with you of the gift of eternal life, as that nothing will hinder your prayers,"* Peter 3:1-6. Husbands, one of the benefits for treating your wife as Christ treated the church and gave His life for it; is that your prayers will not be hindered. This is one of the few reasons why prayer is not answered and thus the only one spoken of to the husband within the marital relationship. Remember husbands, your wife is heirs with you of the gift of eternal life; therefore, you do not want to do anything that may hinder your salvation or your communications with God.

Marital Struggle for headship

"And the Lord God commanded the man, saying, Of every tree of the garden thou mayest freely eat: But of the tree of the knowledge of good and evil, thou shalt not eat of it: for in the day that thou eateth thereof thou shalt surely die," (Genesis 2:16, 17).

God spoke to Adam. God gave instructions (commandments) to Adam. *"The Lord God commanded the man,"* God is a God of divine order and purpose. Therefore confusion should not exist, or struggles of power or false interpretations of God's divine order, will or purpose. Man is the head of the woman and also the head of God's order on earth. God spoke to the man in the Garden and gave him instructions to follow. God allowed man (Adam) to name all the things God had created including "woman." God did not make woman first, nor did He give her instructions in the Garden, moreover, God did not allow woman to name all the things He had created. Therefore, there was divine purpose for God speaking and authorizing man to have dominion over all the earth that he shares with the woman.

This brief exegesis of Genesis 2:16, 17 is important because there exists in relationships today such a challenge of power, control and headship. In addition, because of this relational dysfunction, relationships (married or unmarried) now exist, not in unity but in friction; independence and struggle for the right to lead and affirm. A Brother that understands his role and responsibilities within the marital relationship often times will come under challenge by his wife. Some wives feel the need to express a sense of authority within marital relationships out of fear of losing their identity. The natural order of things given by God has been seemingly replaced in the Black family by the dysfunctional views by both the husband and the wife. These views have placed the Black family in the crisis state of disharmony. There are multiple reasons for this:

First, as I've indicated, is the challenge of control, power and headship by the woman. I believe this challenge by some wives is the result of several factors. The women's movement have created in the minds and hearts of some women, confrontational attitudes and views that not only usurp what God has said in Scripture, but has also contributed to generational cognitive dysfunctions (problems in our thinking handed down to other generations). Some women believe that all men only seek to dominate and suppress the many wonderful facets of a woman. These facets include intellect, leadership abilities and organizational skills. These various dynamics I'll place in the category of entrepreneurial. Women want to and do compete in today's business world. No longer will woman be treated as second class citizens in the world. Therefore a part of the women's movement taught women to think and behave like men in order to compete and be accepted in a man's world; the business world.

Another facet of the women's movement impressed upon women to reconsider being subjective to the authority of men, not only in the business world, but also at home. Women don't want to stay at home and just have babies and be content with being a housewife. Women, like many of us, have hopes, dreams, aspirations, and goals. Women want a rich, fulfilling and rewarding life just as men do. That's not the problem; the problem comes into play when a well defined order or structure within the family system must be established. The independent spirit of some women will not allow them to be in a position of subjection to their husband or anyone else, "that was so last century." Because of this imbalance within the family structure, no real order or alignment exists.

Perhaps one of the reasons why there exists so much friction and battle for power in marriage and family relations is due to the fact of what happened in the Garden. Chapter three of Geneses describes the encounter between the serpent and Eve. Eve knew what she was supposed to do, but in conversing with the serpent, she allowed the serpent to convince her to betray her loyalty to God. Geneses 3:5-6 *"For God doth know that in the day ye eat thereof, they your eyes shall be opened, and ye shall be as gods, knowing good and evil. 6. And when the woman saw that the tree was good for food, and that it was pleasant to the eyes, and a tree to be desired to make one wise, she took of the fruit thereof, and did eat, and gave also unto her husband with her; and he did eat."*

Scripture suggests to us that the woman was taken in by the possibility of becoming wise and like a god. Scripture states that the woman saw that the tree was good for food, and that is was pleasant to the eyes, *and a tree to be desired to make one wise,"* (Italics mine). The woman was motivated either by the cunningness of the serpent, her own desires, or both. Either way she was motivated to become wiser and be like a god, knowing both good and evil. The woman was not satisfied with her role, thus she sought after more than she was given. And because of her disobedience and dissatisfaction with her role, God punished her. Now the Scripture says in Geneses 3:9 *"And the Lord God called unto Adam, and said unto him, Where art thou?"* After Eve and Adam disobeyed God they realized they were both naked, they hid themselves from God. God called to Adam, not Eve. Because God had set the structure and order, God did not call to Eve, but instead called to Adam and asked Adam where he was. This is an important point in consideration to whom it is that holds the responsibility for leadership in the marriage and family, the husband.

Genesis 3:15 *"And I will put enmity between thee and the woman, and between thy seed and her seed; it shall bruise thy head, and thou shalt bruise his heel."*

God said to the serpent and Eve, He will put conflict between Satan and the woman; He will bring hostility between Satan and the woman's offspring, Jesus. God is speaking about the battle of good versus evil that will be played out in humanity for the reconciliation of mankind. God goes on to say that man will rule over her (suggesting that before this event occurred, both man and woman shared more equality) as punishment in which she will experience trouble and anguish.
The text also suggests a natural hostility between man and woman (Husband and wife), as a result of disobedience by both. We must also look at the possibility that Eve was not satisfied with all God had given her (perfection), and in your heart she was convinced that she could gain an advantage over her disposition in the Garden.

Therefore, a very brief theological exegesis of the above text strongly suggests that men and women naturally share a struggle for headship, power, authority and unity; hence the term "friction." Moreover the text suggests that perhaps women may be prone to sinful persuasion and feelings of dissatisfaction. Wives, if your husband's are God fearing, God believing, servant leader, and obedient man of God, then you should be content with where you are in your relationship with your husband. The story of Eve in the garden is suggesting that Eve was not satisfied where God had her and thus she availed herself to the trickery of Satan. Please think about this point for a minute. If God made you perfect; I'll use the term "complete." If God made you complete, and according to Scripture He had; and when we think of what it means to be complete, we think about being made whole or perfect, so when we think about what it means to be whole, we come back to the term perfect or complete.

In other words, no matter how we look at it and no matter what terms we use, all the terms used represent perfection, completeness, without need or want. Eve did not stand in need of anything that God had not already provided for her. Therefore, there was no need for Eve to desire anything additional. According to Scriptural interpretation of the text, I have reached the understanding that Eve was not satisfied with where God had her in life and therefore her will was not equal to God's will and thus she subjected herself to the craftiness of Satan. Satan cannot tempt those that have a strong constitution of faith and commitment to God. What Eve should have done, is say to Satan: *"Get the behind me."* But she did not; she allowed Satan the opportunity to motivate her to do what was already in her heart. Please understand that God did not place deception or dissatisfaction in Eve's heart; God gave Eve a will and Eve decided herself to utilize her will to satisfy her own curiosity by eating from the forbidden tree. Moreover, Eve encouraged Adam to partake of the forbidden tree as well, and because Adam refused to follow God's instructions, all were punished. If there was ever a time that man should have put his foot down; the garden was it! Man was disobedient; he failed to do what God said then, and it continues today!

Why am I making the suggestion that some women are dealing with a spirit of dissatisfaction? Christian husbands I talk to in and out of my practice always make this reference to their wives seemingly insatiable thirst for more of… Husbands complain that no matter what they do and how often they do it, their wives are never satisfied and some husband's have threatened to stop doing what their doing. These husband's don't feel appreciated nor do they feel as if they can ever satisfy their wives. Scripture teaches both husband and wife in 1 Peter 3:8 *"You must live in harmony. Be sympathetic and loving as brothers."* Moreover, Scripture also says in 1 Peter 3:2 *"Wives your behavior must be righteous with a profound respect for God."* And 1 Peter 3:11 *"You must turn away from sin and live a righteous life that is pleasing to God. You must seek and pursue peace with all."* The writer of Hebrews 13:5 says *"Let your conversation be without covetousness; and be content with such things as ye have…"*

Wives, I'm not suggesting that all women are dissatisfied. I am suggesting however, that if you follow the desires of your flesh, you'll never be satisfied; but if you lean and depend on God for all of your good and perfect gifts, you'll have contentment in life. Scripture reveal to us that everything is possible, but not everything is permissible. This takes me to my next point, "nagging." Proverbs 19:13 *"A foolish son is his father's ruin, and a quarrelsome wife is like a constant dripping."* Husbands often complain about their wife's nagging. The referenced Scripture is suggesting that it is not good for a wife to stir up dissension through arguing. Proverbs 21:9 *"Better to live on a corner of the roof than share a house with a quarrelsome wife."* And Proverbs says in 21:19 *"Better to live in a desert than with a quarrelsome and ill-tempered wife."* God is not pleased with those of us who seek to destroy peace by attempting to meet our personal and often selfish needs or wants by quarreling with others. James 4:1-2 says *"What causes fights and quarrels among you? Don't they come form your desires that battle within you? You want something but don't get it. You kill and covet, but you cannot have what you want. You quarrel and fight. You do not have, because you do not ask God."*

Wives, no man is fond of a bitter, argumentative and disagreeable wife. If there is something you need, ask. If there is something you desire, ask. If there is something you don't agree with, make your point known in a profound respectful manner, but don't nag. Husbands, your wives need to talk with you; make yourself available to have a not-rushed conversation that does not interfere with the basketball game. No one appreciates multi-tasking more than I do; however, multi-tasking has its benefits and drawbacks. When your wife needs to talk, you should set aside devoted time to your wife and your wife only; not giving your time and attention to communication could land you in a quarrelsome situation. Wives sometimes nag because husbands will not give them the time and attention we all need to address our feelings.

Another facet of the women's movement that has affected relationships is through the vehicle of siblings. Because of the abusiveness, the domination and lack of respect for many women in marriages by their husbands, women have taught their daughters to become more dependent on themselves and less dependent on a man. This type of relational learned thinking and behaving have placed future Black women into a continued mindset of viewing the family as less of a healthy structure than their mom's before them. Thus, the future of the Black family is in greater peril than it is today because women do not view a husband and a family as something they want to commit to. The issue I've been describing I feel is an issue of "Identity."

Why do so many women, Black or White, get married today with hyphened names? I asked some women this question. The answer I got was what I expected. The women I asked said to me that it was important for them not to lose their identity. Many women today view marriage as a lost of identity. Women view themselves giving up so much to become united with someone else who doesn't have to give up the same things. Therefore, friction within the order of the marriage is imminent. If some women feel as if they're losing themselves in marriage, why get married? Marriage is not a lost, but a gain! The world has taught women, along with many of our dysfunctional men, that being subjective to a man is no longer the status quo. Women have rights today! Women don't have to be quiet anymore, they have a voice now and they're not giving it up. This is the thoughts of many of our women today. These attitudes when expressed in selfish ways have led to a further separation of unity and connectedness in what few Black marriages we still have and thus the Black family.

I encourage women and men to read and study "Who can find a virtuous woman," found in Proverbs 31:10-31. This is the Biblical story of a wife and mother who is an entrepreneur. This woman has everything going on for her. She is a noble wife to her husband, children and the town. She takes care of home and the office. This woman is seen by others as a very special person. Her husband is well respected and her children call her blessed. This is the story of a Christian wife and mother who has kept the order and structure of the family intact while accomplishing her entrepreneurial goals. The woman in the story was not concerned with a dysfunctional sinful identity that separated her from her family, instead she was concerned with order, structure, commitment, unity, priority and most of all Christian identity. Moreover, the Bible says "Who can find a virtuous woman." Women, this story represents a great example of balance.

God did not intend for His creation (humankind) to be out of relationship (balance) with Him or each other. But He did set the rules for how the relationship with Him and each other must go if we're to be blessed. God is a God of balance. To all you bruised, battered, angry, confused and rejected women who feel you must do things alone. You can't do anything alone. Scripture teaches us: *"I can do all things through Christ that strengthens me."* Without Christ we can't breathe, walk or talk. Women, I strongly encourage you to grieve out many of your hurtful pasts and forgive those who have hurt you. Not all Brothers are dogs and Brothers, not all Sisters are B... Joy, peace and fulfillment only comes through a state of balance with Christ. Through Christ you have an identity; you don't need to hold on to a dysfunctional ideology. Marriage and a family is not a lost, but *"I count it all gain."*

Secondly, disharmony in marriage and the Black family is strongly influenced by the performance of the Black man in marriage and the family. Women are looking at men and measuring their performance. Based on marriage and family indicators, Brothers we're not doing very well. Let me say, that I believe the problem with Black marriages and the family stems not from the dysfunctions of women, but clearly the primary dysfunction comes from men. God spoke to the man first and gave man His instructions.

Genesis 2:16-17 *"And the Lord God commanded the man, saying, of every tree of the garden thou mayest freely eat: But of the tree of the knowledge of good and evil, thou shalt not eat of it: for in the day that thou eatest thereof thou shalt surely die."*

Scripture clearly reveals to us that God spoke and gave Adam the instructions for the tree of knowledge of good and evil. (Adam) man did not rebuke his wife when she offered him what they both knew they could not partake of. Instead, Adam (Man) was persuaded to disobey God. The text suggests that man then and now, has not lived up to the expectations God has set for us. Black men are not living up to the expectations God has set for us. Just as Adam blamed Eve for his lack of leadership, many women are blaming men for the same today. In addition, there are many women continuing to choose alternate roles other than the supportive role God has ordained in the Marriage and family. Because so many of us men have yet to step up to the plate, the women have gone on without us, prompting them to leave many of us behind. Because of this, many women have expressed the disappointment in the quality of Black men, and even more so stated some of them, that they don't need us. Clearly Black women are grieving the loss of Black men, and unfortunately statistics have supported this view.

But, in all fairness to Brothers, Brothers report that even where there exist a stable, healthy relationship (as stable as possible), wives continue to challenge their husband's leadership instead of supporting him. Let me say right here, that having a difference of opinion by the wife does not constitute a negative challenge. I'm defining a negative challenge as disrespectfully disagreeing; a superimposing of self-righteousness and selfishness into the process of decision making.

The one thing that really speaks volumes to the institution of marriage today is the fact that we see so many Christian marriages ending in divorce. Even more so, we hear on the news media and by word of mouth (Gossip) that Pastors, ministers, and other clergy are getting divorced. What's up with that! The day is now upon us where our church leaders are not getting along with their wives or husbands. This trend represents a serious problem within the sanctity of the marital covenant.

Why is the Pastor divorcing his wife? What is so wrong in the marriage that reconciliation is not possible? Have the Pastor been counseled by a Christian counselor? What happened to "Till death do us apart." If the Pastor's are divorcing, what is that saying to the rest of us? Why is it that Christians give more power and authority to Satan and this world than to God and His covenants? What happened to commitments? What happened to agape Love? What happened to the fear of the Lord is the beginning of wisdom? I don't know what's going on in some of these marriages involving clergy; I can only tell you as a Christian reconciler, God is not pleased! I believe it is God's expectations that we reconcile our differences.

Husbands and wives allow too much selfishness to enter into the place designed for the *"Two becoming one flesh."* Many relationships move from a stage of "Chivalry to quivery." Let me explain what I mean. While we are dating and trying to impress and win over our spouse, men are very agreeable and accommodating; the same thing goes for the woman as well. However, this usually does not last. Once the honey moon is over and each spouse becomes comfortable within the relationship, each spouse begins to assert their personal will in a greater fashion, thus moving from 'chivalry to quivery'. During the quivery stage the spouses begin to quiver at the thought of having to integrate so many of their desires, instead of having things their own way. Again, this is the process of moving from being united and connected to being separated and dysfunctional; all due to selfishness.

Women, stop fighting your husband's (the good ones) for the head of the family. God ordained only one head in the family, and it is not you (unless you have no husband). Please remember that you can have everything your hearts desire, if you approach it according to God's rules (Remember the virtuous woman).

On the other side of the coin, I have met some wives who are not challenging the headship of their husband; instead they're promoting it, but he won't take it. There are some husbands who don't know how to be effective, servant leaders to their wives and families. And because some of these husbands refuse to take the leadership role, there exists dysfunction, disharmony, and discontentment. Please Brothers and Sisters; I don't want you to think that just because you're a Christian, you know everything there is to know about how to be a husband and wife, in my experience that's just not true. Many believers and unbelievers are unprepared for marriage (pre-marital counseling) and many do not understand what their roles and responsibilities are within the marriage, therefore couples are making mistakes out of ignorance of the Word of God. This is why the church needs to utilize Christian counselors.

To Serve; Not to be Served

The question that is usually asked by marital couples is how am I to get my needs met? And I have to ask them the question: why are you trying to meet your own needs? This response from me usually gets me the "I'm confused" look. The question must be asked, who's responsibility is it to see that your needs are being met?

1 Corinthians 7:3-6
"The husband should fulfill his marital duty to his wife, and likewise the wife to her husband. The wife's body does not belong to her alone but also to her husband. In the same way the husband's body does not belong to him alone but also to his wife. Do not deprive each other except by mutual consent and for a time, so that you may devote yourselves to prayer. Then come together again so that Satan will not tempt you because of your lack of self-control."

The way each spouse gets their needs met is through the other spouse. This command is also a marital principle to be applied to the fulfillment of the marriage. Neither spouse can lay claim to their body or their very lives. First and foremost each redeemed believer has been bought with the price by Jesus' blood, so we are not our own. Secondly, in marriage our body is not our own, but it is for the spouse. A husband is a servant leader to his wife, and the wife is a servant to her husband. When I use the term servant, I do not apply this term to be used as "slavery,' but as serving unto the Lord. The wife's needs must be communicated to her husband, and the husband should make every attempt to fulfill all righteous needs of his wife. The same principle applies from the wife to her husband. When spouses utilize this commandment and principle to serve out of love for the other, the majority of marital needs should be met.

In addition wives, you cannot use sex as a weapon, a manipulative device, a controlling tactic or as punishment, because your body does not belong to you, but it belongs to your husband. According to Scripture, an oversexed (3 plus times a week?) husband is entitled to stick his hand in the cookie jar as he pleases. This same principle applies to the husband. The exception of this rule is applied when the wife is on her monthly menstruation cycle and when both spouses agree to withhold from each other for the purpose of prayer. Now Brothers, let's be real about what the Scripture is saying. If your wife have the flu and she's throwing up from both ends. If she's coughing and sneezing and has chills and a fever; I do believe Scripture wants us to use wisdom and common sense. However, neither spouse should be untrue about the way they feel, just to avoid giving yourself to the other. This principle should be applied to every area of the marital relationship. If this principle becomes a mindset, you will find spouses that are super caring, sensitive, responsive, sympathetic, communicative, compassionate, serving, unselfish and very loving. The premise of Scripture in this matter is to get spouses to not think of pleasing themselves (selfishness), but to think (serve) of pleasing their spouse as Jesus serves the church and gave His life for it.

What about Me!

The opposite of serving your spouse' needs are the serving of your own needs. The major problem in marital relationships today is no longer dysfunctional communications; however it is still a primary focus, but the primary problem as I see it is selfishness.

Selfishness says to the relationship that the honeymoon is now over and its time for my true personality and temperaments to kick in. During the courting and early marriage phase of the relationship, both spouses put on a mask. This mask is a mask of dishonesty. This mask that many couples wear is simply a mirage of who they really are on the inside. It is very important for couples during the courting and early marriage phase to please their partner. I often hear in the counseling office this statement by the wife: "My husband is not the same man I fell in love with, he's changed." This statement says volumes to me. This statement is not a statement primarily used by the wife, but also by the husband. This statement says to me that the mask of the relationship has now come off, and the true self is now appearing. "Things are not always as they seem."

Why do we feel we have to lie about who we really are on the inside? Is this because we don't want our partner to really get to know the truth about who we are? Or is it that by getting to know the truth about who we really are, they won't like us? The fact is, the truth never changes, it is constant and it will not represent a mask. On the other hand a lie takes a lot of work to maintain. A lie not only represents the untruth, it also represents the unknown. A lie cannot represent the truth; it can only mask the truth and misrepresent the truth, thus leaving the truth unknown. The big problem with a lie is that sooner or later the lie will fail and the truth will eventually be known, in most cases. When a lie is exposed, the impact of the lie quickly engages the emotional component of truth and creates confrontation. Confrontation leads to either more lies or the truth. Either way, confrontation leads to separation of trust, and separation of trust leads to marital disharmony.

Why not just tell the truth? Be who God made you to be. If a person does not like you for who you truly are; then they surely won't like you for being someone you're not. We as a people must stop playing the "player game." Being a player creates so much distrust and hurt feelings that either party in the relationship will be devastated; unless they're playing the same game. The 'player game' often times finds a truly open, honest, and sincere Christian person, who will end up completely devastated and misused because the commitment, integrity and honesty was all an illusion schemed up by the player to get what he or she wants without ever availing a true commitment. Have you ever wondered why seemingly so many African American males and females are trying alternate lifestyles? Have you ever wondered how many of our Brothers and Sisters have been emotionally devastated by a player?

Why is it so important to so many of us playing these emotional games with peoples lives, to trick people into giving us what we want, not necessarily what we need? It's all one big game to see how much money, sex, and stuff, we can trick people out of. Many of us are so busy playing the "What about me," game that seemingly nobody can be trusted with a serious commitment, so we all the play the game to some degree. While so many of us are out there playing games with others lives, our children are going to hell because of us and the Black family continues to deteriorate! Check and mate!

Jesus said: *"And ye shall know the truth, and the truth shall make you free"* John 8:32. People today are attempting to find that one someone they can trust. The truth is, we will never fully know each other, no matter how intimate we become with each other. Scripture tells us that no man knows his heart. Therefore, we don't know what we're capable of doing or becoming. Such as we are, we must live *"In spirit and in truth."* I believe people today are tired of all the games and dramatics. People today are looking for truth. In truth there is commitment, integrity, reality, and an unveiling of the mask. "The truth simply mirrors itself; where a lie simply mirrors an image of what the truth could look like." The image represents what you want people to see and know about you whereas a lie is an attempt to hide who you are and what you could become. All men and women interested in seriously developing a relationship first seek to know the truth. We've all been affected by a lie once, twice or even three or more times by someone claiming to be connected as one with us, only to find out the whole thing was simply a lie. No more lies, no more games, no more players; we must encourage the truth if we're to have any hope of two people joining in unity and in connectedness.

Relationship Baggage

Another component to the truth in relationships involves prior relationships. Many of us are not yet out of one bad relationship before we place ourselves into a new, bad relationship. Thus we bring yesterday's relationship woes into our new relationship without ever effectively dealing with the issues of yesterday's relationships. We must not involve ourselves in any new relationships until we have adequately dealt with a past relationship. Unfortunately, many of us have never dealt with any dynamics of our past broken relationships and thus we bring yesterday's baggage into today's attempt at a new relationship. Marital or relationship grief is my diagnosis for misdealt with relationship baggage. In long term grief, a person may experience anger, bitterness, disappointment, uncertainty, depression, anxiety, sexual dysfunction and related stress. These various components can become entangled with emotions often found in the courting phase of a new relationship. Thus what you have is two opposing forces battling for supremacy. What is observed by others is a series of strange reactions and encounters.

Before we get involved in new relationships we must identify those feelings that have emerged or were a part of the dysfunction in the prior relationship. Failing to deal with these feelings will result in a series of complex battles of emotional warfare of the heart and mind. We must allow ourselves the time needed to heal and reconcile our emotions prior to starting a new relationship. Otherwise, what we feel now, will only carry into the next relationship and a new set of the old problems will emerge once again. Anger is often a primary emotion of love. When we get to the point of loving someone we exhibit emotions and physical reactions associated with feelings of love. Likewise, when we fall out of love, just the opposite of these emotions are experienced. Love becomes hate, joy becomes sadness, and euphoria becomes depression and so on.

We must acknowledge the natural process of loss called grief. We must allow ourselves every opportunity to properly grieve through our emotions. By grieving our emotions, we gain strength and knowledge into some things we could have done differently and some things we were OK with. Either way, we allow ourselves time to reflect and analyze past relationships and our role within them. We must know that God made us all with strengths and weaknesses. In relationships both personal strengths and weaknesses can create resistance with our spouse. Allowing ourselves to grieve also cleanses us from maladaptive emotions that can and will create dysfunction in future relationships. We must go into new relationships with a clear mind, heart and spirit. Thus, a primary component to relationship loss (grief) involves the process of letting go and healing called "Forgiveness."

Forgiveness is that aspect of God's character within us that releases those whom have caused us pain. Just as God forgives us when we sin, we must in turn forgive others who sin against us. It's not so much the question of who's right or wrong, but simply an act involving a greater expression of love through the position of releasing painful expressions. Remember God will not forgive us when we ask Him, if we don't in turn forgive others. Biblical forgiveness involves the process of letting go of those human emotions that have caused us emotional bondage. Eventually we must turn the key to the shackles and free ourselves and others of bondage caused through various expressions of humanity. Experiencing forgiveness is also a sign indicating the fact that we have begun properly grieving a broken relationship. Biblical forgiveness states that you can be reminded by stimulus of a broken relationship and yet experience no associated pain or discomfort by it. In biblical forgiveness we also become aware of our own unhealthy and maladaptive traits that led toward conflict and dysfunction. Biblical forgiveness must involve self-reflection and self-analysis. We cannot truly forgive others if we don't know what and why we are seeking forgiveness. Moreover, we won't know what we need to be forgiving of if we don't take ownership for our own shortcomings. Through this process of healing and truth seeking, we gain a closer understanding of who God is; who we are and how we can improve upon our relationship with God, ourselves and others. This is how you know if you're ready to engage in a new relationship. In this way you do not attempt to develop a new relationship carrying sacks of emotional and behavioral dysfunction with you that will only repeat itself again.

Yielding Control

Ephesians 5:18 *"Husband's do not get filled on the ways of the world, but be filled by God's Holy Spirit. God's Spirit will fill you of your desires. Let God control you; don't be controlled by the ways of the world."*

Husband's we live in a time where being a man often means representing your manhood in ways that are not pleasing to God and can lead us to jail or a hospital. God wants men to know that we must make better choices than we've had in the past. Jesus was a "Servant Leader." A servant leader is a person that understands what it means to give of themselves in all they do. A servant leader does not care about prestige, honor, fame, status and money. Nor is a servant leader motivated by foolish pride and control, but delights in nurturing the resources within others. A servant leader also understands the importance of acknowledging personal limitations and weaknesses. A servant leader is always concerned for the safety and well being of others and themselves; after all, if the servant leader is seriously dysfunctional, how can others depend on him? Servant leaders exercise wisdom and humility in their approaches to situations. Servant leaders also understand the importance of giving and receiving proper counsel (advice). Brothers, please exercise care when listening to the counsel of others. Listening to the wrong person may influence you to make bad decisions with terrible consequences aligned with them.

Christians are to listen to the voice of our Heavenly Father. Scripture teaches us that we the sheep of God knows God's voice and will respond to His voice; but those who know not God, does not recognize His voice and will not follow Him. Thus we must listen and hear the voice of God which is primarily heard through Scripture. Many of the decisions we make today must meet with the approval of

Scripture; if they don't, the consequences could be devastating. This is a very powerful point, because often times in marital relationships, dysfunctions occur because of whom we choose to listen to (advice). Society today is not short on its opinions for your life. Wives may prefer to hear the voice of their mother; husbands may want to listen to the voice of their friends. But please remember that you did not marry your mother or your friends. You must go to God in prayer, together both husband and wife must seek direction for your life through Scripture, and then converse with a truly gifted Christian pastor, counselor or friend.

Brothers, don't let your little head give you advice that may ruin the rest of your body, spirit and soul. The only time your little head should be enjoying itself is in the confines of a united, connected, and committed marriage. Married Brothers, you should not need to cheat on your wife. Infidelity is a serious problem in so-called committed relationships today. The problem is so common; wives have decided to play along as well. So now, we've got husbands and wives all getting their freak on with someone else beside their covenant marital partner. Moreover, some of our marriages have begun to explore extra marital committed partners in activities such as orgies for married people, wives and or husband swapping, threesomes, and many other sexual games. **Newsflash**; these freak fests are not Scriptural. In my understanding of the Bible, the Bible does not place prohibitions on sexual expression within the confines of marriage. However, outside the confines of marriage it is not tolerated. Society today has become so freaky and perverted. Men and women, girls and boys, and seniors too; we're all involved in all kind of sexual gratifications. I believe society today is dealing with a higher number of sexual addictions than are being communicated.

Media in American seemingly cannot market a product without having a pair of breast or buttocks attached to it. Where can the sexually addicted person go for relief? Because of America's sex craze and the elevated levels of temptation all around us, both men and women are struggling within their marriages to stay faithful.

Nakedness is all over the television, magazines, cartoons, cinemas and it's being expressed in fashion everyday. You only have to open your blinds at home and look out of the window. Young ladies are wearing outfits that will send a normal God loving man into a perverted frenzy. Thus some men and women are complaining about the lack of sexual excitement in their marriage because they are so stimulated by what society deems normal. There's nothing normal about the whole society becoming hyper sexually aroused to the point where it's led society into a host of clinically dysfunctional and disruptive lifestyles. It seems to me that America is trying its best to resurrect the sinful cities of Sodom and Gomorrah. Moreover, this hyper sexual arousal has led to greater incidents of date rape, marital rape, molestations of all kinds, sexual abductions, prostitution, gay and lesbianism, sexual identity confusion and a host of mental and emotional dysfunctions.

We must pray and refrain from the world's attempts to steal us away from holiness and into worldliness. Brothers and Sisters, we must protect our minds, our hearts and our emotions from the dangers of high sexual arousal and gratification. I remember once when I was much younger. I was at a local bar with my best friend and his girl friend. His girl friend leaned over and asked me if I wanted to have a threesome because she could not get enough. I don't have to tell you my answer do I? I was not saved and had not been called into the ministry yet. Even with that, my buddy still said no! His girlfriend could not get enough sex. My friend revealed to me that she was a nymphomaniac and that he had to break up with her because she was wearing him out. The point is; this type of over sexual stimulation is happening everywhere today and it's causing serious problems. I strongly recommend to any spouse having uncontrolled desires for sexual gratification to seek out a Christian therapist. Someone that can help you define the genesis of your desires and how to begin working toward establishing control and reducing the associated anxiety. Sexual addiction is no different than a crack-cocaine addiction. All addictions have the same characteristics and thus they create similar problems in a persons life; the lost of control. God wants us to be in balance with Him, our selves and others. He does not want us obsessing over anything, including Him. So please be very careful who you're listening to and what is being said. Not all advice is good advice unless it aligns itself to the Word of God, and God has spoken into that advice. All of us must come to the point in our lives when we are yielding all of our control to God, knowing that God uses His control to perfect and edify us.

Chapter Eight
Raising Children for the Lord

There are so many philosophies and formulas about parenting floating around book stores and on television, radio and other forms of media. Why are Christians listening to what some famous secular professional is saying to us about raising our children? If we need advice on raising children we ought to go to the Word of God and the Christian church for answers. Well, one of the shortcomings of the Black Christian church today relies in the fact that we don't have very many of these types of ministries. Many of our church leaders don't see the need, but we'll stand behind the holy desk (pulpit) and preach to folks about how to raise and discipline our children, but rarely do we go any further with it. Church leaders must understand that effective ministry cannot be done in only two hours on Sunday. Effective ministry's understands the needs of the congregation and prepares to address them. Ministry is at least a six days a week operation with dessert being served in praise and worship on Sunday. The administration of a six-day a week operation does not mean the Pastor has to be their everyday. Effective church leadership is one that educates and nurtures spiritual gifts and special skills within congregants, and prepares believers to serve in ministry for the edification of the body of Christ.

Christian Parenting

Let's take a look at the famous Scripture that just about everyone knows: Ephesians 6:*1 "Children obey your parents as obeying the Lord, for this is right."*

There's not a lot to say concerning this Scripture. The Scripture is plain and easily comprehended; right? Then why do our children have so many problems fulfilling these Scriptural commands? One reason spoken by teens in the counseling office is "What mom wants is stupid" (many times the family is led by a single mother). These teens say things like: "Why should I have to do that; my mom doesn't do that." This is clearly an issue related to an old school thought that states "Do as I say; not as I do." Christian parents, if you're still using this parenting philosophy, you're in trouble.

Let me share with you another Scripture that I believe speaks to this old school philosophy: "You reap what you sow." Parenting is about modeling holy and acceptable instructions before children and living those instructions. We as parents cannot demand of our children not to do something, while we in turn do what we asked them not to do. And since children are so perceptive, they clearly see that there is a clear cut distinction in the rules. This distinction creates conflict between parent (s) and child. Which takes me to this Scripture: *"Fathers do not provoke your children to become sharp toned, disagreeable, resentful, and cynical or inflict undo pain upon them. If you do they will become discouraged,"* Colossians 3:21. And Ephesians 6:4 *"Fathers, do not irritate or anger your children; do not be unreasonable; instead, nurture them in the training and instruction of the Lord."*

Parents, our job is to instruct our children in righteousness. Of course we cannot be effective in doing this if we're not living it! That is why the old school thought of "do what I say and not what I do" just doesn't fly anymore. If we want our children to grow up being respectful toward us, then we must be respectful toward them. We must practice what we preach. If we don't, our children will become frustrated with us and they will rebel. Children will not only clearly see the unfairness in what we as parents say and do, but they'll also see how to use our inconsistencies to support their rebellion. Children who rebel at parental authority will soon begin to exhibit signs of moodiness, anger, hostility and minor depression. Children also will lax in their academic performance, athletic performance, duties and other responsibilities around the house and elsewhere. Also, at more advanced stages, depression can become more severe. Children may even begin to experiment with smoking cigarettes, marijuana, other drugs, alcohol, sex, gangs and unruly behaviors ending in minor law infractions. Of course, as these symptoms continue, so do the level of judicial and parenting offenses.

This is why we as parents do not want to exhibit a confusing and improper set of rules before our children. We as parents must raise our children in the admonition of the Lord. To admonish a child in the Lord is to provide a mild disapproval of the Lord when a child violates a righteous rule. Parents must not only teach basic life skills but also Biblical commandments at every age level. Discipline must be appropriate to the level of the offense. To withhold physical punishment from a child is to set that child up for death. This is a strong statement I know, but this is what Scripture have to say about it.

Proverbs 13:24- *"He who spares the rod hates his son, but he who loves him is careful to discipline him."*
Proverbs 19:18-*"Discipline your son, for in that there is hope; do not be a willing party to his death."*
Proverbs 19:20- *"Listen to advice and accept instruction, and in the end you will be wise."*
Proverbs 15:31, 32- *"He who listens to a life giving rebuke will be at home among the wise. He who ignores discipline despises himself, but whoever heeds correction gains understanding."*
Proverbs 23:13, 14- *"Do not withhold discipline from a child; if you punish him with the rod, he will not die. Punish him with the rod and save his soul from death."*
Proverbs 22:15- *"Folly is bound up in the heart of a child, but the rod of discipline will drive it far from him."*

I hope you can begin to see that if you withhold the rod, you'll create more problems for your children as they age and develop. I have heard some parents tell me that "Not every child needs to be beaten." I totally agree with that statement. Slaves were beaten, animals are beaten, our dirty rugs get beaten, but children are not to be punished by being beaten, they are to be nurtured through discipline. We don't punish our children for doing something wrong; we discipline them so they won't do it again. Discipline is meant to be future oriented, while punishment is past-oriented. Punishment is paying your child back for hurting you in some way. Punishment says, "You ruined my life, so I'm going to ruin yours." Punishment is revenge. Parents must never seek revenge on their children. Scripture teaches us in Romans 12:19 *"Do not take revenge, my friends."* Here are some suggestions for child discipline from the National Christian Counselors Association.

"In communication with your children, speak to them on their own level of understanding, making it clear what you expect of them. Do not punish them in anger. Set the example you wan them to follow, remembering that what you do will be more effective than what you say. When you establish guidelines for children, stick to them. Take your children with you to church and let them see you worship God in prayer.

Recognize and teach a child that parental responsibilities extend over public school education, club, group, or any organization's efforts or influences. Parents or guardians must be faithful to teach a child about Jesus Christ."

The rules of discipline should be:

1. Never discipline in anger
2. Always explain why you are disciplining the child
3. Demonstrate your love afterwards
4. Always express forgiveness afterwards
5. Never mention the subject again, treat the child as if it never happened
6. Follow through with discipline. Make sure a command is obeyed
7. Discipline disobedience

How many times do you have to say "Stop?" After several times of saying stop, the very next parental response should be a stronger form of communication involving a hand, a shoe, a stick, a belt or some other appropriate tool.

In America, school teachers are attempting to teach academics and morality. Morality includes appropriate measures of discipline. The reason why children are not learning in many of our urban school systems comes directly from a lack of parental discipline. A lack of appropriate discipline results in children growing up with no fear of retribution by anyone. This includes law enforcement, elders, teachers, other parents, clergy and many others. Our children grow up with what is called O.D.D. or Oppositional Defiant Disorder. In other words, our children have no respect for authority. A child without respect is the most dangerous weapon in society. You only have to look around you. Many of the teenagers on our streets have absolutely no respect for anyone but other thugs like them. When was the last time you saw a young person help a senior across the street or carry their grocery bags without beating them up and robbing them.

Teenagers today are abusing their single mothers. In addition, they're robbing from us, stealing from us, raping us, selling drugs to us, killing us, and demoralizing us. They're dropping out of school and having babies, they're committing suicide and suffering from major depression and attracting AIDS. You can contribute all of these social and family ills to a lack of parental discipline. I know single moms; many of you are doing the best you can. I know many of you are fed up with your own children. The fact is: our single moms need these children's dads. Children have a greater fear for their dads than they do they're mom. But if mom has done all she can, what more can we expect her to do. So these bad children end up in a cycle of drugs and crime, because dad was not there to do his part in raising his children. So not only does mom suffers but the children and all society suffers with them.

Please don't get me wrong; I have no problem with a verbal time out. A verbal time out can be an appropriate level of discipline; however, the discipline must meet the level of infraction. If it does not, the child will sense the inappropriateness and rebel. Parents don't drink alcohol in front of your children and say to them you cannot drink, it's a sin. Remember, as infants on, we learn by watching. So please make sure your words match your actions or you're in for a struggle. Parents must model all righteous attitudes and behaviors if children are going to learn righteousness. It is therefore, parent's responsibility to teach their children that *"The fear of the Lord is the beginning of wisdom."*

According to the Diagnostic Statistical Manual for Mental Disorders- 4, the following represents information on Oppositional Defiant Disorder.

Oppositional Defiant Disorder:

A pattern of negativistic, hostile, and defiant behavior lasting at least 6 months, during which four (or more) of the following are present:

1. often loses temper
2. often argues with adults
3. often actively defies or refuses to comply with adults' requests or rules
4. often deliberately annoys people
5. often blames others for his or her mistakes or misbehavior
6. is often touchy or easily annoyed by others
7. is often angry and resentful
8. is often spiteful or vindictive

The impact of stress is a tremendous concern upon children and especially on today's teenagers. Today's teen's face a unique set of pressures. Information is so vividly available to them that they can be motivated to engage in activities before they are ready. As Christians we have to remember that we are the minority, not the majority, therefore society presents what it wants to and for its own purposes. The world enforces promiscuity, violence, alcoholism, marital separation, smoking, and many other non-Christian values. Morality is something that the world fails to present; therefore, we as Christians must keep these three psychological developments in mind when it comes to our teens.

1. Teens need to develop a sense of personal identity, to find out who they are and what makes them unique.
   (This is a struggle for parents, because this struggle for personal identity involves the pulling away from the parental

relationship. It is very important that Christians express and demonstrate a Christian identity before their teen children)
2. Teens need to begin the process of establishing relationships that are characterized by commitment and intimacy. (Christian parents must have already modeled a Christian relational commitment before their children, in order for their children to have an understanding of Christian expectations)
3. Teens need to begin making decisions leading toward training and entry into a particular occupation. (It must be said at this point, that parents must be careful not to push their children into areas of interest that they themselves have interest in and their child does not. Parents must not attempt to live out their unfulfilled lives through their children. Children often times are not interested in the same things as their parents. Parents must allow their children to seek out their own interests; otherwise the child may rebel, causing a rift in the parent-child relationship).

Parents we must remember that children are a gift from God, and God will hold us accountable for how we treat them. Hebrews 12:5, 6 *"And you have forgotten that word of encouragement that addresses you as sons: "My son, do not make light of the Lord's discipline, and do not lose heart when he rebukes you, because the Lord disciplines those he loves, and he punishes everyone he accepts as a son."*
God disciplines parents too!

Hebrews 12:10, 11 *"Our fathers discipline us for a little while as they thought best; but God disciplines us for our good, that we may share in his holiness. No discipline seems pleasant at the time, but painful. Later on, however, it produces a harvest of righteousness and peace for those who have been trained by it."*

Discipline is good! Without discipline, parents will not have peace in their lives. Peace comes from proper nurturing and training of our children. Properly disciplining children may keep parents from watching children face a judge or claiming their cold body in the morgue. Proper discipline is an expression of love for our children, in the same way God disciplines us out of love to teach and perfect us. But if you want a preacher like me to officiate over your child's home going service, continue to withhold discipline; but I don't think God will withhold His. Proper discipline will teach our children a healthy fear (respect) for God and a sense of obedience to Him and His Word.

N.C.C.A. offers Nine Ways to be Your Child's Best Friend:

1. Let the discipline fit the infraction
2. Never best or bully your child into submission
3. Use action-oriented methods whenever possible
4. Always try to be consistent
5. Emphasize order and need for order
6. Always require your child to be accountable and responsible for his or her actions
7. Always communicate to your child that he or she is good even though the behavior may have been irresponsible
8. Always give your child choices that reinforce cooperation but not competition
9. If spanking is necessary it should be done when you're in control of your emotions. It should always be followed by explanations for why the spanking was necessary, followed with "I love you."

Obedience is Better than Death

"Children, obey your parents in the Lord: for this is right. Honor thy father and mother; which is the first commandment with promise, that it may be well with thee, and thou mayest live long on the earth." Ephesians 6:1-3.

Young adults, you may not like what I'm going to say, but it's intended to be a blessing to you, even though you may disagree with me. "Young adults, I know some of you have it pretty rough. I understand that many of you don't have the loving, nurturing,

supporting family home life that you should have. I also understand that you're dealing with a lot, and for many of you to not have a dad around is even tougher, not to mention the financial strains placed on your family. Many of you are facing extremely stressful situations of life, and many issues older generations did not have to deal with, or their level of dealing was less. However, in spite of your situation and circumstances, you must move past yesterday and live for today! Moreover, you cannot stew in the crap that's been dealt to you; you must take the responsibility to rise above your situation and circumstances in spite of what you need and don't have; in spite of your anger and disappointment; in spite of the rough road and stormy seas. You can and must not turn away from God; He's the only one who has the power and the everlasting love to help you. You must become obedient to God in all your ways, or I fear that many of you will continue on the road you're already on; the road of destruction!
"You can do all things through Christ that strengthens you,"
Philippians 4:13; If you only believe you can?"

The sad fact is that the level of parenting is not as good as it was in earlier generations. In generations of the past, our parents got married, had children, worked and cared for the needs of the family; although our fore-parents did not have a lot of money or the technology we have today. We may have greater "stuff" today, but we don't have the same commitment to the family as we had yesterday. Earlier generations found mom in the kitchen cooking homemade meals for her family. The question for today's moms is: how many of you know how to work the stove? Not the microwave; but the stove? This is a sad fact of today. There are many young women and adults that have never been taught how to cook and bake. Many of these women, don't want to learn how either. Many of these women rely solely on someone else to cook for them, or they'll eat out often. There is nothing wrong with dining out; however, dining out was never meant to be the primary source of family dining.

I know of both young and mature ladies who can't cook and won't cook. I'm sorry; I cannot eat McDonald's everyday. A sad reality exist, that many of our ladies (young and not so young) are too lazy to cook or learn how. Let someone else do it, they say, and mean it too. Many of our ladies now believe that it is a demeaning task to have to cook, clean the house, sew clothing and care for the needs of the family and the house. How is the Black family to exist on fast foods; especially since it is a family heritage to come together over the dinner table. You have watched the television series "Soul Food?" The family dinner table is so much more than eating. It is through the family dinner table that families come together to talk, socialize, debate, share, renew friendships, problem solve, bond, and spiritually mature. Psychological, relational, behavioral, spiritual and emotional maturation takes place around the dinner table. More than anything else, in my opinion, the family dinner table is where people learn to lean and depend on family. The family dinner table is where the Black family comes together as a family and stays together as a family. There's only one exception to the family dinner table and that's the church; but afterwards, it's back to the family dinner table.

A family without a family dinner table is missing so much learning. Fast food and other restaurants cannot provide the same influence on the family as the family dinner table can. So young ladies, as you grow and mature into women, get married and have children, where are you going to share your stories, if you can't cook? And how are you going to prepare your children to take care of themselves, if you can't provide for yourself? You can take this same point and extend it to washing, sewing and other very important skills of providing for the family. When I was in junior high school, they had classes you could take for cooking, sewing and other home economics. I want you to know that I participated in all of those courses, since I did not have any sisters in my family; my mom taught her boys how to care for ourselves. So when I hear that a grown woman cannot cook, sew, garden, clean house, do laundry, pay bills and more, I just shake my head. Home economics are skills that the world has gotten away from, and so have we. We have come to rely too much on instant everything, from foods to clothing, to relationships, everything is quick, fast and in a hurry, but I've digressed.

Children, exhibit a high regard and respect for your parents. As I shared with you my abbreviated story of my father, I can say that it was very hard during those tough days with him to love him and respect him. It's hard to demonstrate respect for someone who does not demonstrate love and respect for you, or the ones you love. Respect is a two way street, right? Isn't that what we always say? If you want respect; you have to give respect. Well, according to Ephesians 6:1-3, that is not true. Great parents deserve to receive a high regard and respect. What about our not so great parents? Do they also deserve to receive high regard and a profound respect?

Who can figure out the mind of God? God wants all children to demonstrate to their parents a high regard. Let's first come to understand what a high regard means. Webster's define regard as: "Consideration; concern, respect and affection; to hold in affection and respect." You mean to tell me that my no-good for nothing father, who won't pay child support or come and see me; I'm supposed to do what? I'm not the one telling you this; the Bible is. Scripture tells all children to have a high consideration, a high concern, a high sense of respect and affection for our dad and mom; although in our mind they have done very little, if anything to deserve it. I believe we call this grace!

What is grace? Theologically, the term is defined as "The unmerited favor of God." Grace states that no one can earn it or deserves it. God give us his unmerited favor called grace. If you remember your Bible, the new testament of Jesus Christ is a relationship founded upon His grace. The primary qualification for Christ's grace is acceptance of Him. The Bible teaches believers that God's grace is sufficient. So, just as Christ died on Calvary's cross for people who did not love Him and accept Him, He paid the ultimate price to redeem us back to our heavenly Father. It is grace that sent Jesus to the cross. It is this same grace that God asks hurting children to demonstrate to sometime, unworthy parents. But there again; who is worthy? Some of our parents don't deserve our grace; but don't forget we don't deserve God's grace either. But for the grace of God, we would be dead in our sins.

Grace is that part of God's character He abundantly gives to us over and over again. God's grace covers a multitude of our sins and shortcomings. Grace is not deserved, nor can it be earned, therefore as lovers of God through Christ Jesus, we must give grace to those we have judged unworthy of our love and respect. The strange thing about God and Christianity is that Christ wants all of his followers to do those things that are right, even in the midst of displeasure. You see, Scripture teach us that there is none righteous; so we all stand in need of grace. Another aspect of grace is forgiveness. As Jesus was dying on the cross, He said *"Father forgive them for they know not what they do."* Jesus was praying to His Father to forgive mankind for what we have done against the triune God; our disobedience. There is no greater expression of true Christianity than to offer forgiveness. Forgiveness is love, grace, mercy, patience, long suffering, and hope, all rolled into one. Jesus gave us forgiveness; we must in turn follow His example and offer forgiveness to "All others" whether they are deserving of it or not. We must release them of their sins against us, just as God releases us of ours when we ask Him.

"Children obey your parents in the Lord." As we think of this word "Obey," we find that Scripture is very clear in its direction to children. As children we are to do whatever our parents tell us to do. This means first and foremost that parents must not ask, demand or require their children to do anything that would first of all displease or shame God. Now, with that said, children "obey your parents". When we think of the term "obey", we think about being in agreement with parents, but that's not the case. Webster's define the term obey as to: "carry out the orders of," parents. This does not mean that as children, we don't have an opinion about what's being asked of us, but it does mean acknowledging, respecting and fulfilling the requirements of those orders while maintaining discipline. Children do not have the authority to debate, refuse, analyze or have third party mediation.

Theologically, the word "obey" or "obedience' means to demonstrate love and the knowledge, favor, and the blessings of God. Obedience is the way by which believers experience the grace, righteousness and life through Christ. Obedience is not sacrifice, but the will of subjection. God asks all His children to obey Him. God does not ask us to obey what He commands because He commands it; He does expect us to obey Him because we love Him, and in loving Him we choose to obey Him. This is the same formula God asks of children towards their parents. When you really think about it, and you're honest with yourself; you don't agree with everything God has asked any of us to do. But that's not the point of it; the point is to do what has been asked. Why do we do things we don't agree with? The answer is simple; "Love." Because I love God and I know He loves me, I trust Him. And trusting Him means giving my decision making authority to Him, because I know that everything He does is perfect and good for me, even though I don't agree with it or see it. Parents don't have quite the same kind of perfection, but the relationship mirrors the relationship and authority of God.

So children obey your parents, honor both of your parents, God commands you to do this. God also gives children a blessing (favor), found in a promise for doing what he asks. God says *"That it may be well with thee,"* (Ephesians 6:1-3). I believe God is saying to children in the Scripture to do what He said, to obey and honor your parents, if you'll do this, I'll bless you. Originally this text was meant for the Israelites. If the Israelites obeyed God, He promised to fulfill the promise He made with their ancestors; to give them a land that flowed with milk and honey. Now the text is general in its meaning, God will provide for your needs. As children grow up, we will stand in need of schooling, clothing, food, shelter, health, relationships, and so many other things. God promises to fulfill all these things in the life of His young children if they remain obedient to Him by being obedient and honoring their parents.

The second part of the promise to children for obeying God is His promise for long life. The Bible promises believers who are obedient to the commandments of God a life as long as three score and ten, or seventy years of life. God even goes beyond His promise of seventy years and states that some people will even live as long as eighty years with good health. God is a God of abundance, God promises one thing and then He goes the extra mile for us and gives us even more than He already promised. This is the reason why today, so many of us are living longer lives. So children, you may not want to obey and honor both your parents because one of them may not be worthy to receive your obedience, your respect and your love; but God is. And because it is my prayer and hope that all who read this book would either strengthen their relationship with God or initiate a relationship with God. God is the only way we can have peace, joy, health and strength and abundance.

Youth and Anger

Let's first define the term anger. "Anger is both the outward and inward expressions of unfulfilled needs and or desires of the heart." Let's look at some Scripture regarding the heart:

- ➢ Proverbs 4:23 *"Above all else, guard your heart for it is the wellspring of life."*
- ➢ Matthew 15:18-20 *"But the things that come out of the mouth come from the heart, and these make a man unclean. For out of the heart come evil thoughts, murder, adultery, sexual immorality, theft, false testimony, slander. These are what make a man unclean."*
- ➢ James 4:1 *"What causes fights and quarrels among you? Don't they come from your desires that battle within you?*

These three Scriptures reference human emotions, attitudes and motivations that come from within each person, and can be found in the heart. A person's heart is the center of all of their emotions, attitudes and beliefs. Therefore, when I speak of the issue of anger in young adults and children, I'm speaking about the unmet desires that are centralized in a person's heart. Anger, then, is the motivation behind what's already in a person's heart. When I consider anger issues of Black children and youths, I find myself asking the question.

What could children and youths be so angry about? Let me identify some of the more common areas of dissatisfaction among children and youths today.

- No father or a dysfunctional father
- No mother or a dysfunctional mother
- Economics
- Education
- Parent-child conflict
- Inter-family relational conflict (outside the family)
- Intra-family relational conflict (inside the family)
- Pre-addiction or addictions
- Health concerns
- The natural pulling away process of adolescence
- Identity concerns
- Stress of all kind

In my opinion and based upon statistics, I believe the number one problems with Black children and youths today is the dysfunction of the Black father. As I talk with children, the one question I always ask them is "how is your relationship with your father?" In females, I begin to see them cry or become angry. In young men, I begin to see them go inside (not talk about it), attempt to brush off the question, tear up, become angry, or a host of various emotional responses. As I continue to understand the young person's emotions, I come to find out the same story practically every time. The child is exhibiting negative behaviors because he or she is feeling abandoned and rejected by their natural father, which has led them to exhibit symptoms of long-term grief, detachment issues, and personality disorders and so on. Some of these young people are suffering with various levels of depression, but all of them have a story to tell and it ends the same. The story ends with young people exhibiting negative behaviors because of a primary need in their lives that have gone unfulfilled; these young people want and need their dad!

Within the process of long-term grief, many of these young people experience symptoms such as:

- Anger
- Disconnectedness
- Emptiness
- Frustration
- Confusion
- Inability to communicate their feelings
- Sadness
- Aggressive behaviors
- Attention seeking behaviors
- Bullying
- Minor issues with the law
- Gang participation
- Drugs and alcohol
- Pre-marital sex
- Change in eating patterns
- Change in sleeping patterns
- Inability to concentrate
- Short-tempered
- Hopelessness
- Lost of normal interests
- Suicidal ideations
- Change in academic functioning in school
- Fighting
- Increased arguing at home; among other symptoms.

I've described for you some of the primary symptoms of grief and depression. Anger is a reactive response to an event. Others can see that something's wrong when a normal event triggers an abnormal response of anger, hostility and mood swings. Anger within itself has multiple layers. Anger can escalate to hostility, aggression and to a full-blown temporary psychosis where the person totally loses control and thus is capable of massive destruction. Afterwards, once the person has calmed down, physically and chemically from the event, sometimes they'll suffer problems remembering what set them off and how they reacted. Some of the other reasons why children get angry:

- Anger serves as a protection and a warning signal that something is happening emotionally.
- Anger is alerting the person to la problem and is often a reaction to hurt, fear, or frustration.
- An in itself is an involuntary response used to shield us from impending danger.
- Anger is a negative perspective on life that will result in irritability, withdrawal, self-isolation, resistance to being told what to do, school chores, or whatever the child wants to resist.

Anger as a learned response

Anger is not only a defense mechanism, an emotional mechanism or a responsive mechanism of our emotions, but anger is also a learned response system. As we grow through the infancy stage of life towards school age of life around six years of age, we are putting the final touches of our personality development. Therefore, we learn to copy our parents' behavior patterns. Through our parents modeling we learn to automatically do what we saw our parents do. If we saw our parents repress their anger, we will tend to repress our anger. If we saw our parents use physical violence, then we too will have the tendency to get physical. If we saw our parents get physically ill or depressed just to gain attention; then guess what; we may do the same also. Parents during this critical stage of personality development must model before their children righteous behaviors and attitudes. So when we think about issues of anger, we must focus on two primary reasons for anger; pent-up anger and brooding.

Pent-up anger is the result of not expressing one's feelings, emotions, attitudes and beliefs. Some of us are more introverted in our personality than others, and thus we have the tendency not to speak up for ourselves, thus disallowing our emotions to be expressed in a healthy format. The other reason for harmful anger is the result of brooding. Brooding is basically holding on to a grudge. A child with a passive personality will refrain from exhibiting healthy expressions of emotions, thus creating both pent-up emotions and grudges. Either way, this type of person will eventually pop his/her lid and express perhaps years of pent up emotions in a very unhealthy way. We must talk through our issues in a respectful manner that does not impose upon the personal rights and privileges of others, but neither should it disallow us to be more forthright in expressing ours. This type of person is often referred to as having a "passive-aggressive personality."

Here are some general helpful tips in dealing with issues of anger from the N.C.C.A.

1. The feeling of anger should never be denied; help the child learn to express and drain it.
2. Encourage the child to talk it out, not act it out.
3. Be a good listener and help the child express his feelings which will help resolve the anger.
4. Give him or her time to discuss what he or she is experiencing and feeling.
5. Create a stable environment. The greater the change the greater the stress and discomfort to the child.
6. Give positive feedback to the child and build the child's sense of self-confidence.
7. Both parents need to give constant and equal amounts of love.
8. Do not allow his or her anger to rule you.
9. Discipline must be agreed on by both parents.

Many of our young persons today do not understand how to deal with their feelings. The unfortunate consequence of many of the decisions made by young people will leave young people with a life time of permanent life changes. Our young ladies look for sexual encounters to feel the love, affection and sense of relationship they miss from a loving father. Our young ladies who make this unwise decision may very well end up pregnant and caring for a young child without the assistance of its adolescent or older father. This same young lady will experience difficulty in school attendance and academic performance. She will experience road blocks when deciding to go away for college; she'll experience difficulties with employment, finances, housing, self-esteem, respect, a support system and short/long term lifestyle changes brought on by the caring of a newborn child and immaturity.

Our young ladies did not ask for all of this, they just wanted someone to notice them, someone to talk to, someone to formulate a relationship with, someone to lean on and receive encouragement and support. Many times our young ladies are only masking the lack of nurturing from dad and mom. Parental nurturing cannot be obtained through a boyfriend/girlfriend, or the taking care of a baby. But that's the result of misguided decisions brought on by an unfulfilled heart. So all of us, no matter what age or race we are, we will attempt to meet our needs the best way we know how. The problem with this is that many times we don't know what our needs are. And other times, we have problems distinguishing between needs and wants. We only know that we want it and that's enough. So our motivations are misguided and thus the decisions we make to meet our perceived needs and wants lead us into a path of the "I didn't intend for that to happen blues."

I want you to know that our young ladies not only look for love in all the wrong places, but today our young ladies are doing the exact same things as our misguided young men. Both our boys and girls are sharing in a host of like misbehaviors. Both are engaging in sex, drugs, violence, gangs, scrimmages with the law, educational concerns, robbing, raping, abusing, destruction of property, disobedience, devalue of life and a genuine disrespect for authority figures including the parent at home. In addition, the girls are articulating filth just as well as the boys are. One of the worse things for me to view is a pretty young lady sounding like a drunken sailor. Why do young people feel the need to speak very nasty, vile, disrespectful and inappropriate words to ever roll off a human tongue? Why do young ladies feel the need to compete with misguided and unruly teen boys? What ever happened to self respect? Not to mention the way some young ladies dress. It's getting harder and harder to look at a young lady without getting aroused. Everything that makes a female different from a male is being exposed, in tight, loose and limited clothing. What happened to imagination? The Bible says that a tree is known by the fruit it bares. In other words, young ladies, if you don't like being called a hoe, don't dress like one!

My young Brothers; I know many of you are hurting. It's totally all right to be truthful with yourself. No one wants you to grow up and repeat the same mistakes your dad or mom may have made to you. Don't we have enough Brothers in juvenile lockup's, jails and prisons? Don't we have enough Brothers dropping out of school and becoming drug pushers and users? Don't we have enough Brothers being shot and killed by people looking just like you? Don't we have enough mortuaries taking care of our dead bodies? Don't we have enough preachers trying to find something good to say about you at your funeral? Don't we have enough mothers crying over another dead son? Don't we have enough? When is enough, enough?

Step Families

One of the problems all families have is issues associated with blended families. In today's world, adults are more and more likely to marry a second or third time. With each new marriage the likelihood of introducing step-children into the new marriage is becoming a standard. Or as statistics confirm for the Black family, we may not be married, but that don't stop us from shacking up as one happy dysfunctional and confused family. Either way, there's a new adult relationship with both adults introducing their children into the relationship as live-in parents, with a new family dynamic and a new set of issues, concerns and conflict. One obvious problem with this new dynamic stems from the simple fact that **"we're not married,"** and two, neither party in the relationship talked about how the dynamics of this new family were going to be handled. If we're ineffectively communicating before we get married; what's the chance of us effectively communicating while we're living together?

Parents of step or blended families introduce into their new living arrangement issues associated with the handling dynamics of each other's children. One primary problem I hear in the counseling office is from the husband/dad. He usually appears frustrated with his spouse because he cannot discipline all the children as he sees fit. The wife/mother wants her spouse to express leadership in the home, but at the same time, she does not allow him to fully discipline her children. Thus the problem begins within this relationship over areas of control. The husband/father feels as if he does not have control over all of his family, just his natural children. The step-children within the relationships quickly learn how to manipulate dad and mom to get what they want. These children know when to be nice and when to act a fool.

The problem as stated in step or blended families is communication. Parents must communicate first with each other and then with all the children. Ground rules must be set by the parents. But I caution parents during the early stages of developing relationships with step children to give the children time, space and opportunity. Give the children time to get adjusted to you. Give the children space to internalize this brand new mode of life for them and lastly, give the children every opportunity to develop a parental friendship with the step-parent. A part of building a sense of family with step-children is first building the step-parent relationship. Step parents must build a friendship, a bond, a trust, camaraderie with step children. This phase of the relationship with step parents and children should be done in the courting phase, prior to agreeing to move in with one another or getting married to each other (obviously moving in with one another is not preferred over marrying one another). Children have feelings too, and to ignore their feelings is to set the step-parent up for future problems of trust and obedience.

Wives/mothers you cannot play favoritism. If you're going to allow your husband/father to be your covering, then you must give him complete authority over all matters of the family including your children. Parents of blended families must not and cannot allow their natural children to manipulate them into doing something for them and not for the other children. Separation or favoritism must not exist between the parents and children. Parents must treat every child equally. Each child assigned to do chores, must do them with the same expectations of performance as everyone else. As children become older they should be allowed certain privileges afforded to them. Any other alteration amongst the children will result in the children rebelling against parental authority.

I wish I could guarantee to children that they'll never hurt again, that they'll never be disappointed again; that they'll never be made to feel as if their in the way. But I can't, and you can't either. But what we can do is learn to move past our shortcomings. Many people both young and old are living respectful, happy and fulfilled lives with out some of the things they feel they need. Do any of us truly have all the things we feel we need, probably not? But such as we have, we give God thanks for it. God will provide for all of our needs, if we belong to Him. Even with this promise from God, He's not going to do all the work for us. God is expecting us to do some things to help ourselves. The more committed we are to trying to live right, the more I believe God blesses us. But we must make the choice in what we're going to do. It's up to us to decide which road we'll cross today and what direction we'll take tomorrow; but there is help, there is hope, and His name is Jesus Christ and He's already giving us parental instructions through His Word, the Holy Bible.

My Brothers, to run from Jesus is to run directly into the face of Hell! Jesus says to everyone: *"Come unto me all ye who are weary and heavy laden and I will give you rest."* My Brothers and Sisters please stop running away from your help and hope and begin to walk toward your help and hope. It's time for a change; but only you can decide when? The answers we seek, both individually and for the

Black family lye through a personal relationship with Jesus Christ. The problems with drugs, sex, aggression and all the rest is found through a relationship with Christ. Black folks have become a misdirected group of God's creation. We have attempted to meet our needs without God.

Parents here are 12 Rules for Bringing up Children by the N.C.C.A.

1. Remember each child is an individual and should be permitted to be himself. Do not attempt to mod them in the image of you.
2. Do not crush a child's spirit when he fails and never compare him with others who have done better.
3. Remember that anger and hostility are natural emotions. Help your child find other outlets for these feelings, or they may be turned inward and create physical or emotional problems.
4. Discipline your child with firmness and reason. Do not let your anger throw you off balance. Make sure the punishment fits "the crime." Even they youngest child has a keen sense of justice.
5. Present a united front. Never join with your child against your husband or wife. This creates emotional conflicts and generated confusion and insecurity.
6. Do not give your child everything his little heart desires. Permit him to know the thrill that comes from earning something.
7. Do not set yourself up as a model of perfection. The child knows that parents do make mistakes.
8. Do not make threats in anger or glowing promises when you are in a good mood. Threaten or promise only what you can deliver.
9. Do not smother your child with gifts and lavish surprises. The purest and the healthiest love express itself in day-in, day-out discipline. Consistency builds self-confidence, trust, and a strong base for character development.
10. Teach your child there is dignity in hard work.

11. Do not try to protect your child against every blow and disappointment. Allow him to get a few lumps. Adversity strengthens character and makes us compassionate.
12. Teach your child to love God. Do not <u>send</u> your child to church<u>, take</u> him there. Children learn by example. Faith in God can be his strength and light when all else fails.

Parent's here is a Bible study on raising children for God:

HOW TO RAISE A CHILD FOR GOD

<u>Study the following principles and circle the ones where you're failing.</u>

1. Examine your expectations for your child. Are they realistic? Evaluate them in the light of the bible (1 Cor. 13:11; Matt. 18:10; Gen. 33:12-14).
2. Love him unconditionally (Dt. 7:7; 1 Jn. 4:10, 19).
3. Look for opportunities in which you can commend him. Express appreciation for him frequently (Phil. 1:3; 1 Thess. 1:2; 2 Thess. 1:3).
4. Seldom criticize without first expressing appreciation for good points (1 Cor. 1:3-13).
5. Give him freedom to make decisions where serious issues are not a stake. Your goal should be to bring your child to maturity in Christ and not to dependence on you (Eph. 4:13-15; 6:4; Prov. 22:6; col. 1:17, 28).
6. Do not compare him with others (Gal. 6:4; 2 Cor. 10:12, 13; 1 Cor. 12:4-11).
7. Never mock him or make fun of him. Do not demean or belittle your child. Beware of calling him dumb or clumsy or stupid (Matt. 7:12; Eph. 4:29, 30; Col. 4:6; Prov. 12:18; 16:24).
8. Do not scold him in front of others (Matt. 16:22, 23; 18:15; 1 Cor. 16:14).
9. Never make threats or promises that you do not intend to keep (Matt. 5:37; Js. 5:12; Col. 3:9).

10. Don't be afraid to say "no," and when you say it, mean it (Prov. 22:15; 29; 15; 1 Sam. 3:13; Gen. 18:19).
11. When your child has problems or is a problem, do not overreact or lose control of yourself. Do not yell or shout or scream at him (Eph. 4:26, 27; 1 Cor.16:14; 2 Tim. 2:24, 25; 1 Tim. 5:1, 2).
12. Communicate optimism and expectancy. Do not communicate by word or action that you have given up on your child and are resigned to his being a failure (Philem. 21; 2 Cor. 9:1, 2: 1 Cor. 13:7).
13. Make sure your child knows exactly what is expected of him. Most of the book of Proverbs is specific counsel from a father to his son.
14. Ask his advice—include him in some of the family planning (Rom. 1:11, 12; 2 Tim. 4:11; 1 Tim. 4:12; Jn. 6:5).
15. When you make a mistake with your child, admit it and ask your child for forgiveness (Matt. 5:23, 24; Js. 5:16).
16. Have family conferences where you discuss:
    a. Family goals
    b. Family projects
    c. Vacations
    d. Devotions
    e. Chores
    f. Discipline
    g. Complaints
    h. Suggestions
    i. Problems

    Welcome contributions from your child (Ps. 128; Js. 1:19; 3:13-18; Titus 1:6-8; Prov. 15:22).
17. Assess his areas of strength and then encourage him to develop them. Begin with one and encourage him to really develop in this area (2 Tim. 1:16; 4:5; 1 Pet. 4:10).
18. Give him plenty of tender loving care. Be free in your expression of love by word and deed (1 Cor.13:1-8; 16:14; Jn. 13:34; 1 Thess. 2:7, 8).

19. Practice selective reinforcement. When your child does something will, commend him. Especially let him know when his attitude and effort are what they should be (1 Thess. 1:3-10; Phil. 1:3-5; Col. 1:3, 4; Eph. 1:15).
20. Be more concerned about Christian attitudes and character than you are about performance or athletic skills or clothing or external beauty or intelligence (1 Sam. 16:7; Gal. 5:22, 23: 1 Pet. 3:4, 5; Prov. 4:23; Matt. 23:25-28).
21. Have a lot of fun with your child. Plan to have many fun times and many special events with your child. Make a list of fun things your family can do (Ps. 128; Prov. 5:15-18; 15:13; 14:22; Eph. 6:4; Col. 3:21; Eccles. 3:4; Lk. 15:22-24).
22. Help your child to learn responsibility by administering discipline fairly, consistently, lovingly, and promptly (1 Sam. 3:13; Prov. 13:24; 18:18; 22:15).
23. Look upon your child as a human *becoming* as well as a human being. Look upon the task of raising children as a process which takes 18-19 years to complete (Eph. 6:4; Prov. 22:6; Gal. 6:9; 1 Cor. 15:58; Isa. 28:9, 10).
24. Live your convictions consistently. Your child will learn more by observing your example than he will by listening to your words (Dt. 6:4-9; 1 Thess. 2:10-12; Phil. 4:9; 2 Tim. 1:5, 7).
25. Recognize that you are responsible to prepare your child for life in this world and in the world to come (Eph. 6:4; Dt. 6:4-9; Ps. 78:5-7; 2 Tim. 3:15-17).
26. Be very sensitive to the needs, feelings, fears, and opinions of your child (Matt. 18:10; Col. 3:21).
27. Treat the child as though he is important to you and accepted by you (Matt. 18:5-6).
28. Avoid the use of words expressing anger or exasperation (Prov. 15:1; Eph. 4:31, 32).
29. Maintain the practice of daily Bible reading, discussions, and prayer (Dt. 6:4-9; 2 Tim. 3:15; Eph. 6:4; Ps. 1:1-3; 78:5-8; 119:9, 11).
30. Become thoroughly involved as a family in a biblical church (Heb. 10:24, 25; Eph. 4:11-16).

31. Make your home a center of Christian hospitality, where your child will be brought into frequent contact with many Christians (Rom. 12:13; Heb. 13:1, 2; 2 Kings 4:8-37).
32. Make it easy for your child to approach you with problems, difficulties, and concerns. Learn to be a good listener when he needs you. Give your child your undivided attention. Avoid being a mind reader or an interrupter or a critic. Show an interest in whatever interests your child. Make yourself available when your child needs you=-even if you are busy (Js. 1:19, 20; 3:16-18; 1 Jn. 3:16-18; 1 Cor. 9:19-23; Phil. 2:3, 4).
33. Seek to bring your child to a saving knowledge of Jesus Christ. Become all things to your child that you might win your child to Christ. God, of course, must do the saving, bring conviction, and give repentance and faith. You, however, may provide the environment in which God saves-by your prayers, godly speech and example, family devotions, and involvement in a sound biblical church (2 Tim. 1:5-7; 3:14-17; Eph. 6:4; Dt. 6:4-9; Mk 10:13, 14; Rom. 10:13-17; 1 Cor. 1:18-21).

Chapter Nine
"Reconciliation"

"Therefore if any man be in Christ, he is a new creature: old things are passed away; behold, all things are become new. And all things are of God, who hath reconciled us to himself by Jesus Christ, and hath given to us the ministry of reconciliation; To wit, that God was in Christ, reconciling the world unto himself, not imputing their trespasses unto them; and hath committed unto us the word of reconciliation. Now then we are ambassadors for Christ, as though God did beseech you by us: we pray you in Christ's stead, be ye reconciled to God. For he hath made him to be sin for us, who knew no sin; that we might be made the righteousness of God in him." 2 Corinthians 5:17-21.

    Why do we seek after the ways of this world; don't we know that they are all temporary. Don't we know that the wages of sin is still death? The world has so much to offer us; yet we choose only those things that are not good for us. Satan was kicked out of heaven and sent down to earth; woe to the earth. Satan's own mission is to steal, kill and destroy. As you have read through the pages of this book, I hope you saw this reality that has long since manifested itself in the flesh of all human beings everywhere. The statements, applications and Scriptural guidance offered in this book are for all God's people to share; for I believe it speaks to situations of mankind. However, my mission and purpose was to present a picture through the lens of both historical and current relevance to the stated mission of Satan and his influence upon the Black people of God.

The Black Plague

    The Black family is in a state of crisis; the Black church is in a state of crisis. You cannot separate the Black family and the church. We are a people that have strong roots in the church and thus the two are inseparable. From the great rich nation of Africa, we came. Not willingly, but nonetheless we're here. I personally do not know Africa. I was born in the USA. But I understand where it all began. Black Americans were once stacked together in their own urine, feces and blood, as we were stacked together like sardines on a boat to Europe, America and other places. We were sold into a culture and into a land that we did not know and did not want to know. We were beaten, misused, abused, neglected, raped, ridiculed, and considered less than dung. After all, Blacks were not even considered human beings. But some four-hundred plus years later, after many freedom fighters and many brave, strong, faithful men and women died for a cause of liberty, justice and the American way. We find the Black man now in 2006, back in chains, back in a depressive state of life; we find Black brothers and sisters living apart from each other as if each other had the Black plague. We, the Black people of God who were once forced into slavery has now become the willing slaves of selfishness, irresponsibility, hostility, laziness and most of all, we have become enslaved by sin; that great oppressor of the people. Black folks don't need Satan to enslave us, we've enslaved ourselves.

Unfortunately, it seems that many of us have contracted a form of the Black plague. It is called sin. A form of plague that not only seeks to steal, kill and destroy everything in its pathway, it also enjoys the work it does. Why do we have to give in to sin's desires?

This form of Black plague has and continues to pull apart the fabric of society called the family. God ordained the family to emulate His own; yet, we have brought Him nothing but sin and shame. This form of Black plague has touched the lips of many of our Black men, both young and old. The fruit of the vine has been the destruction of many. Alcohol in its many varieties, flavors, colors, content and price; continues to eat away at the hearts and minds through the lips of Black men; and now Black women.

This form of Black plague has and continues to fill the Black noses of both the young and the old with crack-cocaine. This misty white rock represents the blackness of the grave, the color of death and destruction, and the loss of light which is life. All those who dare to partake of its crystal like rock form also partakes in its growth to other Black noses; yet this small but very might rock continues destroying and conquering and separating life from death and responsibility to irresponsibility; from love to hatred; from service to disservice; from joy to sorrow and shame; from righteousness to unrighteousness. This form of Black plague is talking to the hearts of many Black men, telling them to serve it; lie for it, steal for it, and kill for it.

    This form of Black plague is worse than any living nightmare ever imagined. As young Black children lay their heads down on their pillows at night with great anticipation of a new day. These beautiful, innocent Black children fall asleep only to enter into a nightmare. They dream their daddy were no longer their daddy; the boogie man called sin had whist their daddy away to a far, far, away place called prison; called the street corner, called the sister down the street's house. These Black children begin to cry as their dream shifts the spotlight onto their mother, as she pleads with their daddy to spend more time with the children, but the boogie man of irresponsibility continued to pull and tug at daddy until the boogie man of disrespect joined into the tug of war for daddy's soul and his place in his family. Daddy shouts obscenities, not at the boogie man, but at mommy. Daddy calls mommy all kinds of names God did not give or make her to be. Then all of a sudden, these beautiful Black children hurriedly awake horrified, yet relieved that it was only a dream; or was it?

    This form of Black plague is not one that is spreading, but disappearing. The great absence of the Black man in the Family is vastly becoming a reality. With more Black Brothers in jail than in college, the Black plague is becoming a reality with Black children being the number one race of children in need of foster parents and adoption services. The Black plague is becoming a reality, with greater and greater numbers of Black youths committing suicide and dropping out of high school and becoming chemically addicted and filling more than half of all juvenile jail cells, the Black plague is becoming a reality. If half of the prisoners in state, federal and juvenile jail cells are Black and the majority of them are addicted to drugs, then who's left to tend to the Black family? Who's left to play with sister or brother? Is this one hell of an illusion; or is this a mirror of reality?

What about the children? Where are the Black men who made these Black babies? Who's training young Black men to be men? Why is it that young Black men and women have seemingly lost their minds today? Why is it that eligible Black youths see no appeal to marriage? Why are so many Black youths being arrested for petty crimes? Why are so many Black youths trying to get so high on weed, crack and anything else they can get high on? What are these youths running away from? Why do so many Black female youths dress like prostitutes and curse like sailors? Why are there so many Black grandparents at age 35? Who's taking care of the children? Who's taking care of the single mother struggling to care for her babies without a father, let alone a husband? What's happening to Black marriages? What's destroying the Black family? Where are all the good Black men? Have Black women begun to inherit the Black plague as well? What's up with homosexuality?

What is Freedom?

I can come up with more questions than I have the time or the energy to attempt to answer at any length. I don't have all the answers, but I believe I have the solution. Black men and women (obviously not all of us) have run and run very successfully from God. This answer does not take years of research to answer or degrees on top of degrees to affirm. The answer is all around us today. It is not only the primary factor in the demise of the Black family, but it is the demise of these United States of America. Whether you're Black, White, Latino, Indian, Alaskan, Asian or any other race of human being created by God; the answer to the world's problems and your personal salvation, rests not with God, but with each of you. Your answer to why life is so hard is because you made it that away. You chose all the liberties and freedoms of the world, and in your partaking of freedoms you forgot about God.

The fact is: none of us have total freedom. Either we are in some form of bondage here on earth or we'll be in eternal bondage when Jesus judges us and sends us to hell. True freedom comes with restrictions. True freedom says I'm willing to give up my earthly freedom of choice, in light of God's freedom of will. I choose God's freedom over the world's freedom. God's freedom is spelled out for me in His Word, but the world's freedom keeps on changing and the fact is; the only freedom the world has will be eventually taken away by God and restored to the way God intended and designed it to be in the first place. So although I think I have total freedom now, ultimately my freedom must demand of me a decision to whose freedom I rather have.

The only true freedom I have on earth is the freedom to make decisions. God gave me the ability to make my own choices, and it is that freedom that I will ultimately have to use if I am to choose where I will spend eternity. But until the time God calls my body back to the dust from where it came and my spirit and soul back to Him, I have continued freedom to make choices. First and foremost, I need to get right with God. My life is not pleasing to God, it doesn't even please me. I understand that I've been trying to live this thing called life without God, and I need to get back with God, because He's the only one that can ever truly free me. I understand that I must confess Christ and draw closer to Him.

Secondly, I need to accept who God made me to be and subjectively place myself back in that position, so I will receive blessings from God while I'm still alive. God made me a man/woman. In being a man/woman God has set the structure for how I am to interact with Him and each other. God said to men to leave your father and mother and take a wife. Men are either to marry or stay single for the Lord. Men, if you decide that sex is something you want, then you must marry. Marriage is a good thing! God created it, and all that God created including man; He said is very good. Marriage is a holy covenant between a man and a woman with God overseeing it through His son Jesus Christ and the assistance of His Holy Spirit. So Secondly, I need to get in where God said I to fit in; God wants me to reconcile with my children (if any), my wife (if possible), my family, friends and the church. But more so, God wants me to reconcile with Him.

As a husband and father, I understand that the relationship with my wife is my primary duty. I am a holy covering for her and my children. I provide her with servant leadership and love, as Christ demonstrated to the church till death. Secondly, I understand that the nurturing and development of my children is my second priority in my family. I also understand that my family obligations come before any ministry obligations at church. I understand that if my family is not together, I'm not to assist the church in pulling its ministries together. As a husband and father, I further understand that God gave me and my wife dominion over all the earth, thus I am to treat what God gave me with respect as I demonstrate reverence (a profound respect) to God.

As a servant leader in my family, I understand that love does not mean that I have the authority to imprison my wife but support and motivate her to fulfill her dreams and goals while maintaining family integrity. I also understand that God gave me a wife for companionship; He did not give her to me to beat on, curse at, misuse and abuse or enslave. I understand that if my relationship with my wife is not right because of me, God will not answer my prayers. I further understand that as the Apostle Paul presented in 1 Corinthians 13:4-8 (love), Paul gave me an example of the characteristics of relational love to use in my marriage and as a general rule to live by.

Paul Wrote: (NIV) 1 Corinthians 13:4-8

- ✝ Love is patient
- ✝ Love is kind
- ✝ It does not envy
- ✝ It does not boast
- ✝ It is not proud
- ✝ It is not rude
- ✝ It is not self seeking
- ✝ It is not easily angered

- ♰ It keeps no record of wrongs
- ♰ Love does not delight in evil
- ♰ But rejoices with the truth
- ♰ It always protect
- ♰ Always trusts
- ♰ Always hopes
- ♰ Always persevere
- ♰ Love never fails

Love is responsible. It was love that came from glory to set the captives free. It was love that reconciled all men from the grip of death. It was love that loosed our shackles and unlocked our chains. It was love that God demonstrated more than His anger when He sent His only begotten Son to the Cross. It was and it is LOVE! It is love that looks past yesterday and welcomes with open arms today.

Ephesians 2:16- *"And in this one body to reconcile both of them to God through the cross, by which he put to death their hostility."*

Christ reconciled us from the judgment of His Father, and it is only Christ that reconciles us from ourselves. There is no longer any need to be separated by disagreements and hostility. Christ took all of that to the cross with Him and buried it there. You and I can freely come and be reconciled both to Him and each other. We have been made alive through Christ. We should no longer carry the burdens, the grief, the pain, the anguish, the disappointment and remembrance of yesterday in our heart and minds; because today is the day of reconciliation. We don't need the world's devices to make us feel better, we only need Christ. Through a personal relationship with Christ we can get our needs met, not through the world; but from the one who created the world. Then we'll come to understand what it means to live in the world; but not be of the world.

In my opinion, there's no greater need in the world, than that of the unification of the family; father, mother, children. We all understand that both men and women of child bearing age produce sperm. Sperm is the DNA of life. Sperm produces life, but it does not produce responsibility. Sperm produces life; irresponsibility hinders and destroys life. A title such as 'father' or 'mother' is a means of identification. However, it is not acceptance of the duties of the position. Children today are hurting; men are hurting; women are hurting; we're all hurting one another. It is not the world's fault for what happens; it is our fault (mankind's), we are the one's making the decisions for the planet. Each of our decisions affects someone else or something else. If we don't put oil in our automobile's engine, it will eventually become dry and the motor will freeze up, thus leaving the automobile inoperable. We would stand in need of a brand new engine. Our families are no different. Our families are standing in the need of nurturing, love and direction. Without these vital components, we too, just like the automobile, will be inoperable.

Is reconciliation easy? No way! Reconciliation demands love, and love demands trust and trust demands a sacrifice and a sacrifice demands acceptance and acceptance demands patience and patience demands time and time demands a decision and a decision demands encouragement and encouragement demands support and support demands perseverance. Reconciliation involves initiation; we must bring initiation into practice. Reconciliation is a process of forgiveness and re-establishment. Mankind has and is still fallen from perfection and is now cursed with a curse because of our disobedience to God in the Garden (Adam and Eve). Because of our disobedience God became very angry with us and separated Himself from us. Because God's love for us is greater than His anger towards us, God initiated a plan to reconcile us back to Himself. God sent His Son (the reconciler) Jesus. Jesus demonstrated love in what He said and what He did. The people could trust that Jesus would do what He said He'll do. Ultimately, Jesus had to demonstrate His father's love through a sacrifice on Calvary's cross, where Jesus buried all of mankind's sins and transgressions against His father. Now, we can experience full reconciliation by denouncing sin and accepting Christ, our reconciler. God Himself knowing all things understands that He must be patient with us while many of us go through the difficulties of life. Many of us desire time to make this all important decision, and God is patient. But please don't use patience as a crutch to maintain irresponsibility. Jesus states in His Word: Find me while I may be found (paraphrased).

In this same way I have demonstrated parts to the process of reconciliation. We have sinned against God and against one another, and because of this we are now separated from each other. This is the part we've done thus far. The most important parts or reconciliation has yet to be attempted. We must forgive each other of our transgressions against each other. There are many Black men today that are on the outside looking in because of what they've done to others. I strongly encourage you brothers to please take that step of faith and take the initiative to start the process of reconciliation. If God, having all power and seeing all things and knowing all things; if He's willing to forgive us, why can't we be willing to forgive each other. Forgiveness is a process. Forgiveness says to you and me, that I will take the pain of what you did and I'll place it under my feet. I'll decide that I will no longer allow what you did to affect me anymore. I cannot forget what you did, but I can stop brooding over what you did and let it go from my heart. Forgiveness says I'll give you another chance. Forgiveness says I'll release you from the debt you owe me for hurting me. Forgiveness says I'll be patient and kind with you as you get your act together. Forgiveness says today is more important than yesterday. Forgiveness says when I think on yesterday, I will no longer feel pain. Forgiveness says I love you more than my anger against you. Forgiveness says we have all sinned and come short and I won't hold you shortcomings against you. Forgiveness says get up and get back in the game.

Isn't this what Jesus did for us all? Didn't God through His Son Jesus say to you and me, I forgive you; and I want you back. You do understand that we were and are the one's that messed up. We are the one's that have disobeyed God; we are the one's that have turned our backs to God. Yet, even in the midst of God's greatest joy in making mankind, God got angry with us, He cursed us. But even in His righteous anger, He also created a plan to redeem us from the grips of

Satan and ourselves. God wants us reconciled back to Him. With reconciliation through Jesus everything is possible. However, I fully understand that this book may touch someone (I pray it does); I also understand that many will never pick it up to read. Many others will read it only to ridicule it. Others will denounce it. The greatest book ever written has suffered these and many other remarks; the Holy Bible.

Satan has his grip on many of you. Many of you will never change. Many of you don't want to change. Many of you don't see yourselves as a problem. I pray that before you take your last breath, you'll change your mind. Until then, as my daddy always said; "keep living and don't die." For those of you who are tired of living not knowing what your children are doing; what they look like; what's their favorite color; what's their favorite food. Mothers, let these children's daddy try to reconcile with them. Full reconciliation may not be possible with some of you sisters because you have entered into a new relationship or you're married now. I understand this. Reconciliation at any level is great progress. Ultimately, reconciliation must occur if the next generation of parents is to form a true family unit as husband and wife. Let's begin to do the right thing. We've messed it up for so long now, it's time to do things the right way; God's way.

Study Guide for Healing Broken Relationships
(Ephesians 4:2, 3)

Philippians 4: 2, 3 indicates that Euodias and Syntyche had once gotten along well, but something had happened to break the close relationship between the two of them.

1. Make a list of the main people with whom you do not have as good a relationship as you once did. (These people might include your husband or wife, a child, your parents, your neighbor, your pastor, a church member, your boss, etc.)
2. Study Philippians 4:2, 3 and list several things that Euodias and Syntyche had in common. Now make a list of what you have in common with the people you listed under assignment number 1.
3. Use your sanctified imagination and list some possible cause for the break in the relationship between Euodias and Syntyche. Now make a specific list of what caused the rift between you and the people previously mentioned. (Example: He criticized me; he ignored me; he disagreed with me; he hurt me, etc.)
4. Problems between us and others become enlarged when we handle them in a wrong way. Study the following Scripture verses and record what should not be done when a problem arises between you and another person.

   Proverbs 15:1   Colossians 3:8, 9
   Proverbs 29:11, 20, 22   James 4:1-2, 11
   Romans 12:17, 19   1 Peter 2:1
   Ephesians 4:25- 27   1 Peter 3:8, 9
   Ephesians 4:29-30

5. Study Philippians 4:2, 3 and answer the following questions:
   a. How do these verses encourage us to think that fractured relationships can be healed?
   b. What does the fact that Paul speaks to both people indicate about solving interpersonal relationships? List how you would have been at fault in reference to the people previously mentioned.
   c. What does it mean to "be of the same mind in the Lord"? Study Philippians 2:1-8 before you answer this question. Study Matthew 5:21-48; Luke 6:32-35; Romans 12:17,18, 20, 21; Colossians 3:12-16; 1 Corinthians 13:4-8; 1 Peter 2:18-3:6, 8, 9; Proverbs 15:1; 16:24, 32; 17:14, 27, 28; 18:6, 7, 8,23; 21:23; 25:15; 29:11 and make a list of what God wants you to do and how you may serve other people to whom you are not as close.
   d. According to Philippians 4:3, what is often needed to solve interpersonal conflict? (also study Proverbs 12:15; 11:14; 15:22; Rom. 15:14; Gal.6:1, 2) Plan now from whom you will seek God's kind of help and make an appointment to seek Christian counsel.

BIBLICAL FORGIVENESS MODEL

1. **Admit your wrongs (sins);** Admit to yourself that you harbor sin in your heart for what someone said and or did to you, or what you said or did to someone else.
    A. (John 8:31-32) Truth gives freedom
2. **Admit to God your sin and seek His forgiveness**
    A. (Mark 11:25) Reconcile your walk with the Lord.
    B. Psalm 51:1-4 Admit your sin to God and seek His forgiveness
3. **Seek reconciliation of the relationship**
    A. Matthew 18:15
4. **Forgive as often as God forgives you**
    A. Matthew 18:21-22; Luke 17:3-4
5. If possible, when doing so does not cause further harm, **seek to pay restitution for any physical damages inflicted**
    A. Lamentations 3:40 Set things right
    B. Exodus 21:33-36 Take responsibility for any damages
6. **Release the anger in your heart**
    A. Hosea 14:4
    B. Micah 7:18
7. **Put off hurtful feelings**, thoughts and memories and replace them with the love of God
    A. Ephesians 4:22-5:2
8. **Forgive the offender of sorrow and pain**
    A. 2 Corinthians 2:5-11
9. **Renew your heart and mind**
    A. Philippians 4:8-9
    B. Romans 12:2
10. **Seek spiritual cleansing and inner peace**
    A. Psalm 51:2, 7
    B. Psalm 139:23, 24
11. **Be patient with human forgiveness**, remember only God can wipe away the memory of sin, humans may take a little longer.
    A. Colossians 1:11 Endure everything with patience
    B. John 5:1-8 Patiently wait for your healing
    C. Hebrews 6:12 Wait patiently on the promise of God

Prepared by Rev. Dr. Avery Bolden
Dove of Peace Christian Counseling Min. LLC.

I would be remiss to talk so much about reconciliation throughout the pages of this book and not offer you the ultimate way that leads to reconciliation with God through His Son Jesus. Let me share with you the Romans road to salvation.

- ✞ Romans 3:23-*"For all have sinned and fall short of the glory of God."*
- ✞ Romans 5:8-*"But God demonstrates his own love for us in this: While we wee still sinners, Christ died for us."*
- ✞ Romans 6:23-*"For the wages of sin is death, but the gift of God is eternal life in Christ Jesus our Lord."*
- ✞ Romans 10:9-*"That if you confess with your mouth, Jesus is Lord, and believe in your heart that God raised him from the dead, you will be saved."*
- ✞ Romans 10:13-*"For Everyone who calls on the name of the Lord will be saved."*

Romans 10:10 says *"For it is with your heart that you believe and are justified, and it is with your mouth that you confess and are saved."* If you are ready for reconciliation right now, all you have to do is pray this prayer to God.

Lord Jesus, I have sinned against you. Please forgive me of all of my sins and come into my life; be my lord and my savior. I give my life to you right now. I promise to serve you to the best of my human ability. I believe you are Lord and I believe God raised you from the dead. I thank you Lord Jesus for salvation and for coming into my life. In Jesus name I pray, Amen.

If you said that prayer and really meant it in your heart, the angels in heaven are now rejoicing. Upon your acceptance of salvation, you have now received the Lord's Holy Spirit. You're never alone in this world anymore. God is always with you. I encourage you to seek out a good Bible teaching, preaching and believing church to fellowship with and grow in the Lord. Let the lord lead you as you journey through the process of reconciliation. Read your Bible everyday and get into a

Beginners Bible study group to learn how to read and understand your Bible. I'm very proud of each and every one of you who took this much needed first step in the process of reconciliation.

This Is My Prayer For All Of You:

Father God in heaven, I thank you for the opportunity to touch the lives of your people. I pray for each person who picks up this book and reads it. I pray that your Holy Spirit will touch them as they read the words. I pray that you would speak into their minds, their hearts and into their spirits. We have all sinned against you, oh Lord. Please forgive us all. Restore unto us our estranged loved ones. I pray that you would help us to seek reconciliation; seek peace; seek joy; seek after righteousness. Lead us Father God how you would desire us to proceed. Give us patience, give us fortitude, and give us direction. Please help us to understand how we are to live according to your Word, so that we may be blessed. I pray for conviction of your Holy Spirit even though many are imprisoned now. Free us from within our hearts, minds, spirits and souls. Help us to live for righteousness and for peace. Help us Jesus to mend broken relationships starting with you. Help us to understand how important it is for us to do all that we rightfully can, so we can become the Man/Woman of God that you want us to be. I pray that we may find favor with you and with those we seek to reconcile with. I thank you Lord for your patience, for your mercy and your grace. To God be the glory for the things He has done. I love you Lord.
This is my prayer for you in Jesus name. Amen.

Rev. Avery Bolden PhD.
Licensed Clinical Christian Counselor-Advanced
NBCCT Board Certified Clinical Supervisor

References

1. Africans in America Web site. WGBH Interactive for PBS Online. 1998, 1999 WGBH Educational Foundation.
2. Nelson's New Illustrated Bible Dictionary. Ronald F. Youngblood. 1995 Thomas Nelson Publishers.
3. The History of the Black Church. Lutz, Norma Jean. Chelsea House Publishers. 2001
4. Slave Young, Slave Long. Meg Greene. Lerner Publications 1999
5. Overview of findings from the 2004 National Survey on Drug Use and Health, pgs 26-29
6. Overview of findings from the 2004 National Survey on Drug Use and Health, Pg 11
7. National Survey on Drug Use and Health, Issue 3 pg 1
8. National Survey on Drug Use and Health, Issue 16 pgs 1-4
9. National Survey on Drug Use and Health-Youth Marijuana Admission by Race and Ethnicity, August 9, 2002. Pages 1-2
10. National Survey on Drug Use and Health-Adolescent Treatment Admissions: 1992-2002
11. Mental Health: Culture, Race, Ethnicity-Fact Sheet- www.mentalhealth.somhsa.gov/cre/fact1.asp
12. National Survey on Drug Use and Health-Smoked Cocaine vs. Non-Smoked Cocaine Admissions: 2002
13. The Stages of Grief- www.memorialhospital.org/library/general/stress
14. Coping With Grief- www.oquinnpeebles.com/coping%20with%20grief.htm
15. Stages Of Grief In Children- www.oquinnpeebles.com/stages_of_grief%20in%20children.htm
16. Fathers.com-Nurturing: Three A's
17. Semen-Wikipedia, the free encyclopedia- http://en.wikipedia.org/wiki/Semen

18. fathers.com- The Extent of Fatherlessness
19. Fathers.com- The Consequences of Fatherlessness
20. Child Trends, A Research Brief-What Do Fathers Contribute to Children's Well-Being? www.childtrends.org
21. Institute for American Values-Black Fathers in Contemporary American Society Strengths, Weaknesses, and Strategies for Change-AmericanValues.org
22. Holy Scriptures were quoted from: The Holy Bible; NKJV, NIV, and KJV
23. Personal Poem-Barbara Winder
24. National Christian Counselor Association-Christian Psychology and Counseling. Terry D King Ph.D., Debra L. King Ph.D., Richard G. Arno, Ph. D., Phyllis J. Arno, Ph. D.
25. Help With Herpes-American Social Health Association
26. HPV-American Social Health Association
27. The Emotional Effects of Sex-1995 Channing L. Bete Co., Inc.
28. Young People Get HIV-1997 Channing L. Bete Co., Inc.
29. U.S. Department of Justice-Substance Dependence, Abuse, and Treatment of Jail Inmates, 2002
30. Centers for Disease Control and Prevention-Sexually Transmitted Diseases 2004
31. U.S. Census Bureau-We the People: Blacks in the United States
32. Internet article-Divorce: Psychological Impact. www.to-agree.com
33. Internet article-Effects of Divorce on Children. www.to-agree.com
34. Internet article-Impact of Divorce on Kids. www.troubledwith.com
35. Internet Dictionary-Religious Coming of Age. Wikipedia, the free encyclopedia
36. Internet dictionary-Age of Accountability. Wikipedia, the free encyclopedia

www.ingramcontent.com/pod-product-compliance
Lightning Source LLC
Chambersburg PA
CBHW031625160426
43196CB00006B/279